Nathaniel Hendricks

THEODORE E. BURTON: American Statesman

Theodore E. Burton

American Statesman

BY

FORREST CRISSEY

THE WORLD PUBLISHING COMPANY

CLEVELAND AND NEW YORK

Library of Congress catalog card number: 56-10430

FIRST EDITION

Contents

CONTENTS

Introduction

Theodore E. Burton was, I believe, our greatest American legislative statesman. Certainly he towered above all others in his Congressional statesmanship of his time. Nor was his statesmanship limited to legislative activities.

If we include the two years as a member of the Cleveland City Council, twenty-eight years as a member of the House of Representatives, and two terms as a Senator, his span of legislative service stretched over forty years. So much did he feel that his best service to his country was in the legislative hall that he refused to leave it for offers to the Federal bench or position in the Cabinet.

His interests and service spread over the whole field of American life.

Widely traveled and with acquaintance with leaders over the whole world, he exerted great influence for constructive legislation on foreign affairs. And at all times he was the advocate of constructive measures for peace.

As an economist of the highest order and the author of the most important book of his time on the business cycle of booms and slumps, he contributed hugely to the great legislative economic measures, including the Sherman Anti-Trust Act and the control of banking and currency.

As long the Chairman of the House Committee on Rivers and Harbors and as a member of that Senate Committee, he was the father of our modern inland waterways system and at the same time the implacable foe of "pork-barrel" legislation.

His legislative career was an unceasing crusade against the spoils system and for the upbuilding of the non-partisan civil service.

Although my acquaintance with Theodore Burton began in earlier years, our deep friendship began in 1923 when he was a representative of the Congress as a member of the World War Debt Commission and I was a representative of the Administration. Had his sage advice been accepted at that time, the United States would have profited and also avoided much foreign antagonism.

The greatest loss I suffered in my Administration was his passing in 1929, for he had understanding of our problems of those times as did no other Senator.

In sum we can say of Theodore Burton that the world is a better place for his having lived and worked to upbuild it.

HERBERT HOOVER

THEODORE E. BURTON: American Statesman

CHAPTER I

Torch-bearers—Gift-bearers

ACK OF EVERY MAN AND WOMAN is a shadowy procession of
ancestors, each bestowing legacies more intimate and personal
than lands, chattels, or money—weak lungs or an iron will, a
sluggish body or a driving ambition, an eye for beauty or an urge
for knowledge, a timid heart or a valiant courage. These legacies
are embedded in the very being of "beneficiaries" without their
choice or consent.

The forebears of Senator Theodore Elijah Burton were torch-
bearers of learning, statesmanship, and religion. They were deeply
concerned with the advancement of the generations of Americans
to follow them; they thought in terms of schools, colleges, churches,
town meetings, legislatures, and the protection and expansion of
human liberties. They took their civic and educational responsibilities as seriously as they did their religion, which was to them a
living daily reality and the only form of emotional stimulation and
expression not subjected to restraints and repressions. They slaked
their thirst for spiritual, social, and emotional refreshment at the
house of God, where sermons, songs, and prayers were fervent and
moving.

The most remote figure in the ancestral procession of Burtons
is that of a man with his legs firmly clamped in the village stocks,
taking his punishment along with the village drunkard and the Sab-
bath-breaker—an offender against the law as administered by the
court of Salem, in 1661. This first Burton in America deliberately
brought punishment upon himself. His trouble was that he had a
disturbing sense of justice and a courage which impelled him to

13

"speak out" when silence before the court was the height of discretion.

Every adult citizen of Salem who strolled past to see how he took his punishment knew that John Burton was fortunate not to have been sent to the gallows instead of the stocks for defying the High Court, defending the persecuted, and berating the ecclesiastical justices as they had never before been denounced in all New England.

In his *Salem Witchcraft*, Charles W. Upham presents a graphic picture of the courageous and justice-loving John, who returned from another state to tell the justices what he thought of them and their oppressions and spread upon the records of savage and superstitious Salem a plea for religious tolerance. This account says:

> John Burton came to Salem early, by way of Barbados. He combined the pursuits of farmer and tanner. He was a sturdy old Englishman who, while probably holding the theological sentiments that prevailed in that day, abhorred the spirit of persecution and was unwilling to live where it was allowed to have sway. He does not appear to have been a Quaker, but sympathized with all who suffered wrong.
>
> In 1658 he went off with them to Rhode Island, sharing their banishment. But his conscience would not let him rest in voluntary flight. He came back, in 1661, to bear his testimony against oppression. He was brought before the Court as an abettor and shelterer of Quakers. He told the Justices that they were "robbers and destroyers of the widows and the fatherless, that their priests divined for money, and that their worship was not the worship of God." They commanded him to keep silent. He commanded them to keep silent. They thought best to bring the colloquy to a close by ordering him to the stocks. They finally concluded upon the whole to let him alone, and he remained here the rest of his life.

A worthy founder of an American line was this valiant old John, who had "the vision of the day when it belongeth not to the magistrate to compel religion, to plant churches of [by] power and force submission to ecclesiastical government by laws and penalties!" *

It is now almost impossible to realize the intellectual penetration and independence required, back in 1661, to see through the fog of superstition which enveloped New England and especially Salem —a murky atmosphere thickly peopled with witches and devils. But

---

* Carl L. Becker, *Beginnings of the American People*. Boston, 1915.

John Burton had the vision to discern the unreality of these fantastic shapes and to abhor the cruelties and crimes committed in the name of the Christian religion as measures of protection against these imaginary "forces of darkness."

The almost scandalous number of candles burning one evening in 1770 in the home of another Burton—Jacob—in the little settlement of Burton Plains, of the New Hampshire Grants, indicated to his few and scattered neighbors that there must be important company in the first frame house of the village. No other man of the town—which was later to become Norwich, Vermont—could afford such extravagant illumination. Jacob Burton was a "man of substance," and a leading benefactor of the settlement. He had built the first sawmill in the community and this had brought an expanding prosperity. His townsmen regarded him not only as a far-sighted man in business affairs, but also as a leader in spiritual, educational, and civic interests. His impressive array of candles lighted the deliberations of the first meeting of the Corporation of Dartmouth College. Other meetings of the founders at his home followed.

His earliest training as a public servant began in 1765, when he became a selectman of the village. He was elected a delegate to the historic convention held at Windsor, on January 15, 1777, where he was chosen one of the committee empowered to frame a declaration of independence and establish the new and independent State of Vermont. In 1926, in a letter addressed to the "Westminster Celebration," President Coolidge wrote: "Such men as Ira Allen, Nathan Clark, Ebenezer Hoizington, Jacob Burnham, Thomas Chittenden, and Jacob Burton represented the best of New England character."

The Honorable Jacob Burton was made Judge of the Shire of Newbury (county court) in 1778. In the same year, and later in 1785, he was elected a member of the Vermont legislature.

At the age of forty-nine, having been married twenty-four years and having become the father of eleven children, he had decided to leave the pleasant and well-settled colony of Connecticut and strike out for the wild country of the New Hampshire Grants. Therefore, in 1765, only two years after the British had ended the long French and Indian War and dispossessed the French of Canada, he began his career in the wilderness.

Judge Jacob Burton, the great-great-uncle of Theodore, was a typical Burton in his intellectuality, keenly conscious of his obligation to promote learning, right living, straight thinking, and sound government.

Visitors to the old village cemetery at Norwich, Vermont, will find there a slate tablet inscribed as simply and tersely as if written by Calvin Coolidge. It reads:

HON. JACOB BURTON

B. SEPT. 14, 1715, PRESTON, CONN.

D. JUNE 12, 1798, NORWICH, VERMONT

IN HIS 83D. YEAR

A FOUNDER OF THIS TOWN, 1764–1765.

ONE OF THE FIVE FRAMERS OF VERMONT

DECLARATION OF INDEPENDENCE, JAN. 1777.

MEMBER OF THE JUNE, JULY AND DECEMBER

CONVENTIONS, 1777, WHICH ADOPTED THE

NAME VERMONT AND THE STATE CONSTITUTION,

OF WHICH HE WAS A SIGNER.

NORWICH'S REPRESENTATIVE IN THE FIRST

GENERAL ASSEMBLY OF VERMONT, 1778.

JUDGE OF THE COURT OF NEWBURYSHIRE,

TOWN SUPERVISOR AND FIRST SELECTMAN.

IN HIS HOUSE (THE FIRST FRAME DWELLING

ERECTED IN THE TOWN) WAS HELD THE

MEETING OF THE TRUSTEES OF DARTMOUTH

COLLEGE, 1770, AT WHICH THE LOCATION

OF THAT INSTITUTION WAS DECIDED ON AND

TO WHICH HE DONATED 67 ACRES OF LAND.

Asa Burton, Jacob Burton's son, worked incessantly "to fell trees, cut them into logs and then by hand roll them with levers into heaps to burn them, and help carry logs to make into log fences, as they had no oxen for two or three years." He threw down his ax when he was twenty and took up a Latin grammar instead. On his twenty-first birthday he was admitted to Dartmouth College, was graduated two years later, and became a preacher, holding one pastorate for fifty years.

The pioneer spirit ran strong in the Burton blood and, in 1788, another Jacob—grandfather of Theodore—responded to its call. Immediately after his marriage to courageous young Keturah Palmer, in Preston, Connecticut, he took his bride and followed the

example of his uncle, the Honorable Jacob, already famous as a
pioneer statesman, and struck northward for Norwich. In his eyes,
this kinsman was a hero who, twenty years before, had helped to
found a small principality and later a sovereign state independent
of king or congress. Why should not he, also, become a landed
"proprietor" and join with his relatives in Norwich in securing
another township grant not far from Burton Plains? Here was a
means of providing himself with a domain he could not hope to
secure in a lifetime in "crowded Connecticut."

The younger Jacob and his bride made this wedding journey into
the Vermont wilderness by ox cart. They paused at Norwich and
held a family council. There they found awaiting them, as by an
act of Providence, the ambitious pioneering opportunity of which
they had dreamed. About eight years before, a grant had been
made to Major Elisha Burton and sixty-four associates of a township north of Norwich, containing 23,040 acres. This new Township of Washington was not so crowded as to prevent Jacob the
Younger from acquiring a "share" on practically the same terms
enjoyed by the original proprietors. The adventurous bride and
groom pressed on to their new domain in eagerness to begin their
pioneering by building a log house in the great hemlock forest. The
cabin was up and roofed with hemlock bark in time to shelter the
birth of their oldest child, William, who became the father of
Senator Burton.

In 1793 the township was regularly organized and Jacob was
elected its clerk. Every day of felling huge hemlocks and digging
out their stumps to secure patches of land for tillage became more
discouraging to Jacob, who was not especially rugged and had not,
like "The Honorable," come into the wilderness with strong sons
to help him. However, he demonstrated the characteristic Burton
trait of stubborn persistence. This was his special gift to his grandson, Theodore.

At eighteen years of age, William Burton succeeded in convincing his father that he should pursue his scholarly bent and was
permitted to attend a good school at Barre to prepare for the
ministry. As a minister William Burton combined a somewhat con-
tradictory assortment of traits and tastes. He preached the whole
repertoire of Calvinistic doctrines with eloquence and conviction—
and then played the fiddle, to the scandal of some of his people.
He concealed his softer emotions under a cloak of austerity—and

secretly wrote a novel of love, mystery, and revolutionary adventure. He was positive and intolerant in his opinions—but became so beloved by his parishioners that they spoke of him as "Father Burton."

His first pastorate was in Connecticut, but ill health caused him to go south and in 1819 he was engaged by a family to teach seven miles out of Richmond, Virginia, earning his board and five hundred dollars a year in salary. Later, however, he again pushed on southward, stopping here and there in the aristocratic homes of the Old South where his obvious culture, piety, and social acceptability won him ready welcome.

Eventually, he responded to Ohio's call for settlers and came up from the South in the company of descendants of the early Cavaliers—an odd circumstance considering his Pilgrim-Puritan background. He located in lower Ohio because he was able to secure a pastorate in Circleville, "on the Great Canal," which he believed would soon develop that settlement into a city of importance.

In less than two years after his arrival in Circleville, William Burton married Margaret Hughs. Her span of happiness, however, was comparatively brief. She died on New Year's Day, 1835, about ten years after her marriage and three years after the younger of her two daughters was born. The two little girls, serious Lavinia and gay Margaret, were temporarily taken into the home of a relative.

An achievement which brought William Burton especial reputation and respect was the building of a brick church in 1828. Until then the congregation had been housed in the county court house. Judged by New England standards, the new church was an unpretentious house of worship, but seen through frontier eyes it had an amplitude which gave it distinction. It symbolized the higher ideals that had been brought to the community by the scholarly young preacher who held that a congregation which was content to continue indefinitely under a borrowed shelter, simply because it was free, could not expect to command respect. To arouse the community to contribute money and labor sufficient to build a brick church was an outstanding achievement. It signified outstanding qualities of leadership.

The death of his young wife was the main cause of the termination of William's successful pastorate in Circleville. He sold his household goods in March, 1835, and became "Agent of the General Assembly's Board of Education," a post offered because of the reputation he had made in Circleville. At the time he wrote his brother, Stephen:

"As to property I have done better than I could if I had remained in New England. I have now $2,500 in bank stock, yielding ten per cent per annum, and $1,000 loaned on sufficient security at six per cent, besides some other property. While I continue in the agency I can lay up nearly a thousand dollars a year and this I think I shall do for a few years. . . . My health has improved by traveling." The affluence represented by a cash capital of $3,500 in 1835, in rural Ohio, is difficult to realize today.

At the end of a year, however, William "found the work of the agency irksome" and impulsively left it for the pastorate of the Presbyterian Church at Athens, Ohio, the seat of the state university. He was lonely and anxious about his two little girls. While in this mood he met Miss Elizabeth Grant, principal of the Young Ladies' Seminary of Granville, to whom he was immediately attracted. He knew at once that he wanted her for his wife. His wooing was swift and resourceful, but he did not find his conquest an easy one.

Elizabeth Grant's life had been dedicated from girlhood, with almost nunlike exclusiveness, to the task of broadening the intellectual and educational horizon of young womanhood. However, the shy, dignified, intellectual Elizabeth was both feminine and human and at last she surrendered to the spirited siege of her sweetheart, who readily agreed that she should be permitted to continue in her educational work as long as she wished. They were married in Granville, Ohio, on September 12, 1836.

Since each human life involves the merging of two ancestral lines, it is interesting to turn from the ancestral company of Burtons to the ancestors of Elizabeth, the mother of Theodore. In their independence of thought and action, clearness and breadth of mental vision, in their ability to "stand fast" in justification of their convictions, and in their devotion to the intellectual, spiritual, and civic interests of their country, the Grants were well entitled to form an alliance with the Burton line. They belonged by right of natural endowment to the same rank of intellectual aristocracy.

Like brave John Burton, of Salem, who denounced the justices and clergy for their oppressions and superstitions, the first Grant in America was a Puritan who left England to find religious freedom in the New World—and met with sore disappointment. In 1630 Matthew Grant left Plymouth, England, on the ship *Mary and John*. Soon he discovered that the government of the Massachusetts Bay Colony was almost as intolerant and oppressive as that from which he had fled.

In Dorchester, Massachusetts, where he first settled and was made a freeman, on May 18, 1631, he soon recognized that he was a freeman in name only; that there was little or no separation between Church and State; that civil law and religious law were administered by the same court; that liberty of conscience was almost as restricted as in Old Plymouth.

Matthew Grant was a quiet, thoughtful man—a carpenter and surveyor by trade—of great personal independence. He believed profoundly that the people of any state or colony should be free to govern their own civil and religious affairs without interference from any higher authority. His mind was especially occupied with the problems of representative government.

Five years after he landed at Boston harbor he was ready to start upon his second adventure in search of the liberty becoming to a "Freeman." In October, 1635, with a company of his neighbors and friends who shared his views, he started for the Connecticut River, there to establish a new colony unhampered by the restrictions of a Royal Charter. It was a slow march through a wilderness of virgin forests.

The most conspicuous gifts which Matthew passed on to his descendants were rigid honesty, a devotion to the development of liberty, democracy, and intellectual progress, and a strain of personal reticence. The reticence has been consistently transmitted from one generation to another, and notably to Senator Burton. It was, indeed, one of his greatest handicaps in political life.

The children of Joel Grant, great-grandfather of Theodore Burton, attended school in an unpainted, one-story house devoid of blackboards, crayons, wall maps, or any other of the simplest physical furnishings of a schoolroom. As was the custom, the entrance was in the rear of the house. By the light of a blazing log in the big fireplace, with the New Testament as a first reader and Webster's Dictionary as a speller, their education progressed rapidly. The only formal school textbook was Lindley Murray's

Abridgement of English Grammar. This was the foundation of their grammatical training—riveted in their minds by diligent parsing. The instruction in that schoolroom was rare, individual, distinctive—even for those days when education was unstandardized. Each pupil worked in his or her own way in applying the principles explained by the teacher. The work was unhurried and special help was given only to those in special need of it. Not a few pupils in that old school "finished arithmetic without assistance and without recitation." They were their own pathfinders.

Elijah Grant, grandfather of Theodore, gave early proof of a memory which made him a community oracle regarding dates, names, and the time and place of local happenings. Because of his reputation for honesty and a high sense of justice, he became a local court of arbitration which made "going to law" relatively infrequent among his townsmen.

That Elijah Grant handed on to his grandson Theodore an inheritance in the form of a remarkable memory is evident. It was a gift of great usefulness to the Ohio statesman.

Elijah Grant, who inherited the care of his father's family when he was still an adolescent, had a deep affection for his sister Zilpah Polly, born when he was twelve. As she grew to girlhood a close attachment developed between them.

On long winter evenings, when it was impossible for him to work, he would help Zilpah by Socratic discussions on many subjects. This was almost the only recreation he knew—and he could think of none more stimulating. The free development of her mind, of her capacity to "think things out" for herself, became one of the first considerations of this discerning and devoted older brother.

The nineteenth century was then in its early infancy, and the mentality of womankind was commonly regarded from almost a feudal viewpoint. Therefore the attitude of Elijah Grant toward his young sister was as unusual as the mind of the child which challenged him.

Woman teachers of ordinary elementary schools were then almost unknown. Teaching the children of farmers and artisans was considered a man's job, but Zilpah Polly Grant announced her determination to teach school and Elijah could not deny that she was qualified to do so. She also declared that the money to be earned as a teacher was much needed in the family and that she should be self-supporting.

This Elijah could not deny. But the most convincing argument for her plea was one which Elijah himself furnished. He wanted to see her "try her hand." Probably no other girl of her years could have secured the engagement to teach in the little log schoolhouse—but she was Zilpah Polly Grant and Elijah Grant stood back of her, so she was given the position.

While her engagement as a teacher was supposed to involve only temporary self-support and incidental assistance to the family, it opened for her the door to many visions and aspirations. Education became a sacred thing to this shy slip of a girl. Not even the reticence of the Grant blood could quell the intensity of her revolt against almost universal schoolroom methods which stifled the mental development of pupils.

She gained her first experience as a teacher in the little log schoolhouse in East Norfolk when she was only fifteen. The primitive building had one door, a stone chimney, four half-sash windows, and a dungeon beneath, into which troublesome pupils were supposed to be deposited through a trap door. The dungeon, however, remained unused because this form of punishment was revolting to Zilpah. In fact, all punishments then in vogue were contrary to her educational code.

In this school more than one graduate of Yale received his first lessons from her lips. Her first period as a teacher covered seven years and gave her the conviction that the prevailing theory of school government-by-fear was a stupid fallacy. Also she refused to receive without challenge and analysis any of the theories of teaching then generally accepted. Her schoolroom became a laboratory for the testing of her own courageous and independent educational methods. She held to the theory that the object of teaching was not the forcing of facts into the minds of pupils, but the development of their mental faculties.

Zilpah clearly saw her need of more education to fit her for service in this field of intellectual pioneering. Finally, her brother Elijah told her he would spare what he could from the meager family funds to enable her to attend the unique school at Byfield conducted by James Emerson, an outstanding educational progressive of his day.

There, in Emerson's classroom, Zilpah met Mary Lyon, three years her junior—redheaded, impulsive, fun-loving—the temperamental opposite of herself. This contact made history for the future education and intellectual freedom of women in America.

As the head of Derry Academy, Miss Grant secured Mary Lyon as her assistant. So far as history reveals, this school, in 1823, issued the first diploma for a "finished course" ever given a "female" in this country.

Zilpah Grant and Mary Lyon planned an institution at Ipswich which should be the greatest and most liberal for the education of women in the country, if not in the world. It was to be, in fact, a modern college for women, with dormitories, a library, and spacious and beautiful grounds. When, about 1835, Zilpah's health began to fail, Miss Lyon carried on the work of the institution. Her letters of that period repeatedly express her intellectual debt to Zilpah Polly Grant.

To this school came Elizabeth Grant, the daughter of Elijah. Instantly she caught the spirit of her Aunt Zilpah's work and determined to share it. Elizabeth dedicated her life to carrying on the cause of liberalized education for women as completely as if she had taken vows.

In 1839 Zilpah Grant's state of health became so precarious that she took an indefinite leave of absence and, with a companion, started upon an extended tour of the South. On her return to New England, several years later, she found the school which she and Mary Lyon had planned a realized ideal. It was, however, at South Hadley, Massachusetts, not at Ipswich. The Mount Holyoke Female Seminary, now Mount Holyoke College, lacked nothing of what they had so carefully planned, and it had the additional feature of allowing the students to perform the domestic work of the school family, thus reducing the expense of their education. Edward Hitchcock, President of Amherst College (1845–54), said:

"No one reading the life of Mary Lyon can fail to see that Miss Grant's plans and counsels formed the foundation and framework of Mount Holyoke. Many of the buildings were planned and drawings for them made by Miss Grant's own hand."

Through Zilpah's influence, Elizabeth Grant was selected by the Female Academy of Granville, Ohio, as principal. Thus, in 1834, young Elizabeth started on her own daring adventure as a missionary of the new liberated education for young women.

Perhaps the proudest distinction which came to Elizabeth was an invitation to become a member of the faculty at Ipswich and later

at Mount Holyoke. When she yielded to the importunities of the
Reverend William Burton, it was at the sacrifice of a career which
she had expected never to relinquish and for which she was ad-
mirably prepared.

The transition from torch-bearer to child-bearer could scarcely
have been an easy one for Elizabeth Grant Burton. She was, for
her day, singularly unprepared for the role of housewife, being
almost wholly untrained in even the simplest household duties.
And she had a generous portion of surprises and disillusionments. A
spirit of restlessness seemed to take possession of her husband, who
moved from one charge to another in quick succession. Their
oldest child, Mary, who became Mrs. Giles Shurtleff, of Oberlin,
Ohio, was born in Florence, Washington County, Pennsylvania, a
little more than a year after their marriage. Soon the Reverend
Burton moved to East Liberty, Ohio, near Pittsburgh. A few
months later he bought a large farm near Piketon and combined
farming with light ministerial duties.

Here Elizabeth exchanged the school platform for the kitchen
sink and the stove. With characteristic thoroughness she promptly
mastered the details of the work of a farmer's wife in a pioneer
country. In addition to cooking and cleaning, this diverted missionary of higher education prepared the wool from the farm flock for
spinning, spun it into yarn or thread, made the soft soap, and the
dipped candles, cared for the milk, prepared the home-cured meats,
did all the family sewing by hand, and dried bushels of fruit—wild
berries, cherries, plums, and peaches—for winter use.

Also, in the ten years of her voluntary servitude as a farm woman,
she gave her husband three sons—Philander, Edward, and William.
In this period she did not know an idle moment. She looked back
upon her student and teaching days as times of almost miraculous
leisure and delight. Physical weariness and bodily pains, however,
could not subjugate her intellectual activity. An open book was
braced on a shelf where her eyes could follow its lines as she plied
the churn dasher and, by a similar arrangement, she read as she
spun the home-grown wool into yarn for the family garments,
socks, blankets, and carpets.

Her teaching faculties were not permitted to rust from disuse.
She insisted that her children attend the district school rain or
shine, but only as a proof of the family's identification with the
community, not as an educational measure. In fact, the older Burton

children were better instructed than the teacher—who cracked and ate hickory nuts while hearing recitations and whose pronunciation was often ludicrous. It was a task requiring no little diplomacy for Elizabeth Burton to correct at home the faulty training which her children received in the schoolroom.

At the age of seven, Mary and her younger brother Phil began their education at the nearest district school, a small log building a mile away. This long mile of sticky mud afforded constant excitement. Some shoes were pulled off and others lost in trying to locate them. Mary attributed a slight deafness from which she suffered to her being obliged to sit with wet feet all day—and long were those old-time school days, beginning at eight and lasting until five.

In 1848 Rev. William Burton and his wife Elizabeth went back to New England for a visit; William also visited his old home at Washington, Vermont, and Dartmouth College, from which he had graduated years before. Renewed contact with his own people evidently made a profound impression upon him, for in the following year he made the important decision to move to the Western Reserve of Ohio, "a bit of transplanted New England." He wished to be assured that, in case of his death, his family would be left among "their own kind of people." A journey of reconnaissance into the Reserve led him to choose Jefferson, Ohio, as their future home. It was the center of the antislavery movement, it had good schools and its leading inhabitants were, he believed, sound representatives of the New England school of thought.

The exit of the Reverend Burton and his family from Pike County, one autumn morning in 1849, held a touch of almost baronial magnificence. A group of neighbors and friends gathered to bid them farewell. Leading the caravan was a splendid coach. How it came into the possession of a preacher from New England is a mystery unsolved by family records, but its design was "elegant," its proportions impressive, and its decorations elaborate. Such coaches were seldom seen on the more quiet roads off the great pikes.

Dr. Burton, his wife, his daughter Margaret, and the youngest of the boys occupied the coach's spacious and comfortable interior, which would easily have accommodated the entire family. The two older boys, however, preferred to ride with the drivers of the two covered wagons containing the household goods. Mary, a slender girl of eleven, brought up the rear, mounted on her favorite horse,

Drommy. This act registered her rebellion against the coach, which she considered "gaudy and unseemly."

Dr. Burton smilingly humored her. As for himself, he was thankful for the coach's comfort.

The time of their pilgrimage had been chosen with respect to road conditions which then dictated all overland movements in the new country. Only the National Pike—the great artery connecting the East with the West—could be traveled regardless of weather conditions.

It was a happy journey for Elizabeth Burton. The dreary farm life was forever behind her. The work of caring for her family in the comfortable village house which her husband had already bought in Jefferson seemed, in prospect and by contrast, a perpetual vacation. Soon she was going to rest and read and entertain cultivated people. Some of the wayside taverns at which they stopped offended the fastidious Margaret by their crudeness, but to Elizabeth Burton they were parts of a gracious processional in which she was moving out of a hateful peasant existence back into her normal sphere of life.

CHAPTER 2

Theodore: Town Crier of Civil War News

T HE BURTONS HAD SCARCELY SETTLED into the pleasant routine of civilized life in Jefferson when Theodore was born. Their next youngest child was seven years old and their oldest thirteen. Elizabeth was thirty-nine and her husband sixty-three.

Elizabeth had not confessed the prospect of this event to her husband with any happy expectancy and it seems unlikely that the dignified Dr. Burton looked forward with any particular relish to the role of being a cradle-rocker at sixty-three.

However, their attitude apparently changed when the child arrived, on December 20, 1851, for they named him Theodore, meaning "Gift of God." The attending physician remarked that his size at birth was exceptional—and added the prophecy that he would "make a remarkable man."

If adoration could have spoiled his disposition, it would have been wrecked in the first years of his childhood. But, according to family letters and diaries, he was the most serene and the least troublesome of the Burton children. The family life literally revolved about him. His father built for Theodore a little wagon— the pioneer forebear of the modern baby carriage—and the elderly scholar drawing his young son became a familiar sight on the streets of Jefferson.

The future statesman could not have selected the time and place of his birth more fortunately. The ferment of every change in public thought—political, religious, educational, commercial— seemed to be concentrated in Jefferson in the period of Theodore's childhood and boyhood.

Senator Ben Wade, the stalwart leader of the abolition forces in Ohio and Washington, and his eloquent political partner, Joshua R. Giddings, both lived in Jefferson and made it a center of anti-slavery agitation. These two men were national figures. Giddings, his wife, and Mrs. Wade were members of the church to which Dr. Burton had been called. Senator Wade, however, seldom attended and was, in the eyes of Dr. Burton, a dangerous representative of aggressively liberal thought.

While the atmosphere of Jefferson, as the center of abolition and antislavery agitation, suited Dr. Burton's political convictions, its prevailing tempo of religious thought disappointed him. He had selected it for his home because he longed for a bit of "transplanted New England." It met this demand more fully than he realized, for, along with the culture brought to it by the later settlers from Vermont, Massachusetts, and Connecticut, went the more liberal religious creeds of the Universalists and Unitarians who had obtained scant root in Puritan soil when he had received his theological training. Also there was in Jefferson a distinct tendency toward "free thought" and even outright atheism.

Peculiar religious sects sprang up by the score in this, as in all other, pioneer sections. The presence of an element of college-trained men—the intellectuals of that day—in communities composed largely of settlers with little or no schooling, but with abundant courage and strong convictions of their own, fed the ferment of ideas. Many of the settlers might have written and read with difficulty but all of them felt qualified to speak on the rights of an American freeman to do his own political and religious thinking.

Jefferson was on a sort of trunk line of the underground railroad for the forwarding of Negro fugitives to the Canadian border and was a station of strategic importance. With this humanitarian enterprise the new minister was in active sympathy.

To Elizabeth Burton, life in Jefferson was a grateful restoration to social and intellectual companionship. The Burton home at once became the town's cultural and social center, and Elizabeth Grant Burton blossomed out in the congenial atmosphere. Her happiest days were those of Theodore's childhood on the Western Reserve.

The presence in the household of her two stepdaughters and her own daughter, Mary, all of them capable, energetic young women and devoted to little "Thedie," made her cares comparatively light.

About three and a half years after coming to Jefferson, Dr. Burton bought a large brick house, which had served as a pioneer tavern, in Austinburg, five miles westward from Jefferson. Around the house were eighty acres of farm land, which, he observed, would furnish work enough to "keep the boys from habits of idleness." Grand River Institute, located there, would give his children fine educational advantages.

Hospitality abounded in the big house at Austinburg. Whole families of relatives from other sections of Ohio would descend upon the Burtons unannounced and would receive a welcome as warm as the fire which blazed in the great dining-room fireplace.

There was also an unfailing supply of ecclesiastical guests—many of them strangers. Dr. Burton began his Austinburg residence by preaching in the little log church at The Center—the oldest church building in the Western Reserve. Its organization had been established, in 1801, by Rev. Joseph Badger, the first missionary to the Reserve.

At the age of five, the Reverend Burton's son Thedie astonished members of the family and the neighbors by inviting them to attend "divine service" in the large attic room which had served as a dance hall in the days when the house was a wayside tavern. The service was well attended, though Thedie's auditors had difficulty in maintaining a semblance of seriousness. He gave evidence that he had been a close observer of his father's pulpit presence. His mother had already secretly dedicated her son of her later years to the Christian ministry.

In the old mansion at Austinburg was a huge wood box, with a broad top, which stood beside the kitchen stove. Here Theodore and Will sat while their father taught them the Ten Commandments. On other occasions Theodore used it for other purposes. It was an excellent vantage point from which to throw his bread and butter through the open window after he had carefully licked the honey from it. Expectant chickens were generally waiting outside this window. No ordinary chickens, these! Thedie called them by quaint names of his own invention and often, on a Sabbath morning, would deliver to them a formal and earnest sermon.

Childhood was a land of enchantment to little Theodore. His first gropings brought him in contact with only friendly, protective hands and alluring experiences. His sister Mary, who supervised his earliest education, wrote of him: "Little Thedie loved the farm life and especially the living creatures on the place. He was a very happy child." His brothers were enough older to make their attitude toward him more paternal than brotherly. Theodore was exempt from the rough treatment which they accorded one another. He was "the young fellow," not to be teased, scared, or fought with, but to be protected and amused. In this protective atmosphere, Thedie unconsciously acquired a guileless, trustful outlook on life, expecting truth and affection in all he met.

He learned to read at four and this achievement brought him endless resources of self-amusement. Precocious, he was something of a philosopher. When urged by a companion to join a party of coasters, he replied that he could not see the sense of sliding downhill when one had to plod back uphill and draw the sled too.

A revealing picture of Theodore at the age of nine is given in a letter to the writer by an older boy who saw much of him:

> Very often mother would suggest: "Don't you want to walk over to Austinburg and stay over night with Thedie?" I was a hearty little animal with an insatiable appetite and knew that I would find unlimited food at the Burtons'. Besides, I liked Thedie. Always he assumed the role of host and played it to my complete satisfaction. First he took me upstairs to a certain bedroom, the floor of which was spread with walnuts, butternuts, hickory nuts and chestnuts—all shucked and cured. We filled our pockets with these and then descended to the kitchen, where we cracked them on a flat-iron. When I had eaten enough nuts, we descended into the cellar, where the apples were stored—Northern Spies, Greenings, Seek-No-Furthers and Russetts. That cellar was a fragrant place! After I had feasted on apples, Thedie would draw glasses of sweet cider from the barrel and give me all I could drink. This would hold me until the family meal.
>
> As the twilight came on, Thedie gave me a feast of quite another sort. Sitting before the fireplace he would bring out a thick quarto volume containing several hundred woodcuts of persons and scenes, and hand it to me with instructions to open it at random, cover all the text with a piece of paper and allow him to glance at the woodcut only. Then he would name the person portrayed and give from memory the story of the exploits or achievements of the man. Of course I followed the text in the book, as best I could, as he

told the story. I was too young fully to appreciate how remarkable a memory feat this was for a boy of nine—but I did realize that Thedie was amazingly "smart."

Dr. Burton took keen satisfaction in the fact that, on his own initiative, Thedie had taken up the study of Latin. At the age of seven he had discovered a Latin grammar and it fascinated him. He carried it about and read it as persistently as other youngsters of his age read *Robinson Crusoe*.

In those days, when growing crops were unfenced and every farmer kept a flock of sheep, the work of shepherding invariably fell to the smaller children of the family—generally to the youngest boy. This was the case in the Burton household. Looking after the sheep called for nothing beyond the occasional attentions required to keep them bunched and out of the crops and gardens. Thedie accepted the role of shepherd without protest. Here was a task which would give him agreeable seclusion and an opportunity to study his Latin grammar without interruption.

The grammar proved even more absorbing than he had expected. He was once suddenly aroused from a conjugation by the shouts of a neighbor whose crops were being invaded by the sheep. But when the man saw that the youngster had allowed the sheep to stray because of his absorption in the study of Latin, he laughed and told the neighbors that not another boy on the Western Reserve would have let his flock stray for the same reason.

In the fall of 1857, Rev. William Burton became interested in the lands which were being opened up to settlers on both sides of the Mississippi River. Land was always alluring to him, and with his son-in-law, Publius Jones, he started in a wagon for Iowa, about the first of October, 1857. During their absence of nearly two months they made a thorough exploration and according to the entries in Mary Burton's diary, acquired "one section of land in Poweshiek County . . . and three quarter sections in Webster County" at the price of $1.25 an acre. The Burtons would hold this empire of prairie land as an anchor to windward for their old age.

After the Iowa trip, William Burton found himself not quite as energetic as usual. His general health, however, gave no warning of the violent illness which, in a few days, resulted in his death, on March 12, 1858.

Seventy years after the event, Senator Burton told the story of the first tragedy in the old Austinburg home to Granville Mooney:

"The passing of my father is as clear to me as though it had taken place yesterday. His going marked a house of desolation. I knew not whither to turn. I went through the house looking for my eldest brother, Phil, who was at this time a grown man. He was nowhere to be found. Finally, looking out, I saw footprints in the snow which led across an open space back toward the woods. Scantily dressed as I was, I started out to follow them, stepping in the larger footprints. This trail led me into the woods and there, on a log, sat my brother, alone. He had gone to seek consolation which was nowhere to be found. Upon seeing me, he took me in his arms and we wept together. Returning to the house, my big brother carried me much of the way."

Jefferson and Austinburg were typical interior settlements of the Western Reserve, characteristic of that day and of the vast stretch of magnificently timbered territory between the Allegheny Mountains and the Mississippi River. This was the heart of the domain of Freedom in which human rights to "life, liberty, and the pursuit of happiness" were guaranteed by the great Ordinance of 1787. When Theodore Burton had occupied his homemade and hooded cradle, Jefferson, according to historian Henry Howe, had had nearly a hundred dwellings, four churches, three stores and a "commodious" tavern, a newspaper of outstanding influence, and a group of lawyers of state-wide reputation. This place and its peculiar atmosphere had a part in forming the character of Theodore Burton.

All newspapers, books, and periodicals that came to the hand of the boy Theodore after his sixth year—and they were many and excellent—were grist to the mill of his devouring mind. This was especially true of those which revealed the splendid panorama of development characteristic of that golden age of our national expansion. While he reveled in Latin, poetry, and the romance of the Colonial period, his mind early showed a practical bent. The story of Eli Whitney's invention of the cotton gin in 1792 was his first lesson on the basic authority of economic law. Whitney's gin had brought almost unlimited wealth to the planters of the South and had made slave labor in the fields the foundation of cotton production.

From the story in his book, Theodore understood why the South felt that slavery was its most precious institution, the foundation of a new agriculture and a new wealth. Men, he observed, were swayed by considerations of property and the opportunities to achieve wealth. Other considerations were secondary. Senators Wade, Sumner, and Seward and Mr. Giddings might argue eloquently and endlessly against the wickedness and cruelty of slavery; so long as cotton was king and slave labor spelled fabulous wealth, the South would fight for the extension of slavery into every state and territory where cotton could be grown. Theodore did not then call economic law by its name, but he realized that here was a force of terrible power which twisted the consciences of men until wrong seemed right to them. His father told him that this had been true from the beginning of history.

Theodore lived in a hotbed of antislavery agitation where the wickedness of the institution of slavery and resistance to the extension of slave territory were topics of discussion everywhere. It was inevitable that this boy, with a mental development far in advance of his years, should early understand the background of "the irrepressible conflict" leading to the formation of the Republican Party in 1856 and, ultimately, to the Civil War.

The Fugitive Slave Act of 1850 was readily understandable to a boy living on one of the busiest lines of the underground railroad. Whenever Theodore entered a barn with his young companions in Austinburg or Jefferson, it was with the feeling that perhaps he might encounter a Negro in hiding, waiting to be carried on, at night, to Ashtabula, the next underground station, there to be stowed away for passage across the lake to Canada and safety. A fleeing slave might be concealed in any loaded wagon or bobsled that passed. In fact, at a home in Jefferson where he spent the night with a boy friend, Theodore was warned that a fugitive slave and his wife were occupying the spare bedroom usually reserved for honored guests.

New things seemed to crowd themselves into the lad's vision in bewildering numbers and a very large portion of them proved to be of almost revolutionary importance. As a boy of eight or nine, he would walk miles into the country to witness the operation of the perfected threshing machine or harvester.

While the opening of the California gold fields occurred two years before his birth, the national excitement caused by the continuous and increasing floods of gold which poured eastward from

California persisted during his boyhood. That output amounted to more than fifty-five million dollars a year of fluid wealth which instantly went into the veins of financial, industrial, and commercial development—particularly into the building of railroads. The nation was awakening to the fact that it was rich and that no man could safely predict the limits of its wealth and development.

Then, too, in the years 1858 to 1859 came the second gold rush—to Colorado—which kindled the belief that the whole mountain region of the Far West was a vast storehouse of gold. Not only did Theodore read everything he could find relating to this outpouring of gold, but he listened attentively to the talk of his father and other local leaders. They discussed the significance of this great discovery of hidden wealth in the West and its meaning to the political life of the country.

From the moment when the boy Theodore began to take an interest in them, an unflagging procession of exciting events, which stirred the passions of his elders, crowded upon his attention. Most of them had a connection with the locality in which he lived. There was John Brown, for example. Men came to the Austinburg store who boasted that they had sold wool to John Brown when he was a peaceable and industrious man, before he had become a bloody guerrilla chieftain in Kansas. Suddenly, in the autumn of 1859, the nation was shocked by the news of John Brown's fanatical raid upon the United States Arsenal at Harpers Ferry.

Theodore acquired a surprising knowledge of the great debates between Abraham Lincoln and Senator Douglas in 1858. He could repeat many of the most striking passages from Lincoln's speeches. Then, in 1860, came the dramatic nomination of Abraham Lincoln as the Republican candidate for the Presidency—accomplished by the change of four votes in the Ohio delegation to Lincoln from Salmon P. Chase. Theodore was proud that Ohio had done this.

Young Theodore performed his first public service at the outbreak of the Civil War. Standing on the freight platform of the general store at the Austinburg "Four Corners," he read to the assembled citizens accounts of President Lincoln's call to arms. This service came about quite naturally, because his father was the only resident of the town who regularly received a weekly newspaper. When the group at the store, which was also the postoffice, saw the paper in his hand there was a call: "Read it, Thedie! Stand up on that box and read it so we can all hear!" He obeyed the command and read in a clear resonant voice. This service was so well performed that, by common consent, he was made the town crier of war news for Austinburg.

As defenders of their country, the descendants of the first John Burton had made a proud record. John's son, Isaac, was a soldier in King Philip's War. One Burton, Israel II, fought for nearly ten years in the French and Indian War; numerous Burtons from Vermont, Connecticut, and Rhode Island were in the Revolutionary War. Two were in the War of 1812 and received grants of land in recognition of their services. Senator Burton's three older brothers were in the Civil War.

Burtons mounted guard in defense of their country as eagerly as they mounted their pulpits or their classroom rostrums in time of peace.

Tearfully, but proudly, Thedie had seen his brothers march away to the music of the fife and drum. The patriotism of this region was conspicuous and the young lad felt that in dispensing the latest war news he was rendering his townspeople the only kind of service he was able to give.

One day, when the situation at the front was tense, the Burton paper from Cleveland failed to arrive. The disappointment of the men at the store was great. Theodore said nothing, but quietly struck out at a swinging lope for Jefferson. A few inquiries there assured him that it had no fresh news from the front. Jefferson was connected with Ashtabula, ten miles to the north, by a plank toll road, then regarded as the most important public improvement of that section as it permitted "rapid" travel at all times, regardless of weather conditions. Theodore was confident that he could find a paper in Ashtabula and started up the plank road.

At Ashtabula he quickly located a copy of the *Cleveland Leader* —edited by Edwin Cowles, who had been born in Austinburg— and was permitted to read it under the watchful eye of its owner. It reported the second battle of Bull Run, on August 30, 1862. Scores of men would seek the privilege of reading that paper before the day was over. Besides, copies of newspapers in those exciting times were carefully kept by their owners for future reference. The young courier from Austinburg read column after column of the dispatches with intense concentration. Then he read with equal care the editorials on the war situation.

His return trip was in double-quick time, behind one of the fastest spans in Jefferson, owned by a family friend. He alighted from the buggy at the road leading to Austinburg. As he neared his home town he announced to everyone he could hail that there had been a great battle in the East and that he was going to tell all about it from the freight platform. Word quickly passed from house to house and penetrated to the outlying farmsteads. Waiting for his audience to assemble gave the spent courier opportunity to catch his wind and rest a bit. When the freight platform was crowded with eager, anxious neighbors, he mounted a box.

Probably Theodore Burton never addressed the House of Representatives or the Senate at Washington with a greater sense of excitement and importance than moved him in recounting to the men and women gathered about him the details of what he had read in the paper at Ashtabula. He realized that he was facing the most exacting memory test to which he had ever been subjected.

After he had finished summarizing the contents of the dispatches, he quietly remarked that he had read the editorial by Mr. Cowles commenting on the battle. There were prompt calls of: "Give it to us, Thedie! Let's hear what Ed wrote!" As he responded, it became evident that he was almost quoting the exact words of the editorial—for the rounded sentences which came from his lips were not in the language of an adolescent boy.

Naturally, the promotion of General Ulysses S. Grant to his first position of leadership was a matter of intense interest to Theodore, for Grant was "one of Mother's people." The family relationship was not close, but it was a real one, and Elizabeth saw in the silent and dogged commander besieging Vicksburg many of the characteristic Grant family traits.

Also Thedie was constantly appealed to respecting the utterances of Cabinet members and leaders in Congress. This experience was a rare training for the future tasks of statesmanship. Hundreds of persons have speculated upon whether Senator Burton's phenomenal memory was the result of training or was a natural gift. The answer seems to be that it was a combination of the two. This Ohio country boy, whose face had not yet known the touch of a razor, had read virtually everything available relating to the history of his country—in books, pamphlets, magazines, and newspapers. The circulating library was rich in histories and biographies, and from it young Theodore probably drew more books than any other person in his town.

The family gatherings in the Burton home were open forums in which the shy Thedie was encouraged to ask questions which received painstaking answers from his elders. In these fireside discussions the boy received an elementary education in the basic principles of just and sound self-government.

Elizabeth Burton played no minor role in this informal education of her son. She prayed for humility when pride in her youngster swelled within her.

Such were the foundations of Theodore Burton's preparation for his career. He lived his most impressionable years in a time when national development struck into an unprecedented pace; when machines supplanted hand labor and the new industrial system brought in mass production; when a flood of useful inventions fascinated the public mind; when the earth began to give up long-hidden riches in coal, oil, and gold in an abundance that staggered belief; when mechanized agriculture multiplied the production of crops; when railways were built as rapidly as were paved highways following the mass production of automobiles.

Many thousands of miles of telegraph lines were flung across the country and Cyrus W. Field connected America with the Old World by laying the Atlantic cable; newspapers and books, printed on swift rotary presses, were multiplied a thousand fold; poor men quickly became rich in industry and commerce and the West began to produce a seed crop of future millionaires; high schools began to dot the country and popular education for the masses was established.

Finally came the colossal catastrophe, the tragic interlude, of the greatest civil war the world had known, costing half a million American lives and more than ten billion dollars. Theodore saw scores of sick and wounded men returned from the battle front, listened to their recitals of war experiences, and witnessed the grief of those whose sons were left on Southern battlefields. He learned the meaning of war—and never forgot it to the end of his days. The safe return of his brothers, who had served through the conflict, moved him profoundly. Possibly at this early period of his life grew the ideas which later made him an outstanding apostle of peace.

Then came the assassination of President Lincoln and the outpouring of a nation's grief—the last act of the great drama of the abolition of slavery and the preservation of the Union.

Shortly Theodore was told that the Austinburg home was to be sold and that he was to go with his brothers Phil and Will to the land in Iowa which their father had bought in 1857. There was said to be an excellent college at Grinnell and Theodore expected to continue his education there. He resolved to study hard and make his western stay as short as possible, for he was determined to make his escape from farm life quick and permanent.

When he boarded the train at Ashtabula—for his first railway ride—he felt himself quite a man; he was leaving the old home and adventuring into the West!

CHAPTER 3

Student and Early Law Days

H IS ABSORPTION in the pursuit of knowledge undoubtedly
saved young Theodore from overwhelming homesickness
in the first months of his life on the Iowa frontier.

He had exchanged the pleasant old mansion at Austinburg, with
its cheer and social activity, for the shelter of a small frame farm-
house six miles out from town. Back in Ohio he had been a local
favorite known to almost everyone as Thedie, the boy authority
on war news, the possessor of a remarkable memory, the best student of his years that Grand River Institute had ever known, and
the son of cultured Dr. Burton. Here, he was merely the new
boy.

At night, instead of the cheerful illumination of the Institute,
the church, the store, and the homes of intimate Austinburg
neighbors, he saw, here and there in the far distance, a few tiny
points of candlelight from windows of the homes of scattered settlers who were total strangers to him. But the loneliest note in the
whole billowing landscape was the poignant night wail of the
prairie wolves.

Wherever he went he carried a book under his arm. He was six
feet tall and walked with a long stride. His brothers owned a large
flock of sheep and in the summer of 1866 Theodore was given the
job of shepherding them. Once established with his flock, he was
lost in the pages of some book.

He entered Grinnell College as a sophomore and is said to have
left behind him the most brilliant record for scholarship ever made
by a student of that institution. As a student at Grinnell he did not
lose interest in current practical affairs. He read the Ashtabula
Sentinel as eagerly as he did his Caesar or Cicero. He heard news of

bluff Senator Ben Wade who belonged to the Radical Republican triumvirate composed of himself, Charles Sumner, and Thaddeus Stevens, all violent proponents of antislavery doctrines riding high and hard to the end of giving the liberated Negroes of the South complete equality.

With the weekly arrival of the home-town paper in the Burton household on the Iowa farm, the family at once went into session as a "Committee of the Whole on the State of the Union." These discussions, of course, were not peculiar to the Burton family. They prevailed in virtually every home in the United States.

Theodore took part in this fireside congress with unfailing eagerness. Naturally his interest was sharpened by the fact that Senator Wade was a familiar figure to him. The impetuous, fearless, hardhitting, and fanatical leader of the fire-eaters dramatized the great struggle to him with intense vividness. As an intensive kindergarten course in politics, these contemporary discussions of the Reconstruction drama became rich contributions to his career.

A considerable part of his four or five years in Iowa was spent in earning money with which to finance his education. He worked in the fields as a harvest hand for two or three summers and taught district school for as many winters. He enjoyed farm work in retrospect only. In the Sixty-ninth Congress, when a member from Iowa taunted him with being unable to understand the farmer's viewpoint, he replied that he could not be accused of lack of sympathy with the farmer as he had been an Iowa farm boy at an earlier time than any Senator or Representative from that state then in Congress.

Deciding upon a college in which to complete his academic education involved a family conflict. A close friend of the family—a woman of wealth—who believed in Theodore's brilliant future as a scholar, offered sufficient funds to finance his education at Yale, the alma mater of many of his mother's people. Theodore wished to attend Yale or Dartmouth more than anything else in the world.

His mother, however, refused to assent to the proposed financial arrangement. It was intolerable to her that he should take help from anyone outside the immediate family circle.

Eventually, he made Oberlin his second choice. His adored sister Mary, who had become the wife of Professor Giles Shurtleff, lived there and he would see her daily.

Virtually every young man in Oberlin in those days was made to feel that the ministry was not only the highest calling to which he could dedicate his life but that, if he failed to enter it, he would be unfaithful to the "spirit of Oberlin." In this atmosphere, it seemed inevitable that Theodore would accept the idea held by his father and mother almost from his birth and become a Christian minister.

The bucksaw and the sawbuck were the twin tools and symbols of self-support in the Oberlin of that day. One of Theodore's friends among the young male students worked his way by sawing 250 cords of wood while in Oberlin. But Theodore had a deep prejudice against bending his long back above a sawbuck. Besides, he was reluctant to admit that he could not make his way through college by the use of his mind rather than his muscles.

Almost immediately he applied for a position as assistant tutor in classical languages in the preparatory department. The late Professor A. W. Burr, then in charge of that work, employed him at thirty-five cents an hour, a rate which was soon more than doubled. When Professor Burr unexpectedly appeared one day in young Burton's classroom to observe how the student from Grinnell was discharging his duties, he witnessed a scene which became both an Oberlin and a Burton tradition.

"The lesson," related Dr. Burr, "was a portion of one of Cicero's orations. As Tutor Burton called the class to order, he laid his Cicero on his desk and did not open it once in the course of the class. And he did not make a single slip. He analyzed one sentence after another, from both a grammatical and a rhetorical viewpoint, revealing to the students its perfection of construction and its distinctive oratorical beauty."

It was at this time that Theodore had his first romance with a beautiful and talented young girl. No engagement was announced but Theodore's devotion was to his friends the equivalent of such an announcement.

Bundles of old letters tied in faded ribbons with dates covering a period of eight years, found after his death, at last told the secret. From them it would seem that many years of happiness would have been possible had Theodore known as much about a woman's heart as he knew of the emotions of the ancients. The opinion that he was more skilled as a tutor than a lover seems conclusive.

Considerable excitement was felt in Oberlin when it was rumored that Theodore Burton, then a "theolog," was going to forsake his ministerial calling and study law. The shock to his mother was unnerving but, as she would have, he met all arguments against such a course with independent thinking. A brief experience as a substitute pastor had brought him disillusionment. He would manage with the sermons but he shrank from the intimacies of pastoral duties involving bedside ministrations to the afflicted and the difficult complications of parish diplomacy.

His student years brought him, as their outstanding benefits, a courageous sense of self-determination, liberation from an inherited professional misplacement, an awakening to the fact that he hungered for practical secular affairs and that he had little relish for the cloistered life of a professional scholar.

They also brought him the conviction that indulged emotions involved costly interferences with ambitions and that the wedding march was too often a prelude to distractions, irritations, and disturbances which no man whose intellectual equipment dominated his emotion could safely invite.

After his college days ended in 1873, Burton left for Chicago to "read law" in the office of ex-Senator Lyman Trumbull, one of the commanding figures of the Illinois bar. This was the same office in which William Jennings Bryan read law later.

"Chicago still showed the scars of the great fire," Burton recalled many years thereafter. "A provision of law required that foreclosed property should be sold at auction at the front door of the court house. The court house had gone up in smoke but we used to go down solemnly to the spot where the front door had been to attend the sales."

Evidently the young law student brought to Chicago a rather surprising fund saved from the proceeds of his tutoring in Oberlin, for he bought two Chicago lots, an investment which netted him a modest profit.

After his formal admission to the bar of Ohio by the court sitting at Mount Giliad, on July 1, 1875, young Burton decided to locate in Cleveland.

One of the most important law firms in that city in the early seventies had as its principals John M. Henderson and John C. Grannis. To their office gravitated the choicest law business. They were cultivated and agreeable gentlemen whose standing in Cleveland society was as select as their standing at the bar. Their friends and families were persons of wealth, culture, and refinement. They were "property lawyers" and held closely to that line.

Young Burton knew that property law not only paid the largest fees but also guaranteed the greatest rewards in the coin of legal and social standing. It was his kind of law and he would follow no other.

For many years Mr. Henderson had been John D. Rockefeller's personal attorney. In 1931 Henderson was still in active practice and related this of Theodore Burton:

"In presenting Mr. Burton—a tall and serious young man—Mr. Grannis asked if it would be agreeable to me if he were given a desk in the office and some work to do. I assented and he became a part of the office force. He received no salary, but certain matters of minor importance coming into the office were turned over to him. He worked them out and received his own fees for them."

Burton's industry was so great that it was something of a problem to keep him occupied. His insatiable capacity for work was not especially soothing to some of the younger members of the office force, who did not enjoy so extreme an example of application.

Although reticent almost to the point of bashfulness and possessing a fine respect for the privacy of others, he soon attached the attention of Mr. Henderson and Mr. Grannis. Meantime he formed many valuable acquaintances. These, however, were highly selective. He was not a natural mixer and he knew it. But he held every acquaintance he made and developed acquaintanceships into friendships.

On entering law practice, he secured a home—not a boarding place—with Erastus Gaylord and his wife. They had no children, were rather lonely, and wished to have in their home the companionship of a young person of correct habits and intellectual tastes. Young Theodore Burton qualified.

The parents of Erastus Gaylord had come to Cleveland when it was a mere hamlet, thus securely establishing the Gaylord name in the list of Cleveland's first families. Once established under the Gaylords' roof, Theodore endeared himself to them. They played euchre, pinochle, and cribbage and talked about books, plays, operas, politics, taxes, the folly and extravagance of Congress, the upward course of Cleveland real estate values, the harassments of the Grant Administration, and the social events in their circle.

A lifelong friend of Senator Burton's gives this pleasant picture of the Gaylords: "All the neighbors and friends called the Gaylords 'Grandpa' and 'Grandma.' Grandpa Gaylord was the only man I ever saw who wore his silver-white hair long and tied with a black ribbon."

Among those to whom the Gaylords introduced Theodore Burton were Anne and Mary Walworth, whose grandfather, John Walworth, had been Cleveland's first postmaster. He was a pioneer who had strong faith in the future of Cleveland. This he demonstrated by acquiring large holdings of real estate direct from the Connecticut Land Company, much of the propery being located on the two trails which are now Broadway and Ontario Streets. This property had become very valuable even as early as 1875.

The Walworth sisters liked the dignified, scholarly young lawyer, he commanded their confidence and they employed him to manage their real estate. This involved selling parcels of land, collecting on mortgages, contracts, and loans, and making new investments.

Being retained by these clients was an important step in Burton's career. There were few lawyers in Cleveland—even those who were well established—who would not have welcomed this business. The public knowledge that he had been selected to handle the substantial Walworth properties was a business-builder for the young attorney.

In the first year of his practice, Theodore Burton earned and collected fees amounting to three thousand dollars. Books were almost his only luxury, although he dressed well, taking as good care of his clothes as he did of his money. He wasted nothing and kept an exact account of his expenditures.

E. A. Paddock, Burton's classmate in Oberlin, later President of the Intermountain Institute of Idaho, has a lively recollection of Theodore Burton's first law case before a Cleveland jury:

"One day, when riding in a Cleveland street car, I heard two men talking about how a young lawyer named Burton had given a large corporation not only a big surprise but a decisive defeat. My curiosity was aroused, and I went to Theodore's office to get from him a full account of the case.

"An old man who had long served a large company—possibly a railway corporation—in a minor position involving the handling of certain funds apparently was short in his accounts of a relatively small amount and was being prosecuted under a criminal charge.

He had brought his case to Mr. Grannis, who passed it on to Theodore with the remark, 'Here's a dead duck for you to practice on.'

"Burton told me that he dug into the case for all he was worth and that the deeper he dug the more he became convinced that the old man deserved acquittal. In other words, his client's shortage was technical rather than criminal. Theodore was not one to allow his sympathies to run away with him. But when he assured me that he believed in the justice of his client's case and the injustice of the prosecution, I accepted that statement without the slightest discount. Intellectually, as well as commercially, Theodore Burton was scrupulously honest. He put as much hard work into the preparation of that case as if it had involved millions of dollars.

"Burton made a masterful presentation of the case. His appeal to the jury was perhaps the most impassioned speech of his life. He had the jury in tears and fully convinced that the old man was the victim of heartless injustice on the part of the big corporation which he had served faithfully for almost a lifetime. Theodore won the case and with it a local reputation.

"The next time I went to see Theodore, in about 1878, I found that he had left Mr. Henderson and Mr. Grannis and opened an office by himself at what was then 218 Superior Avenue, west of West Third Street. Associated with him was a young law student, George I. Dake, with whom he later formed a partnership. Their business soon outgrew this first office and quarters were established in the old Blackstone Building, which was on a quiet street rather removed from the beaten path. I asked him why he had sought such a location and he replied that it was to escape petty and undesirable business; that the clients whom he wished to attract would find him in his secluded location as readily as in any other, and those whose business was inconsequential would not take the trouble to hunt for his office. At this time he told me that he was retained by a number of important firms in the iron-and-steel business and that his practice in the case of estates had grown in a very satisfactory way.

"About the time that Burton tried his first law case, he made his first political speech. One day a young man with whom he had become acquainted in Oberlin called upon Theodore and explained that he was a candidate for the office of Justice of the Peace, that the revenues of that position would be important to him in getting a start in the law, but that he had strong opposition for the post. He was, he said, leaving nothing undone which might help him to be elected and it had occurred to him that perhaps his college friend would consent to address a mass meeting in his behalf.

"Young Burton instantly and cheerfully accepted this appeal from his former college associate and made the principal address at the mass meeting. Like his first plea to a jury, his speech had in it the fire of youth and carried his hearers with him so completely that a member of the audience was overheard to remark to a companion, 'Why does this young man that Burton is talking about bother with the petty office of Justice of the Peace? We ought to send him to Congress.'"

When the Society for Savings Building, the first skyscraper in Cleveland, was erected, the firm of Burton and Dake were the first tenants. Here was the scene of many dramatic political conferences. Burton's campaigns for Congress were all handled from this office. It was here, too, that he made his final decision to be a candidate for Mayor of Cleveland against Tom L. Johnson in 1907; and, later, his campaign for election to the United States Senate was handled from this office. The Burton and Dake partnership lasted for twenty years, until January 11, 1913.

It was while living with the Gaylords that Burton came to realize that a young man could enjoy the atmosphere and comforts of a home without the responsibilities of marriage, and that a bachelor's freedom from domestic ties and accountabilities was a liberty not to be lightly sacrificed. His sweetheart had a right to expect that they would be married, now that he had made a successful start in his profession, and that at last she would be given the joy of starting a home with her campus sweetheart. But he already had a home—a delightful one—which imposed no obligations upon him beyond the prompt payment of his monthly bill for board and lodging. The conclusion was soon reached, on the part of his friends and relatives, that he was permanently "married to his career." And so came to an end their eight-year engagement.

CHAPTER 4

The European Education
of Mr. Burton

THE HABIT-FORMING TRIP which made Theodore Burton an incurable foreign-travel addict was taken in 1880 when his law practice had grown prosperous and he was in a position to relax from the grind of office work. Until then he had been without any absorbing diversion.

For the first time, on the deck of a transatlantic steamer, he suddenly realized that he was a natural nomad; that going places and seeing things was the most agreeable indulgence he had discovered and that he would have the time of his life in getting acquainted with the alluring world he had first met in the years of student reading.

All told, he made twenty-eight trips to Europe—fifty-six Atlantic crossings—in addition to his trips to the countries of the Orient, Australia, and South America. He loved the contacts made in passing, and in the social atmosphere of the first deck relaxed somewhat from his customary aloofness. Neither the salt-water gambler nor the seagoing widow caught him unawares in mid-ocean; he carried his discretion with him as faithfully as he did books. But this did not prevent him from becoming known to most of his fellow passengers as the gracious gentleman who talked so delightfully on any topic of interest. His social pores seemed to open when exposed to the sea air and, in his earlier crossings, he formed some of the pleasantest friendships of his life.

In the course of his twenty-eight visits to the Old World, Burton had scores of contacts with men of international reputation. While it is true that most of them were politicians, statesmen, economists, engineers, and technical authorities in special fields, the wide scope of his intellectual interests is indicated by the fact that he met a considerable number of literary men also. These included poets, novelists, journalists, biographers, historians, and philosophers. His obvious scholarship and dignity served him as a passport into official circles where, in the eighties at least, education and intellectual background were requisites of political preferment.

Burton's interests and sympathies were remarkably wide and catholic. He was greatly interested in the drama and, in his earlier European visits, he came to know many of the leading playwrights and actors. His appreciation of good painting was equally discerning and he seldom visited a European city without making a leisurely and discriminating survey of its art galleries. He was a devoted attendant of the best opera performances and had a good natural ear for music which enabled him to retain in his memory the score of a new opera almost as readily as he could memorize a page of Shakespeare.

In his later years he frequently expressed regret that his duties as a national legislator prevented him from indulging in purely literary reading to the extent which he craved. He had, in fact, a modest idea of his knowledge of literature. He knew Shakespeare and proudly admitted it; his knowledge of Dickens also was unusual and he was more than passably familiar with the works of the best French, British, and American novelists—yet he felt that his reading in creative literature was too limited.

Burton's meeting with Count Tolstoy is an excellent example of the intellectual adventures with which he crowded his foreign travel.

While in Moscow, in the summer of 1892, he made the acquaintance of a banker who proved to be most helpful and congenial. He was a man of culture and had a wide acquaintance among the intellectual leaders of Russia and did much to make the visit of his friend from the United States agreeable. One day, Burton chanced to remark to this man that, above all other things, he would like to meet Count Tolstoy, then generally regarded as the world's greatest living writer. This remark brought to Burton one of the most enjoyable experiences of his life.

In a day or two he received a telegram from Count Tolstoy inviting him, in most cordial terms, to visit at Yasnia Polyana, Tolstoy's summer home 130 miles south of Moscow.

He left the train at Tula, about nine miles from the count's home. Here he secured a carriage and driver and started out over the old military road connecting Moscow and Kiev. Even the imminence of a meeting with Count Tolstoy could not prevent him from taking note of the river which divides Tula, the factories and industrial plants accounting for its reputation as "the Sheffield of Russia," the grotesque range of colors of its buildings, and the fact that the surrounding farming country reminded him of the prairies of Iowa.

When within about a mile of Yasnia Polyana, he saw approaching him a figure which he at once concluded must be the count.

"His appearance was most striking," related Burton in an account published later in the Cleveland *Plain Dealer*. "He seems a well-preserved man about sixty-five years old, with hair and long beard nearly white. His shoulders are bent but he has a muscular build, and his appearance, as I saw him, was that of a man who all his life has been inured to physical labor. He wore, as his wont, a blouse, also a belt, and leaned somewhat upon a cane. We walked together to his home.

"One of the first things he said was that he ascribed his good health to the fact that for some years past he has been a vegetarian. On the way he raised his hat to each of the workingmen whom we met. In walking about his estate, we met a half dozen children starting out to gather mushrooms. He spoke kindly to them as they went upon their way. We had been speaking of the increase of popular education in Russia. Turning about and looking at the children he said, 'Three of those children know how to write and read. The rest have not learned as yet.' "

The traveler found the ancestral residence as odd and picturesque as its owner. One portion of it was new, the remainder virtually as it had been during its occupancy by Tolstoy's forebears for generations. In Burton's eyes, it bore a strong resemblance to a typical plantation house of the South in his own country. The interior he found "neat and roomy" but severe in its plainness.

Naturally, his interest centered on the study in which Tolstoy did his writing. It contained no easy chairs and was guiltless of carpet or floor covering of any kind; it looked to him "more like the workshop of a mechanic" than the studio of a writer of fiction. It was littered with books in Russian, French, and English.

"Count Tolstoi spoke English fluently," Burton related. "Occasionally he would ask his wife the English equivalent for a Russian word; but this seemed rather out of deference to her than because of an imperfect understanding of the language. His wife is a very young-looking woman, and while giving the most careful attention to the matters of the household, she showed very high intellectual attainments and strong character. I am told that she has of late years had full control of the management of his business affairs, including the making of all contracts for the publication of his works and the care of his estate.

"They have nine children, six of whom were at home. The youngest is a boy of about three or four. The oldest sons were absent. His oldest daughter is one of the most interesting members of his family. She appeared to be a woman of very wide reading and marked literary culture. She spoke English with perhaps the least foreign accent of any of the family. I take it that she acts as amanuensis for her father, as he mentioned that she attended to his correspondence.

"While at Yasnia Polyana some member of the family asked me if I had visited a private art collection at Moscow, in which there were numerous works of Vereshchagin and some other Russian painters. I was told that I ought to visit it, and a letter of introduction to the owner was given to me. I found, on calling there on my return to Moscow, that the letter of introduction gained for me an immediate and favorable entrance to the gallery. The Russians, as a people, are intensely national and very proud of the achievements of any of their citizens, whether in the line of literature or in any other direction."

Of Tolstoy's conversation with him, Mr. Burton had this to say:

"We had been speaking of the expression of the popular will in a legislative government, when he said: 'After all, in your form of government, I am not sure that you get at the will of the people. A member of one party introduces a measure. Others of his party take it up. All the members of the other party oppose it. The bill has to be amended, and it is manipulated and changed so that by the time it becomes law I am not sure that you get any nearer to the popular will than we do here in Russia, although we have no legislative body at all.'"

It was a true Burtonian feast, an intellectual conversation which yielded him great pleasure. Apparently the enjoyment of this contact was not one-sided, for Burton recorded that:

"Count Tolstoi showed a great deal of interest in America and, for a Russian, an unusual acquaintance with our history and people. Jefferson and Lincoln seemed to be his heroes among our public men.

"I have never met any one less anxious for display in his conversation or more free from affectation than Count Tolstoi. Whatever he said was spontaneous and sincere. In saying good-bye I could not forbear expressing my pleasure at meeting him in very strong terms, and also my appreciation of the value of his works which I had read. With the authority and impressiveness of an old patriarch he dwelt upon the obligations which we owe to each other. It was with no mock humility that he continued: 'What am I, except what others have made me? What do I know, except what some one has told me?'"

Mark Hanna and Theodore Burton represented the two most conspicuous trends of American civilization immediately preceding the opening of the twentieth century: firstly, the concentration of wealth into relatively few hands and, secondly, the refinement of American life through an increasing knowledge of the elements which made the life of educated people in Europe so full and agreeable.

Perhaps the most intimate of the friendships which Theodore Burton formed in his earlier visits to the Old World was that with James Bryce, author of *The American Commonwealth*, who, at the outset of the twentieth century, made this statement of the American situation: "There is some poverty, many large fortunes, and a greater number of gigantic fortunes than in any other country of the world."

The sweeping mechanization of industry with its accompaniment of mass production was in full swing and the regimentation of capital under corporation control had become country wide. Its long and strong arm reached every form of business in America.

Mark Hanna's enterprises employed thousands of men. He was one of the ablest of the pioneers of modern industrialization. In virtually every particular, he was a typical "captain of industry" of the paternalistic type somewhat fashionable in the period in which his fortune was made. He knew scores of his employees by name and many of them regarded him as their personal friend. They knew of his kindness, the broad scope of his human sympathy, and the tang of his wit. While Hanna's operations were smaller than those of the great financiers and industrialists of the East, he was, notwithstanding, typical of the tribe which was spreading over the entire country.

Theodore Burton was as truly typical of the army of intellectuals in public life who, as Professor Harry Thurston Peck observes, had "discovered Europe" and absorbed much of the intellectual idealism of its leaders of thought.* The door to the pleasant vista of Old World friendships was opened by letters of introduction from American scholars; Burton's own self-evident intellectuality, combined with a reserve of bearing which was better understood in England than in America, widened the scope of his contacts.

He made his way rapidly to a London and European acquaintance of amazing scope and selectiveness. Always he brought back to America a rich cargo of facts and conclusions derived from the best European sources.

These expeditions established in his thought a new standard of living—both intellectual and material—to which his home country might well aspire; a broader sense of civic and cultural responsibility, an expanded definition of the demand upon all to serve the general welfare. Politics in Europe was regarded as an honorable career; the word did not imply the sordid associations which it carried in America. The fortunate and favored must think and legislate for the unfortunate; it was their clearly recognized obligation.

This became Burton's basic code and he loyally lived by it.

* Harry Thurston Peck, *Twenty Years of the Republic*. New York, 1906.

CHAPTER 5

Burton's Maiden Congressional Campaign—1888

THE HOME LEGISLATIVE BODY—the municipal council or
the county board of supervisors—is the standard grade
school of elementary training for public service in American
political life. Theodore Burton made no attempt to avoid this
humble preparation but he did not tarry long in the primary grade.
He became a member of the Cleveland City Council in 1886 and
served one term of two years.

To some extent, Burton's first advance on Washington may
have been dictated by personal ambition, but the keynote of his
public career was his conviction that participation in politics was a
patriotic duty and that those who shirked it denied themselves any
right to complain of the administration of public affairs. The general indifference of young men in America to this obligation was
to him shocking and painful.

Burton's appeal, in his first Congressional campaign, for an
awakened sense of the obligations of citizenship expressed his
strongest convictions. On October 3, 1888, at the age of thirty-
seven, he opened his campaign in Brooklyn, a village near Cleveland. It must have been a great occasion for that village, as it was
for the candidate. Burton, the premier speaker, rode in state in an
open carriage escorted by a platoon of supporters "in uniforms
of blue dress coats, white trousers, and high boots."

A current newspaper account recites that Burton declared that
"a change from a protective tariff to free trade would involve for
the country a greater revolution than a change from a republic to a
monarchy." He also observed that the tax upon land, as urged by

53

Tom Johnson, his Democratic single-tax opponent for Congress, "would result in confiscation of property rights, in a confusion of ownership and finally in Socialism or Communism."

Burton's first appearance as a candidate for Congress was dignified. The remainder of that campaign, however, was a violent baptism in the mud and slime of politics of the most revolting type, in which dignity availed nothing and only Burton's stubbornness enabled him to go through with it and win. This "dirt" was dished up by the Tom Johnson ward heelers.

A typical example was the incident of "the widow Broughton's mortgage." Burton's "persecution" of this widow and her children was dramatized by their exhibition at a labor mass meeting. The producers of this campaign melodrama, however, overplayed their hand and underestimated the widow's regard for truth. The facts of her case, as ultimately revealed by its court records and by her own admission, were:

In 1883, a client of Burton's who had a mortgage on two lots— each with a house—in Newburg, placed in his hands the foreclosure of this mortgage because all payments had ceased and there was no reason to believe that they could ever be made. In December of that year Mr. Broughton died. This made the eventual liquidation of the mortgage appear still more hopeless. There was nothing for Burton's client to do but take over the property, which had greatly depreciated in value, and Burton was retained to see that this was done in a legal manner.

His correspondence with the widow began in December, 1883. She was given ample time to make some disposal of the property which would permit her to get something substantial out of it for herself. Eventually she reported that she could accomplish nothing, and in April, 1885, the property was sold under the mortgage. It was bid in by the mortgagee, represented by Burton, who allowed the widow to continue to live in the house she occupied and to collect and use the rent for the other house. She was not asked to pay taxes or rent and was allowed to retain possession of the property for nearly two years after the mortgagee was legally entitled to take it over. Then she voluntarily abandoned it. On behalf of his client, Burton paid her the expenses of moving her household goods and a modest sum besides.

This attempt to depict Burton as a harsh oppressor of the Widow Broughton proved to be a political boomerang.

Organized labor was solidly arrayed against Burton. It had a force of able and unscrupulous picadors who peppered his flanks with darts calculated to enrage him and drive him to wild and ill-considered action. But he kept his head. He was denounced as "an enemy to labor, a man with a record of hate and enmity to progress and humanity." The basis of this assault was the claim that, in 1886, as a member of the Cleveland City Council he had voted against an eight-hour-day ordinance. He responded with proof that he had voted for such a measure in 1886 but had opposed the ordinance of 1887 because it did not cover all kinds of labor.

A poor mixer, Burton was at as great a disadvantage as Woodrow Wilson would have been in wooing an electorate of mill hands. Even his pleasant initial utterance at Brooklyn developed unpleasant associations as a result of his tariff utterance. The Cleveland *Plain Dealer* promptly branded him a turncoat and editorially remarked: "Burton, publicly, is now a Chinese Wall tariffite, but privately he favors free trade."

As a matter of pure economic theory, free trade has seldom failed to appeal both to professors and the young men of their classrooms. Burton was no exception to this rule. But in the years since he had left college he had come into contact with the realities of practical business. Cleveland had many manufacturers who had to meet the competition of foreign goods, produced under cheap labor conditions impossible in the United States, and he listened attentively to their statements. It was not in his nature to disregard facts.

Then, too, he lent an attentive ear to the oracles of his party. To use his father's pet scriptural phrase, he was "predestined and fore-ordained" to become a Republican; he had absorbed that party's doctrines with his every breath.

His final espousal of moderate protection was, therefore, not necessarily insincere; a host of other men who had left college as free traders had become protectionists.

In his maiden campaign for Congress, Burton was at peculiar disadvantage in having for his opponent a man who was an adroit campaigner and the idol of organized labor in an industrial district. Tom Johnson had every quality that Burton lacked. He was gifted with a genius for mixing, with a ready wit, and with a rare faculty for ridicule. He slapped backs, kissed babies, and jollied the workers with a naturalness which won him the support of foreign-born mill hands who could understand his smile better than his words. Tom Johnson was short, fat, and jolly. He oozed sympathy for the workers at every pore. In 1882 he had come up from Louisville, Kentucky, and bought the small street railway of Brooklyn, Ohio, for the purpose of extending it into Cleveland as an entering wedge into the larger domain then controlled by Mark Hanna, who put all the obstacles possible in his path.

Johnson—a shrewd and adventurous businessman—was a thorn in Burton's side. He did not deny that his considerable fortune had been amassed in street railway operations in which he had felt himself obliged to do many things not in keeping with his later convictions. He had, he implied, turned from the error of his ways, become a convert to the single-tax theories of Henry George and proposed to devote the remainder of his life to lifting from the shoulders of the toilers the burdens placed upon them by an unjust system of taxation and by the oppressive schemes of the rich. The very frankness with which he confessed his capitalistic sins captured the imagination and confidence of the workers. They accepted the conclusion that the man who knew the whole capitalistic bag of tricks was well qualified to fight their battles and they followed his leadership with devotion.

Although Burton was a pathetic failure in his efforts to fraternize with the mill hands of his district, he had a compensating quality. This was a faculty for impressing thoughtful young men with his intellectual power, and the breadth of his outlook upon public affairs. The only flattery in which he indulged was the matter-of-fact assumption that the educated young men with whom he came in contact—many of them law students—shared his high ideals and associated themselves with his organization because they were anxious to promote good government rather than their own interests.

Many of the younger men of his district evidently felt that it was a distinction to be recognized and consulted by this new kind of politician who used Latin with as much facility as other politicians used profanity.

A. N. Rodway tells how he fell under the "Burton spell" when he was scarcely more than a boy.

"One evening I strayed into a political meeting and took a front seat. Theodore E. Burton was the speaker. I had before attended many local political meetings and expected to be entertained with the usual line of rough-and-ready stories, jokes, and personal on-slaughts. But this speaker was amazingly different. He dealt in facts and made them seem very important to the welfare of Cleveland and the people of this country.

"I was charmed by his wonderfully melodious voice and by the simple but stately diction of his address. He gave me the impression that he was tremendously in earnest and knew what he was talking about. A little later I happened to sit beside him in a street car. To my great surprise he spoke to me and said: 'Young man, I remember you. You sat in the front row at the political meeting the other evening.' Of course I was flattered and became his devoted follower.

"However, considerable time passed before we had another personal meeting. By that time my interest in politics had become active as a party worker who enjoyed the competitive element of that kind of contest. Mr. Burton had imbued me with the idea that a young man who didn't take an active part in politics didn't amount to much as a young citizen."

"Burton's Young Men" became his political sponsors. They felt that politics in Ohio should be lifted to a higher level and that the intellectual Burton was the man to lead them. And so, as a politician of a new model, he was sent to Congress, where he was to meet others of the younger generation ambitious to use their education, wealth, and leisure to raise the level of American politics. Here was alluring adventure in the field of good citizenship.

In the years immediately preceding 1900, and in all parts of the country, ardent recruits joined this informal movement. Dashing young Theodore Roosevelt became the nation's most conspicuous leader of the new generation of civic idealists.

The movement was not elaborately organized but rather represented a national trend of thought. If these young crusaders agreed on anything, it was that the tremendous concentration of wealth in the hands of relatively few men must be checked or it would destroy the opportunities of the masses. Special privilege had gone wild with abuses. The divergence of ideas as to how this was to be checked was wide. The important fact was that, in this exciting era, the old order was on the retreat before the forces of Young America.

A conspicuous phase of this trend, which continued throughout

McKinley's first campaign and administration, was a new national interest in economics; the burden of party conflict was passed to younger men who could discuss banking, currency, and corporation control. In this field Theodore Burton was in his element.

There was a strong tendency toward state socialism; but Burton was a natural conservative who could not go to this length. Firm state control of corporations, particularly of public utilities, rather than their public ownership, appealed to him as the sounder course. Individual opportunity should be kept free and open and at the same time capital should receive all reasonable encouragement to develop the resources, wealth, and progress of the country.

And so it was that "Burton's Young Men" symbolized a novel and wholly natural type of campaign organization which accumulated power as his reputation increased. It was a major influence in his election of 1888 by the close margin of 616 votes. This was hailed by the Republicans as a brilliant victory over an adroit and popular opponent who not only had the forces of labor but also the most powerful newspaper of the city on his side.

Despite his conversion to the doctrines of Henry George and to the cause of the toilers, Tom Johnson continued his capitalistic activities until about 1895. In this period he added greatly to his fortune—and to the irritation of Mark Hanna.

Until the Presidential campaign was almost upon the country, the Republicans were in need of an issue on which to make an appeal which would stir the country. The first campaign against Grover Cleveland had been one of personalities on so low a plane that its repetition could not be considered. Cleveland's courage and patriotism had made such a repetition an impossibility.

Suddenly, however, in 1887, Cleveland gave the confused and fumbling Republicans a major issue. He sent to Congress a special message devoted to the patriotic duty of reducing the tariff and thereby reducing the treasury surplus which, it was estimated, would amount to $140,000,000 for the year. This was then regarded as a huge sum in the finances of the nation. Cleveland felt that it would prove a tremendous temptation to Congressional extravagance.

The Democratic leaders to whom Cleveland confided his determination to submit this message to Congress were thrown into consternation. They begged him to abandon such a suicidal course. Why bring this up on the eve of a Presidential election? There was time enough to deal with it after he was re-elected. Did he wish to withhold the sweets of office from thousands of good Democrats who had been denied such nourishment from the days of Franklin Pierce, in the early fifties, until he had broken the long Democratic famine in 1884? They argued that a revision of the tariff had never failed to disturb general business conditions. In the name of his country's good, as well as party expediency, they pleaded that he let the dogs of tariff reform sleep until the votes were counted in 1888.

But it was not in Grover Cleveland's nature to tread softly on any issue involving his personal convictions. Regardless of campaign consequences, he set his whole vast weight upon the tariff reform issue. "It is more important to the country that this message should be delivered to Congress than that I should be elected President," he declared.* Therefore, on December 6, 1887, the fateful message was delivered.

Few candidates for re-election to the Presidency had ever accumulated a more formidable array of handicaps than had Grover Cleveland. His veto of the Dependent Pension Bill had aroused a storm of wrath that had swept the entire North and earned him the vociferous enmity of the G.A.R., which boasted that it could swing a million votes. Then, too, President Cleveland had opposed scores of private pension bills, adding fuel to the fire of veteran resentment. To oppose these bills, which were frequently of doubtful validity, required superb courage—which Cleveland had in abundance.

Then there was his feud with the press. Cleveland had suffered many indignities at its hands and did not hesitate to tell the world how deeply he despised those responsible. In a letter dated December 12, 1885, he confided to Joseph Kettler, editor of *Puck*: "I don't think there ever was a time when newspaper lying was so general and so mean as at present; and there never was a country under the sun where it flourished as it does in this."

In his first administration Cleveland also contrived to offend two powerful elements in his own party—the "Tilden Wing" and Tammany Hall. The belief that Samuel J. Tilden had been cheated of the Presidency back in 1877, when the bipartisan Election Commission awarded the Presidency to Rutherford B. Hayes, was well-nigh universal in Democratic ranks. This gave Mr. Tilden the sympathy and influence which a wronged man generally

* Alexander K. McClure, *Colonel Alexander K. McClure's Recollections of Half a Century*. Salem, 1902.

commands. Undoubtedly Cleveland was largely indebted to Mr. Tilden for his first Presidential nomination. Naturally this carried with it the expectation, in the mind of the cold, calculating Tilden, that he would exert a powerful influence in the Cleveland Administration if the Democratic ticket were elected.

But Mr. Tilden was permitted to name only one Cabinet member, Daniel Manning, his devoted friend, who was made Secretary of the Treasury. Manning was meagerly consulted by the new President and came to feel himself lonely and isolated. He stood this chilling atmosphere for a time and then resigned. It was temperamentally impossible for Grover Cleveland to be subservient to any outside influence. The people had elected him to break the long succession of Republican Presidents starting with Abraham Lincoln and this was mandate enough, in his opinion, to justify him in following his own free will and judgment.

His hatred of Tammany Hall was unconcealed; he regarded it as the pre-eminent Democratic abomination. In the course of his administration, Cleveland did not yield an inch to Tammany or to David B. Hill, the chief beneficiary of the organization in New York State politics.

A veritable plague of strikes and labor disturbances, most of them violent, broke out all over the country. Cleveland's method of dealing with them was interpreted by labor as hostile. He could count organized labor as solidly against him. This was a period of great activity in the labor unions. The railroad traffic of almost the entire West was tied up by strikes and the destruction of railroad property was great. In this experience President Cleveland "showed his teeth." He would not tolerate interference with the movement of the United States mails. This act was timed to take advantage of the great Pullman strike in which about fifty thousand workers participated. The atmosphere of the entire country was charged with dynamite, but President Cleveland did not flinch or sidestep. Apparently he took no thought of the political consequences of his attitude or acts.

In Chicago, on May 4, 1886, the historic Haymarket Riot had been one of the sensational events of Cleveland's first administration. Then, too, during Cleveland's first administration the great Standard Oil monopoly had developed into a national scandal. Naturally this provoked public revolt—the initial result of which was the passage by Congress, in 1887, of the first Interstate Commerce Act forbidding rate discriminations and pools by nominally

competing railroads. This law did not have even a set of baby
teeth, but it was historic as a step in the right direction. It was instantly signed by President Cleveland, who appointed the first
Interstate Commerce commissioners.

In addition to these handicaps with which Cleveland approached
his second campaign, his blunders in the diplomatic field were
many and sad. He had no background to fit him for these responsibilities, never having been outside of his own country; nor had
he been a student of international affairs. Again, there was not a
trace of diplomacy in his nature.

In campaigning for his party against Cleveland, Burton felt restraints which handicapped him. He admired Cleveland immensely.
They stood on common ground in their views of the obligation of
every citizen to place the welfare of the nation above party advantage. Cleveland abhorred the spoils system and the plague of
patronage; his respect for the Constitution amounted to reverence
and he was gifted with a clear legal mind. It was impossible for
Burton to attack Cleveland in the indiscriminate manner of many
of the Republican orators of that campaign. His speeches frankly
expressed his respect for Cleveland's courage, his intellect, and his
patriotism.

Benjamin Harrison was an excellent candidate. In sharp contrast to Cleveland, he had background and traditions. His grandfather was President William Henry Harrison and an earlier forebear was a signer of the Declaration of Independence. He was a
trained lawyer, a cultured gentleman, the possessor of a poised and
unemotional temperament and his platform manner was as winning as his private manner was cold. One term as United States
Senator from Indiana had added to his reputation as a sound and
adroit reasoner. He was pre-eminently a "safe" man and had the
strategic advantage of coming from Indiana, generally regarded
as a doubtful state. His personal character was unassailable.

The Republicans seemed to have secured a slender majority in
the House—though it was too narrow for partisan comfort. Anyhow, the Democrats were out, the Republicans were in, and President Harrison was a "good party man" who could be relied upon
to throw the Democratic job-holders into the discard. Here was a
kind of co-operation certain to count in making the country once
more safe for Republicanism.

Theodore Burton packed his trunk for Washington.

CHAPTER 6

Burton's Congressional Baptism:
"The Famous Fifty-first Congress"

WHEN THEODORE BURTON went to the Capitol in the winter of 1889 to begin his first term as a national Representative, Destiny generously decreed him a novitiate in the most brilliant, dramatic, and historic Congress of his time—"The Famous Fifty-first."

This was the Congress in which Tom Reed led his sensational revolt against ancient forms of procedure, blazed the way for real majority rule, and reset the machinery of legislation in the lower house of Congress to a speed required to deal with the vast volume of business which the expansion of the country was soon to force upon it.

At the time when Burton, the tall, slender, and serious young lawyer, walked down the center aisle of the House and took the oath, he was without legislative experience except for his one uneventful term in the City Council of Cleveland. He had never watched the proceedings of either house of Congress as a gallery spectator. There was in his mind, however, the memory of one legislative scene which had influenced the course of his life.

On a visit to Europe, in the early eighties, he had secured admission to the gallery of the House of Commons in the hope that he might see Gladstone, "The Great Commoner," for whom he had a strong admiration. At this sitting he was privileged to hear one of the most eloquent speeches "The Thunderer" ever delivered.

Young Burton was then enjoying a thriving law practice and had every reason to expect that ultimately the law would yield him fortune, distinction, and probably high judicial honors. But this speech of Gladstone's swept him out of the law and into a legislative career. From that instant, his face was set toward Congress. Mr. Gladstone's address so profoundly impressed him that years later he was able to repeat its peroration, word for word, without having once referred to it in print.

The Fifty-first Congress, which gave Burton his legislative baptism, was a maelstrom of party warfare. The exciting possibilities of his new position revealed themselves almost immediately. He soon received a summons to attend a Republican caucus for the selection of a party candidate for Speaker.

Four men of national reputation were contestants for that honor: Major William McKinley, of Ohio; Joseph G. Cannon, of Illinois; Thomas B. Reed, of Maine, and David B. Henderson, of Iowa. The four were about evenly matched in the number of votes at their command. Since he was from Ohio and had a slight acquaintance with Major McKinley and an immense admiration for him, it was natural that the new member from Cleveland would cast his vote for McKinley. Here was the first test of his party regularity.

In the hours preceding the caucus he had been fascinated by the huge figure, piercing brown eyes, and remarkable poise of Tom Reed. Instantly he recognized that Reed possessed peculiar qualifications for the position of Speaker, particularly in a House having a meager Republican majority and therefore destined to fierce conflict between the representatives of the two leading parties. In Reed Burton saw a fighter of high courage and mental agility. Major McKinley, he knew, was able—but also amiable, almost to the point of gentleness.

Burton felt that the Speaker's chair was not the place in which to enthrone amiability. He wanted to cast his first caucus vote for Tom Reed, but realized that to do so would be an affront to the Republicans of his state. Major McKinley was already regarded as Presidential timber and any move by Burton which did not play up to this possibility would be an act of political suicide.

A few hours before the caucus was to convene, another new member, also undergoing his legislative baptism in "The Famous Fifty-first," was called upon by Theodore Roosevelt, then a Civil Service commissioner, who exclaimed:

"Hansbrough, I met you out in Dakota—remember? By jove, you're *my* Congressman and I want you to vote in the caucus for Tom Reed."

"Yes," responded Hansbrough, "I've seen you busting broncos

at Glendive—and you sure can ride 'em, cowboy! But I've already pledged General Cogswell, of Salem, that I'd cast my first vote for Henderson, of Iowa. However, if Henderson drops out of the running, I'll switch to Reed."

Hansbrough did switch to Reed and carried three other votes with him. This helped in nominating Reed and in depriving McKinley of the Speakership.

In describing this incident to the writer, Senator Hansbrough remarked:

"Shortly before that caucus, Tom Reed slouched down beside me, chatted about various things, but said not a word about the Speakership. I had the feeling that he would have shown this friendliness quite as readily if he had not been a candidate. Politics develop many strange quirks and coincidences. Certainly here was one of them: Roosevelt—destined to become McKinley's running mate at the head of the Republican ticket, in 1896, and to succeed him as President—helped to turn the trick that defeated McKinley for the Speakership in 1889.

"As Chairman of the Ways and Means Committee, McKinley brought out the tariff bill bearing his name which is generally credited with making him the nominee of his party for President. It seems quite probable that if McKinley had been elected Speaker, he would not have been nominated and elected President."

The Cleveland *Leader* carried a graphic story of that memorable day in the life of Theodore Burton—the opening of the Fifty-first Congress on December 2, 1889. In part, the article reads:

Long before noon to-day the spacious galleries of both Senate and House were crowded to their utmost capacity with spectators. . . . In either house the ladies' galleries were filled with the fair sex, attired in the newest winter fashions. The many colors of gown, and wrap, and bonnet, and plume presented a variegated scene that was charming to the eye. . . .

For an hour before the opening, in both halls, men were buzzing about like a swarm of bees, exchanging kindly greetings with old acquaintances and forming new ones among the novices in statesmanship. In all this there was no politics, no North, no South, no East, no West. Lodge, of Massachusetts and Martin, of Texas, Perkins, of Kansas, and Hemphill, of South Carolina, clasped hands in friendly recognition. The friction will come later.

Big "Tom" Reed—as everybody calls him—was the central figure in the crowd that filled the hall of the House. He was on deck early, his fat, round face beaming like a full moon in June. During the hour or two before the opening he shook hands with probably a thousand persons. Republicans and Democrats, with equal cordiality, presented their compliments and congratulations upon his success in the contest for the custodianship of the gavel. Ohio's "young Napoleon," who met his Waterloo on Saturday, and the other defeated candidates for Speaker were all in most gracious mood and enduring with the utmost fortitude the good-natured chaffing of their fellow members. . . .

When the gavel fell, those who were members of the last Congress dropped for the time being into their old seats, the new members distributing themselves around in a miscellaneous way in the seats made vacant by the last Congressional election. . . . Hon. T. E. Burton found a temporary resting place in the back row on the Republican side. . . .

There were no fireworks in the nominations for Speaker. General Henderson, of Illinois, a sturdy old soldier, with gray mustache and black hair, in studied phrase presented the name of Thomas B. Reed, of Maine, whereat there was a clapping of hands on the Republican side. Then McCreary, of Kentucky, smooth-faced and dapper, nominated John G. Carlisle. The Democrats, in greeting the name of their setting sun, very decidedly outdid the Republicans. They clapped their hands loudly and long, again and again. A stranger would have thought that Carlisle was going to be elected. . . .

The Republicans had another inning, when, after the tedious call of the roll, the election of Mr. Reed was declared, and again when, a moment later, he emerged from an anteroom and passed down the main aisle to the desk under convoy of McKinley and Carlisle. . . . The election of a Speaker requires a majority of the whole House, and Reed received precisely the necessary number. . . .

There is always a good deal of fun in the drawing for choice of seats. All the members withdraw to the space behind the last row, while balls the size of small marbles, numbering from 1 to 335, the total of members from the States and Territories, are placed in a box and drawn out one at a time by a blindfolded page. As each number is called the corresponding name is called from an alphabetical list, and that number is then at liberty to chose any seat not already taken. . . .

About half of the Ohio men were called early, and fared well.

Caldwell, of Cincinnati, was first of them, then Grosvenor, and then McKinley, who was vociferously applauded as he went to just the seat he wanted, immediately in front of that formerly occupied by Reed, of Maine. Burton was unlucky, being next to the last of the Ohio men, and within a dozen of the end of the list. He had to content himself with a seat in next to the last row near the wall, flanked on the right by Cheatham, of North Carolina, the only colored member. General Kennedy, of Ohio, was the very last of all, and he had only "Hobson's choice," which was a seat over among the goats on the Democratic side, where they have as little love for him as for any Republican in the House. There was a great laugh when Thomas B. Reed's name was drawn. He appeared to be fully satisfied with the seat he already had in the Speakership chair.

It was fortunate for the freshman Representative from Cleveland that the historic "Quorum Storm" did not break upon the House until late in January, nearly eight weeks after the opening of Congress, for the delay gave Burton opportunity to take stock of the men with whom he would be associated.

On the Democratic side of the aisle were Charles F. Crisp, of Georgia; William M. Springer, of Illinois; John G. Carlisle and William C. P. Breckinridge, of Kentucky; Richard P. Bland, of Missouri; Amos J. Cummings, of New York; Roger Q. Mills and David B. Culberson, of Texas.

On the Republican side the men of conspicuous ability were: Joseph G. Cannon, Robert R. Hitt, and Albert J. Hopkins, of Illinois; William S. Holman, of Indiana; David B. Henderson and Jonathan P. Dolliver, of Iowa; Nelson Dingley and Charles A. Boutelle, of Maine; Henry Cabot Lodge, of Massachusetts; William McKinley and Benjamin Butterworth, of Ohio; William D. Kelley and John Dalzell, of Pennsylvania.

Among those in that House who had not yet won their spurs were perhaps a score who, like Burton himself, were destined ultimately to become Senators and make national reputations. The House in which Burton found himself was exceptionally able.

When Burton attended his first caucus, at the outset of the Fifty-first Congress, the Republicans faced a perilous party situation. On the face of the returns they had a majority of six in the House which, under the rules then operative, was little better than a tie. The members of the minority, by the simple expedient of refusing to answer when their names were called, could force the decision from the Chair that a quorum was not present and that the business of the House could not proceed.

In a word, enforcement of the "no quorum present" rule in the House provided the minority there with an effective weapon for defeating the will of the majority. Today it is difficult to realize the stress then placed upon party loyalty. The success of the party was the supreme consideration of the men on both sides of the aisle. The Civil War was still fresh in the minds of all members of that Congress, most of whom had personally participated in it, in one way or another. They had, therefore, a wartime code of loyalty to "the cause" which required unquestioned obedience to the high command of leaders.

The responsibility of Speaker Reed and his lieutenants was to enable the Republicans to put through the program of legislation which they had been elected to enact. Evidently, there was only one way of doing this—that of exploding the traditional quorum rule. This could not be accomplished unless the number of Republicans in the House was materially increased, which seemed to some an impossibility—but not to Tom Reed.

Reed had courage, audacity, and resourcefulness. Throughout his life, Burton delighted to talk of Reed and spend upon him a wealth of adjectives which he withheld from all others.

For about two months Skipper Reed allowed the Republican ship to drift easily before the wind. No legislation of a party character was put forward, no change in rules was attempted, and the Speaker governed the House by what he was pleased to term "general parliamentary law," instead of specific rules reported and adopted, according to the general practice of the House at the opening of a new Congress.

Meantime, the number of election contests for seats increased. In districts where Democrats had been elected over Republican opponents by slender majorities, the disappointed contestants would appeal to the House commanded by the resourceful Reed. The Republicans had to build up a safe working majority and they did so from these contests, which numbered about thirty.

On January 29, 1890, every Republican was in his seat. The number physically present constituted an actual quorum. Two less than that number responded to the roll call. The matter before the House was a report from the Election Committee unseating a Demo-

crat and giving his place to the contesting Republican. The drive
to provide the Republicans with a working majority in the Fifty-
first Congress had started! In a quiet and almost casual manner the
Speaker said:

"The Chair directs the clerk to record the names of the following
members present and refusing to vote." Almost before the House
realized what was taking place the Speaker had named a considerable number of silent Democrats. The scene which then took place
has been described to the writer by William Tyler Page, at that
time Assistant Keeper of the Archives of the House, and later
Clerk.

"The entire Democratic side of the House arose as one man and
shouted epithets at the Speaker, all of them unparliamentary in
character and most of them unprintable. The mildest of them were:
'Czar!' 'Tyrant!' 'Scoundrel!' 'Autocrat!' Meantime they moved en
masse toward the Speaker's rostrum. There was every indication
that violence to the Speaker might result.

"Meantime the Republican members sat quietly in their seats
watching the mob scene. At the steps the Sergeant-at-arms and his
deputies met the enraged Democrats and turned them back. Before
the retreat, however, the Speaker had looked every one of the
leaders squarely in the eye. Apparently this had quite as much
effect in forcing a retreat as did the presentation of the mace in
the hands of the Sergeant-at-arms and the presence of the strong
force of deputies. Under the spell of that gaze the enraged Democrats one by one turned back and took their seats.

"Then, with both hands grasping the head of his gavel, Speaker
Reed drawled: 'The House will be in order.' This was the signal
for the Republicans to rise and cheer the Speaker for at least five
minutes."

Of course there was an appeal to the House on this revolutionary
ruling and it was bitterly debated. The Speaker's decision rested
upon the fact that the Constitution gave the House the power to
compel the attendance of members and that the exercise of this
power would be an empty gesture if, after a member had been
brought into the Hall of Representatives by an officer of the House,
he was then privileged to be recorded as absent simply by failing to
respond to his name on roll call.

The flood of abuse poured out upon Reed seemed only to add to
his urbanity. No taunt could sting him into any reply which lacked

suavity and judicial poise. He was playing for a great stake—the power of the Republican Party to enact the legislation to which it was pledged. Then, too, there was the possibility that if his daring parliamentary adventure succeeded, it might eventually make him President of the United States. What his followers did not know was that he had all arrangements made, if he failed, to resign immediately and practice law with Elihu Root.*

The debate lasted for about three days and then came the deciding vote. For a time the result was far from certain. But eventually the roll call showed that not a Republican had "deserted the standard."

Then the Committee on Rules, of which the Speaker was chairman, reported a new set of rules framed to kill filibustering in the House and prohibiting the Speaker from entertaining a dilatory motion.

In commenting upon this historic parliamentary battle, William Tyler Page relates:

> It had been a common thing until Reed's time for a minority, political or numerical, to hold up the House in a filibuster by dilatory tactics and by refraining from answering to a roll call for the avowed purpose of breaking a quorum. On one occasion the House was held continuously impotent for two weeks by these filibustering tactics. . . .
>
> The old rules gave privilege to certain motions, made some preferential to others. By the adroit handling of these privileged motions it was possible to construct a labyrinth of interference and delay. Each step involved a roll call which became merely a time-consuming device—for the members of the minority would refuse to answer to their names and thus break a quorum. . . .
>
> This parliamentary warfare would sometimes continue night and day without cessation until a responsible majority would be forced, from sheer physical exhaustion, to capitulate to the minority and enter into a compromise which would permit the transaction of business. What Speaker Reed did in the Fifty-first Congress was to change quorum-counting from a fictional to a factual basis. He established the validity of what he termed a "Constitutional quorum" as distinguished from an "articulate quorum."
>
> One of the amusing incidents of those days when Speaker Reed and his trusty crew were building up a safe Republican majority in the House, was the suddenness with which Democratic members

* Samuel W. McCall, *The Life of Thomas Brackett Reed*. Boston, 1914.

involved in election contests were unseated and Republicans put in their places. . . . The Democrat who, on the face of the returns, had been seated in the House of Representatives found that, in the course of a few moments of relaxation in the cloak room, his seat had been snatched from under him and a Republican firmly planted in it. There was no denying that these cases were decided primarily on political, not judicial, grounds. This wholesale eviction of Democrats was simply a matter of extreme partisan necessity. Of course, in each case the Committee brought in a report which served as a plausible basis for ousting a Democrat and seating the Republican.

I do not think there was any Republican member of the House who enjoyed this violent eviction of Democrats less than did Theodore Burton. . . . "No pleasure in the death of the wicked" would have expressed his feelings rather aptly. . . . The sour and shocked expression of his face indicated his distaste for the unjudicial character of these proceedings. But he was as helpless as a child to do anything about it. . . . Clearly, practical politics as it obtained in the House of Representatives under the rule of Tom Reed was decidedly out of line with his expectations.

Important consequences were involved in Speaker Reed's quorum-counting decision. The legality of all legislation after January 29, 1890, might depend upon the soundness of the reasoning upon which it rested. However, the validity of Reed's device was upheld by the Supreme Court of the United States in connection with an action challenging the McKinley Tariff Bill. The Court held that it could not go beyond the Journal of the House, which recorded that a Constitutional quorum had been present.

Into this Congress flowed a strong current of "wild blood" from the West which exerted a strong influence upon Theodore Burton. Among the friends he made in this Congress was the dashing Henry Clay Hansbrough, of North Dakota, who had been so instrumental in saving the day for Reed. His career as a national legislator was almost uniquely picturesque and stormy. Instantly, the two young tyros of the House became friends. Theirs was the attraction of opposites. One was impulsive, adventurous, and tempestuous; the other cautious, reserved, calculating, but devoted to his carefully reasoned convictions. Hansbrough was a fiery political knight of the new order of Republicanism; Burton, a sober, quiet student of the principles of sound, practical government.

In a letter to the writer, Senator Hansbrough recounted certain incidents of "the Tom Reed Congress" which are revealing as to young Burton's attitude toward problems of that day.

In my contact with Theodore Burton I gained the impression that, elementally, he was inclined to independent thought and action, a bit resentful of arbitrary control on matters offending his strong convictions. . . . This opinion is not based upon anything Burton said in private to members of the western group but rather upon the pleased expression on his face when the Democrats peeled the glamour off the "full dinner pail," and the uneasy attitude when sarcastic John Allen flayed the policy of "creating monopolies with one hand only to knock them down with the other." Of course he referred to the McKinley Tariff measure in the House and the Sherman Antitrust resolution in the Senate. Burton was not the only one on the Republican side who winced and twisted under this thrust. . . .

Anyhow, there were independent-minded Republicans in the Fifty-first Congress, among them no less personages than Tom Reed, Bob La Follette, Tom Carter, and Theodore Burton—not to mention myself. One day, in the Speaker's room, Carter and I sought to quiz Reed in regard to reciprocity. We knew of his predilections in this direction. He believed, as did James G. Blaine, in more liberal trade relations with foreign countries. The independent-minded group were all for making reciprocity the leading feature of the McKinley bill. Reed was upon the point of giving expression to his views when Burton entered.

"Welcome to the conference!" drawled Reed with a laugh. "Perhaps you can tell these gentlemen about the 'Ohio idea,' whatever it may turn out to be."

"The full dinner pail and things like that!" added Carter, with a note of irony.

"But," smilingly responded Burton, "isn't there a bit of danger in overfilling the bucket?"

"There," exclaimed Reed, "you have the answer to your questions!"

Burton's reply to Carter's jab at the full dinner pail has left the impression on my mind that his party shackles were somewhat irksome at times; that he was a man of conviction as well as of discretion. His Cleveland district fairly seethed with high-tariff heat, as did the newly admitted states of the West. No matter what were the innermost sentiments of Senators and Representatives on this subject, to have given public expression to anti-high-tariff ideas would have spelled defeat at the next election.

Mr. Hansbrough's entrance into the House was peculiar in that his political influence was greater, before he took the oath, than that of many a veteran member. He was already a member of the Republican National Committee, had wielded a strong influence in nominating Benjamin Harrison for President, and had led the battle to divide Dakota Territory into two states, thereby bringing into Congress four Republican Senators. These were major political achievements.

Just a year and four months after he was sworn in as a House member, he was privileged to walk up the long corridor into the Senate and be received as a member. There he remained continuously for eighteen years.

One of Hansbrough's achievements greatly impressed Burton. This was the passage of a bill which Hansbrough introduced prohibiting the use of the United States mails by lottery companies. The lottery companies had been driven out of Louisiana, where their operations had debauched the politics of the state and created a national scandal. They needed a new base of operations.

Because the population of North Dakota was relatively small and its people had the tolerant attitude characteristic of most pioneer Western sections, the lottery interests decided to dig in there. It was not difficult for their agents quietly to elect a legislature favorable to their purposes. Settlers were in need of cash and many were easily convinced that it would be a good thing for the state to have millions of dollars pouring into it from all over the country for lottery tickets.

Hansbrough, however, had the vision to see that a franchise to the lotteries would corrupt the politics of the state and give it a bad reputation. Therefore he announced that he would oppose a lottery franchise and would run for the United States Senate in opposition to a Senator who was believed to be in favor of allowing the lotteries to entrench themselves in North Dakota.

But on becoming a member of the House, he learned that his efforts to save his state from this disgrace were likely to fail. Then he had an inspiration. In the older states sentiment against lotteries was stronger than in his own. Therefore, he introduced a bill denying the use of the United States mails to lottery companies.

The strategy of the situation, so far as the lottery interests were concerned, was that when his bill came before the House, if it could be sidetracked or buried in a committee, the legislature of North Dakota would have an opportunity to grant the franchise.

The Cleveland *Plain Dealer* of May 3, 1914, records Burton's recollections of these stirring events of the Fifty-first Congress. "I remember a dramatic incident, in 1890, in the House of Representatives. A bill forbidding the use of the mails by lottery companies was pending. No one opposed it, though a single company engaged in this business would no doubt have paid hundreds of thousands of dollars if the measure could have been defeated. Time for consideration was assigned on a Saturday afternoon—and there was no quorum present.

"When the discussion was completed a viva-voce vote was taken and no one raised his voice in opposition. But two members arose simultaneously and asked for a division—that is, that those who favored the measure should stand up and then those who opposed it. Such a vote would have disclosed the fact that less than a quorum was present and the bill probably would not have been considered again at that session.

"Not a word was said, but in the press gallery reporters for papers were waiting to send the news that these two men had prevented the passage of the bill. The atmosphere was surcharged with suspicion and almost immediately the men who made the request for a division withdrew it. The bill went through and later became a law."

Senator Matthew S. Quay managed the measure in the Senate. Meantime, Hansbrough had announced that he would run for the Senate as an opponent of the lotteries. He was elected and eventually the Senate passed the bill which permanently outlawed lotteries in the United States.

With firm control of the legislative machinery, the Republican majority proceeded to pass legislation of great importance, including the McKinley Tariff Act and the Sherman Antitrust Act. Six states were admitted to the Union—all from the West—North Dakota, South Dakota, Montana, Washington, Idaho, and Wyoming. Evidently Speaker Reed and his followers were of the opinion that these new states would provide a bulwark of strength for the Republican Party in Congress. They were later to learn that they were endowing the Republican Party with endless trouble and dissension within its own ranks. The Senators and Representatives from these new states proved to be thorns in the flesh for Republican leaders.

The most violently debated measure of this Congress was a law offered by Representative Lodge, of Massachusetts, providing for the holding of elections in the "restored" Southern states under the supervision of United States marshals. This bill was a hangover from the black era of Reconstruction. It was the last of the political-control measures directed against the states which had seceded and was known as the Force Bill.

Inevitably, this bill enraged the Southern members, who regarded it as an assault upon the freedom of the ballot in their states and a gratuitous insult to their honor. It was, in their opinion, simply a Northern device to perpetuate the Republican Party in power. A large proportion of the Republican members also regarded it as unnecessarily offensive to the Southern people. In the Republican caucus it secured endorsement by the narrowest possible margin.

Once accepted as a Republican measure, however, it was given full Republican support on the floor of the House and demonstrated the almost perfect control which Speaker Reed exercised over the Republican organization in Congress. By various adroit tactics the Democrats contrived to prolong the consideration of the bill, but they were up against the new Reed Rules and the bill was finally forced to a vote and passed by a small majority. In the Senate, Arthur P. Gorman, of Maryland, began a determined filibuster against it which was finally successful. This made him the hero of the South and no bill of this character was ever again attempted.

Theodore Burton enjoyed such fiery and exciting debates, but was content to keep out of them. His greatest interest in the proceedings of that Congress centered in the preliminary "battle of the metals," the first major engagement between the defenders of the gold standard and the silver crusaders. At that time, most of the members of both houses of Congress were disciples of the doctrine of bimetallism.

Here was a subject which challenged the interest of the economics-minded young member from Cleveland. It was apparent to him that there was an amazing amount of loose thinking in Congress on the subject of national currency and finance. In his opinion, the supremacy of economic law over Congressional enactments was not fully appreciated by national legislators.

Many of the Western states were producing great quantities of silver and looked to the Government of the United States as the Heaven-appointed market for this metal. They were able to have things much their own way because of the general attitude favoring bimetallism. Those Eastern Republicans who had clear convictions that bimetallism was unsound were not in a position to press this conviction and considered it discreet to give the plan a "fair trial" on the theory that the price of farm products would move in sympathy with the market price of silver.

Hence, a bill known in the House as the Conger Bill, but later generally referred to as the Sherman Silver Purchase Act, was passed. It instructed the Secretary of the Treasury to purchase monthly 4,500,000 ounces of silver bullion at the market price, to be coined into silver dollars of 386 grains fineness, and to issue against these silver dollars treasury certificates and treasury notes redeemable in silver or gold at the option of the holder.

This act was a compromise measure framed to appease the advocates of the free coinage of silver, who were extremely strong. President Harrison was a gold-standard man and could have vetoed a measure for the free coinage of silver, but his party did not wish to invite defeat by an act so offensive to the silver states. Therefore Speaker Reed and his Republican lieutenants decided to pass a compromise calculated to soothe the free-silver enthusiasts. This was the bill of which Reed later said:

"That it then and there saved this country from the free coinage for which every Democratic leader was then clamoring and on which they are now silent I do know." *

Of course this law made silver mining immensely profitable and the silver-producing states realized great riches from their output of "white gold." For a time, the prices of farm products followed the price of silver, as had been predicted, and ultimately the price of silver bullion rose to a pinnacle of $1.33 an ounce. Mountains of silver dollars were accumulating in the vaults of the Treasury and the silver certificates and treasury notes issued against them were covering the country like a flood.

The silver purchase clause of the Silver Purchase Act was mandatory and inflexible. The Secretary of the Treasury could not check the tremendous flood of silver—only the repeal of the clause would make that possible. Here, let it be emphasized that the Act

* McCall, *Thomas B. Reed.*

stipulated that holders of silver certificates could demand their redemption in gold if they preferred it to silver. The result was that the gold reserve of the Treasury was raided and depleted. The gold thus passing into the hands of the people immediately went into hoarding and the Secretary of the Treasury was helpless to abate this gold raid. His only means of maintaining the gold reserve was to sell bonds.

William Jennings Bryan, who entered Congress on March 4, 1891, brought forward a demand upon the Secretary of the Treasury that these obligations of the government should be redeemed in silver instead of gold. The Secretary of the Treasury refused to comply with this request on the ground that it would take the nation off the gold standard and place it on a silver basis.

Consternation swept the country. Silver bullion dropped on the open market from the peak of 133 to 38, which automatically converted the government's silver certificates into fiat money, save for the actual market value of the silver bullion which they represented.

This Battle of the Metals which started in the Fifty-first Congress did not reach its climax until 1893, when Grover Cleveland succeeded Benjamin Harrison as President.

Meantime, the general election of 1890 had brought overwhelming defeat to the Republicans and swept Theodore Burton out of his seat. He was succeeded by Tom Johnson, the millionaire single-tax Democrat whom he had defeated in the previous election. The House which followed the Reed Congress contained only eighty-eight Republicans.

This sweeping Democratic victory was a typical panic-depression political revulsion. The Reed Congress, the first in history to spend a billion dollars, was charged with reckless extravagance. To this, Reed made his famous retort that the United States was "a billion dollar country"—a clever and characteristic answer which, for the moment, was widely applauded. But this surge of national self-satisfaction was short lived.

From the first administration of Grover Cleveland the Treasury had inherited a surplus of nearly a hundred million dollars. The probabilities were that this surplus would continue to grow.

It was a temptation to the party in power—as a surplus has always been to politicians of every party. Mr. Reed and his followers so handled the surplus that it would not by any accident fall into the hands of Democrats.

The Dependent Pension Bill, vetoed by President Cleveland in his first administration, was passed and signed by President Harrison. Of this Harry Thurston Peck, in his *Twenty Years of the Republic*, wrote:

"At once the number of pensioners rose from about 350,000 to nearly 550,000 and steadily increased until, ten years later, it had reached a million; while the yearly payments grew from $65,000,000 to $150,000,000, representing nearly half the entire annual budget of the United States."

The main cause of the defeat suffered by the Republicans in the Congressional campaign of 1890 was the instantaneous jump in the price of commodities after the enactment of the McKinley Tariff. The ink of the President's signature on that measure was scarcely dry when the advance in general living costs set in with a terrifying sweep. Vast importing activities started the instant when the enactment of the McKinley Tariff became a certainty. There was a hectic rush to bring into this country every possible shipment of goods before the duties levied in the tariff measure went into effect.

"The Cunard Steamer *Etruria*," says one historian, "reaching the port of New York a few minutes before the hour set for the enforcement of the McKinley Bill, saved by her speed something like a million dollars for the owners of her cargo." [*]

Although merchants loudly proclaimed that their advantage in beating the duty deadline would be passed on to the consuming public, the voters of the country discounted this assurance. They reasoned that by the time these goods could reach them from the shelves of the retailers they would be in luck to have any share in the importers' savings, and the wage advance which they had been promised as the result of this high protection measure did not show the speed of the price advance in commodities. They felt themselves in the grip of a price pinch and therefore they took it out on the Republican Party, which had enacted the highest protective tariff measure in the history of the country.

Republican counsels had been far from unanimous as to the wisdom of a number of the high duties embodied in the McKinley Tariff. James G. Blaine, then Secretary of State in President Har-

[*] Harry Thurston Peck, *Twenty Years of the Republic*. New York, 1906.

rison's Cabinet, had resisted scores of them to the utmost of his power.

Also, he shrewdly urged the adoption of the "reciprocity" principle. Under this, we were to admit without duty certain products of foreign countries which we needed and did not produce—this advantage to be "swapped" for the admission, duty free, into those countries, of certain of our own products which we could export to our profit. Secretary Blaine constantly bombarded Mr. McKinley with appeals to adopt his reciprocity plan, but with little success.

Whenever an important item came up for consideration by his committee, McKinley was likely to receive a frank note from Secretary Blaine. A good example is the following letter.*

Washington, April 10, 1890

Dear Mr. McKinley:

It is a great mistake to take hides from the free list, where they have been for so many years.

It is a slap in the face to the South Americans, with whom we are trying to enlarge our trade. It will benefit the farmer by adding five to eight per cent to the price of his children's shoes.

It will yield a profit to the butcher only—the last man that needs it. The movement is injudicious from beginning to end—in every form and phase.

Pray stop it before it sees light. Such movements as this for protection will protect the Republican Party into a speedy retirement.

Very hastily,

James G. Blaine

All of Mr. Blaine's predictions regarding the prospective revolt of the people against the McKinley Tariff were realized. McKinley, high priest of high protection, was defeated for Congress in 1890 in a district supposed to be burning with admiration for its local statesman.

The Sherman Antitrust Act was one of the most important measures ever enacted by Congress. It was used in disciplining a number of the most powerful and highhanded corporations in the country and in preventing them from crushing their competitors and exercising an autocratic control over prices. Senator John Sherman, from whom this act takes its name, was almost an idol of the Ohio people—including Theodore Burton.

* Gail Hamilton, *Biography of James G. Blaine*. Norwich, Conn., 1895.

Apparently Burton was not proud of his well-disciplined vote for the McKinley Tariff Bill or the Silver Purchase measure, but he had every reason to be of his part in passing the Sherman Antitrust Act and the land legislation of 1890. The latter had rescued a hundred million acres of fertile Western lands from the clutches of the Union Pacific and other Western railroads and restored them to public settlement under the Homestead law. Thus an end was put to the railroads' exploitation of the Government's prodigal generosity of land grants to encourage the building of the first transcontinental railways. This measure met Burton's conception of statesmanship.

Burton's support of the Hansbrough Bill outlawing lotteries was another House enactment of his first term in Congress that gave him satisfaction. While the Senate did not pass this law until he had been swept out of office by the wave of popular resentment following the enactment of the McKinley Tariff, he had done his part in ridding the country of this debauching institution.

In the meantime, Burton was learning that the life of a Congressman was not altogether serene. The committees to which he had been appointed were a disappointment. Only a few weeks after his arrival in Washington he had written to Speaker Reed as follows:

HOUSE OF REPRESENTATIVES U. S.

Washington, D. C. December 16, 1889

Hon. Thomas B. Reed,
My dear Sir:
In accordance with your kind suggestion, I will state my preferences as to assignment upon Committees. I am satisfied the best assignment for me, viewing the condition of things in my own district and my standing at home, would be the Committee on Commerce. It is my decided wish that you may see your way clear to place me upon this Committee. Next in order, I think, would be Post Offices and Post Roads. . . .

Yours very respectfully,
(SIGNED) T. E. Burton

Mr. Reed, however, had other plans for Burton. The young Congressman found himself a member of the Committee on the District of Columbia. Speaker Reed also assigned Burton to the Claims and Expenditures in the Navy Committee.

The Committee on Claims was regarded as the graveyard of committee assignments. However, it was characteristic of Theodore Burton to make his service on this committee the means of gaining the attention and respect of the House. The story of how he accomplished this was related to the writer by William Tyler Page.

Immediately following the assignment of members to committees, Mr. Burton came into my room and in a hesitant and almost diffident manner asked if I knew anything about the claims which had not been disposed of by the Committee of Claims in preceding sessions. I laughed aloud at this question and replied that I thought I could oblige him with quite an accumulation of documents of that character. . . .

Then I explained to him that it was the traditional habit of members unfortunate enough to receive assignments to this committee to treat their responsibilities in this connection as a joke and to make a mere gesture of investigating the hundreds of accumulated claims. . . .

Very quietly he asked me if he might be permitted to take a number of these claims to his desk for examination during the day, returning them to my custody each evening. . . . I confess that I entertained a lively sense of mischief in taking from these shelves stacks of dusty and discolored documents—all I could carry at a load. My idea was to discourage him, at the outset, from wasted industry.

Instead, he smilingly thanked me, seated himself at his desk and took from the top of the huge stack of claims the first one that came to his hand. . . .

Every moment when the proceedings of the House did not demand his attention he applied himself doggedly to the examination of these ancient claims, many of which originated in Civil War times and some of them very much earlier. Here, to me, was a new kind of Congressman! . . .

In one of the few quiet days of that stormy session . . . I saw Mr. Burton arise and ask the Speaker for the privilege of presenting to the House a report from the Committee on Claims. In a clear, melodious voice, easily audible throughout the House, he proceeded to make his report. . . .

Gradually the hum and confusion of the House subsided; the members apparently were reacting to the spell of this new voice. . . . His presentation of each case followed in orderly method: first, a clear, crisp and concise statement of the facts involved and next a brief but logical presentation of his conclusions drawn from these facts. When he sat down, I heard one influential member of the House remark to a little group of his colleagues: "We're going to hear from that young man."

The vote on his recommendations indicated conclusively that this opinion was shared by his colleagues generally. Almost to a man, they were impressed with his ability and his soundness merely from his report on a mass of musty old claims. This was something of a miracle and had, I was told, never happened before in the history of the house. . . .

From that moment Mr. Burton was on a new footing with his colleagues and, apparently, also with Speaker Reed and his chief-lieutenants on the floor. . . .

The documents exhumed from the Claims Committee archives abounded in annals of delays and disappointments which had brought hardship, disaster, and heartache, vividly illustrating the apparent futility of attempts by humble private citizens to secure from the Government payment of claims admittedly just but allowed to drift without final settlement.

Here was the case of a Revolutionary soldier who not only fought for his country, but, out of his savings, lent "considerable sums" of money to the Continental Government. He had been paid, in part, in counterfeit and otherwise worthless Continental currency. Two spinsters, granddaughters of the original claimant, were petitioning their government to give them good money in exchange for the counterfeit which apparently it had unwittingly passed to their soldier ancestor more than a century before.

Another claim was for the bark, *General Berry*, chartered by the United States Government at the outbreak of the Civil War to carry quartermaster's stores from New York to Fortress Monroe. This was captured and destroyed by the Confederate cruiser, *Florida*, in July, 1864. Its value was more than forty thousand dollars. In those days that was quite a substantial fortune—but James Cooper, the owner of the bark, had been obliged to wait twenty-six years for the major part of this amount. Burton reported a bill for his payment.

But the classic example of governmental injustice was the case of Daniel C. Rodman, of Connecticut, who fought for the Union throughout the Civil War and then returned to his native state "to accept the position of Pension Agent, which he filled with that marked integrity which distinguished his whole life. Out of his savings as Pension Agent he purchased a small piece of property, and at the time of his death, in October, 1881, his whole estate inventoried about six thousand dollars." With five others, Colonel Rodman had become a surety on the bond of Ozias Morgan, Registrar of the land office at Tallahassee, Florida. When Morgan went out of office in 1870 his accounts were short $1,942. The Government secured judgment against five of the six sureties on Morgan's bond. One brought in $69.50. "In the other four cases," the record recited, "the District Marshal reported that the defendants were either dead, hopelessly insolvent or had absconded." In his lifetime Colonel Rodman received no official notification of his responsibility for the debt outstanding against Morgan. But twenty years after giving the bond and five years after Colonel Rodman's death, "the Government for the first time made a demand upon his estate to pay the deficit."

In the words of the report, "Now nothing remains on which to realize except the modest little homestead on which the widow lives, worth perhaps two thousand or three thousand dollars. Her pension of thirty dollars a month, together with her skill in sewing, enabled her to support her mother and an invalid sister." In his report that Colonel Rodman's widow be relieved from the claim of the Government against her husband's estate, Burton emphasized "the peculiar hardship to which Colonel Rodman's family would now be subjected" if the Government insisted upon taking its pound of flesh from the widow after it had slept on its technical rights in the matter for twenty years.

Burton was scrupulous and exact in his own business standards and practices; it had never occurred to him that Uncle Sam could be made to appear as either a deadbeat or a Shylock; but the history of many of the claims examined strikingly suggested these roles.

Burton's maiden speech was devoted to the silver question. He advocated the use of silver but opposed its "free and unlimited coinage." It was not a speech he could recall with entire satisfaction a few years later, when the lines between the gold-standard men and the silverites were more sharply drawn. But it should be remembered that bimetallism was then good Republican doctrine and the silver states were tenderly considered in Republican councils. Again, the Silver Purchase Act, then being promoted by Senator Sherman, was not regarded wholly as a matter of party strategy and expediency. The need of a greater volume of currency was pressing and the monetization of silver seemed a good way in which to meet that need.

Furthermore, it should be kept in mind that this "silver issue" was enveloped in confusion and uncertainty. The gold standard was yet to be securely enthroned.

Upon the occasion of Burton's first visit to Cleveland after taking office, his friends gave a reception in his honor. In a speech to his constituents he said that, to him, Cleveland was the dearest place on earth. He hoped that his errors would be considered "of the head and not of the heart." While he did not expect to be as pliable as some men, he desired "to pay the proper respect to the wishes of my constituents."

Following this speech there was, of course, great applause and a vote of endorsement of his record so far in Congress was taken. Generally speaking, Burton's conduct in the Fifty-first Congress had pleased the city of Cleveland.

Measures which he introduced early in the first session are suggestive of the main trend of his public service. These were bills or joint resolutions providing for a survey of a channel through the Great Lakes, for better regulations for the movement of lumber rafts, and for the operation of lighthouses, for the establishment of new lights, and the provision of lightships.

His first term was an intensive short course in political disillusionment. He had not flattered himself that his time, in the beginning, would be entirely absorbed with the larger problems of national and international statesmanship. However, he had not expected to serve his constituents exclusively as an angler for government jobs, a glorified national errand boy, or a Washington guide and entertainer for visiting Buckeyes.

A graphic picture of Burton at this time was given by the Washington correspondent of a Cleveland newspaper who attempted to keep up with him in this distasteful phase of his public service. After stating that Burton "ran his feet off" in chasing about for constituents, this correspondent wrote:

"I don't think I ever saw anybody who could get over more ground in a given time than he did. He didn't spend much money on cabs, but took the street cars when they were going his way, or went afoot. His stride is rather longer than the regulation army step, and unless it is pretty cold weather it will start the perspiration on you to keep up with him. Mr. Burton will find that his locomotive powers will be severely taxed before he gets through with his term. . . ."

Never was a prediction more completely realized. He was frankly disgusted with the demands that doing patronage chores made upon him.

Patronage became his pet aversion. How could a Representative in Congress make any worthwhile contribution to constructive legislation for his country when most of his time was at the mercy of petty office seekers? And the distribution of the larger patronage positions carried a burden of responsibility and worry out of all proportion to their importance in government administration.

In this connection it is interesting to read some of the newspaper comments—not all of them sympathetic by any means—on his appointments:

"Mr. Burton has been harassed by place hunters until his health is undermined."

And another regarding the appointment of postmaster at Berea, Ohio:

"Mr. Burton procured appointment of a civilian who is not a soldier when four of the other candidates equally worthy were members of Berea Post, G.A.R. . . . This action has alienated the support of the Grand Army Post of this district."

A fellow Congressman is quoted as saying: "I notice that Congressman Burton got into trouble over some of his appointments. Offices are dangerous shoals for the Congressman."

In a newspaper interview in 1892 to learn if Burton would again be a Congressional candidate, he was asked if he had enjoyed his first term. He replied:

"In many respects, I liked it, but from the very first . . . I found myself entirely prevented from giving consecutive attention to any other subject, because of the enormous demands made upon me in the way of patronage. Fifty callers each day, coming at all hours, was the rule, rather than the exception. Some of them were importunate, and were inclined to go away in a vindictive mood if their impracticable requests were not immediately complied with. . . .

"I have minutes of applications from thirteen hundred persons who wished me to obtain offices for them, and the actual number of applicants was much greater. The majority, without any specification as to experience, qualifications, or even preferences, simply asked for 'an office.' Those who did express their choice sought a variety of positions from cook at the White House to foreign ambassador. Aside from this there were a large number of claims and private interests of my constituents which involved a great burden and would have taken all my time if I had responded to them. . . .

"There are, on the average, twenty applicants or more for each position to be filled. Nineteen of these, with their friends, must be disappointed. Some of them will take their defeat with a great deal of bitterness."

From early boyhood he had hated "choring"—not because he was physically lazy but because other activities seemed so much more interesting and important. In seeking election to Congress he had not realized that a large part of his time would have to be devoted to this lowly and irksome form of political drudgery. His ingenuous vision of service in Congress was tinged with the glamour of "statesmanship." This viewpoint and ideal never deserted him.

CHAPTER 7

The Pork Barrel Produces
a Statesman

THE REAL APPRENTICESHIP of Theodore Burton as an economic statesman began with his appointment, by Speaker Reed, as a member of the Rivers and Harbors Committee of the Fifty-fourth Congress, on December 21, 1895. Here was solid meat, suited to his taste, into which he set his teeth with zest. Evidently Reed had not forgotten the industry and intelligence with which the young member from Cleveland had dug into the musty archives of the Committee of Claims.

Congressman Burton settled modestly into his chair at the foot of the big oval committee table from which millions of dollars of political fat had been dispensed to the faithful of both parties. He listened quietly to the talk of his seniors, asking an occasional question—otherwise keeping his own counsel.

His associates on the committee regarded him as a freshman who knew his place and would follow their lead without any attempt to upset the well-established routine. In a word, he was "regular." Before he had been with them more than a few weeks he demonstrated an insatiable appetite for information and hard work. His questions revealed that he had somehow acquired, in only a few weeks on the committee, an amazing knowledge of the projects under consideration, the engineers' reports, and the records of public hearings.

He betrayed no signs of bumptiousness, no urge to grab all he could for his own district, no inconvenient impulse to reform the Rivers and Harbors Committee and upset the fine adjustments of political logrolling which it had worked out over years of manipulation.

It seemed that a kind Providence, personified by Speaker Reed, had suddenly provided the committeemen with a research go-getter who was "a hound for facts," asking nothing more than the privilege of running them down, bringing them in, and dropping them on the committee table. Naturally this odd trait made the young recruit popular with his seniors.

He would be of great value in developing the facts of projects being urged upon them. Members of Congress who were not on the committee, "associations" of business interests, and lobbyists were constantly pressing for advantage upon the presumption that the committee members could not, by any possibility, "know everything." There were times when knowledge of the facts would protect the committee from mistakes.

Therefore, Theodore the Digger was a welcome addition to the committee, the older members of which had plenty to do without "wading catfish streams" which were, so the back-home folks hoped, to be transformed into "teeming arteries of water traffic." Here was a recruit of prodigious industry and a consuming desire to probe every creek, bayou, and river of the country and learn at firsthand every vital fact concerning its depth, flow, actual and potential traffic, and the population in its territory.

It is not to be inferred from this picture of the position in which Burton found himself that his associates on this important committee were not, as a rule, concerned with the sound development of the waterways of the country. They were. Undoubtedly they all desired this and would have preferred to do their work without having it complicated with political entanglements. But, in the slang of a later day, they were in a hot spot, in which they were forced to reconcile the interests of constructive expenditures for the upbuilding of commerce by water with the distribution of those expenditures to meet the demands of members of Congress who believed that securing an appropriation for a waterway "improvement" in their districts was essential to their continuation in office.

In many instances their constituents believed, often with good reason, that water commerce in their localities could be developed to an extent which would justify the investment and greatly increase the trade and prosperity of their sections. Of course, their representatives in Congress reflected this faith. Those were the days of large and general belief in water transportation and the miracles which it would perform.

Anti-railroad sentiment had become strong. Railroads charged too high a carrying rate. To secure their construction the United States Government had given the builders of the railroads a vast kingdom of the most fertile land in America and the railroad magnates had been ruthless, wanton, and arrogant in their exploitation of the government and the people. The consistent and country-wide development of water transportation, it was generally believed, would check the rapacity of the railroads and prevent them, through actual or potential water transportation competition, from extortions which threatened the development of extensive sections of the country.

In the main, Burton's apprenticeship on the Rivers and Harbors Committee in the sessions of 1895 and 1897 was devoted to study of the problems and processes of this kind of legislation and to mastering the technique of the task. On its political side it offered a constant exposition of the art of compromise, of placating members of Congress and business organizations who asked support for projects which were obviously absurd or at least momentarily impracticable. This committee was, in a sense, a clearing house of political hopes. It dealt the cards of politics with one hand and of waterway developments with the other—and made a study of synchronizing the two functions.

The record is clear that recognition of this necessity for offsets, adjustments, and compromises in order to achieve practical legislative results of value was a disappointment to Burton's idealistic line of thought. Members of a great legislative body, like the Congress of the United States, should, he felt, be influenced by reason rather than meaner considerations. But, it seemed they generally were not, and such considerations had to be taken into account when securing desirable legislation or when preventing legislation that was clearly undesirable. Repeatedly he heard one or another of his seniors, whose general intellectual honesty commanded his respect, grumble to the effect:

"I hate to hand out a dollar for that worthless Turkey Run project—but what can we do? The member from down there is as determined as the leader of his pack of bear hounds and he's held his seat for years by just this sort of thing. Besides, he's something of a leader of the whole Congressional delegation from his state and we've got to have their votes or there'll be trouble when the bill lands on the floor of the House. It goes against the grain, but I think we'll have to give him a dribble of a hundred thousand or two just to shut him up."

The first conclusion which occurred to Burton was that the method of developing the waterways of the country at an annual expense of millions of dollars should somehow be shifted from a political to a business basis. Also, he felt that the first practical step in accomplishing this was to outlaw "dribble" appropriations. Take the case of the hypothetical "Turkey Run" project, for example. Let it be assumed that it called for a total expenditure of half a million dollars, but its advocates would be content to secure an actual appropriation of $100,000 as a starter—comparatively an insignificant sum in a Rivers and Harbors Bill running high into the millions.

The project would have to come up again when another Rivers and Harbors Bill was framed and was likely to be ultimately abandoned. Meantime, the Congressman especially interested would be able to return to his people with something to pacify them. Also, the total cost of the doubtful project would not evoke criticism. Millions of dollars in future commitments were carried in the bill—and had been in each of its predecessors—in this manner.

When the device for eliminating this tricky and wasteful practice by changing the system of reporting projects and authorizations occurred to the committee's new recruit, he continued to keep his own counsel regarding it. Time enough to talk about it when he had gained a firmer foothold and greater influence.

He tackled it as a long-time job in which the soundest procedure was to make haste slowly, learn the business thoroughly, and be sure of his ground at every step.

Publicity along one line only was regarded by him as safe and helpful. This concerned his knowledge of facts regarding streams, harbors, and watercourse tonnage and his astounding memory. Newspaper correspondents found him indulgently responsive along these lines, but otherwise reticent.

He saw that he needed first to build up the confidence of his associates in his ability, his judgment, his knowledge of waterway problems, and particularly in his leadership.

The difficulties of changing the methods of Rivers and Harbors appropriations from a political basis to a business basis were increased by the fact that this dealing of the cards was, in large measure, a nonpartisan or bipartisan performance, which recog-

nized the brotherhood tie of a common hunger. Partisanship advantages were not supposed to be pressed to the limit in the dis-
pensation of good things at this festive board. The Democratic or
minority members of the committee at this time occupied the position of familiar guests at a family feast to whom generously hos-
pitable courtesies were not to be refused—as they might eventually
become the hosts.

Again, Burton held the conviction that projects were authorized
which would have been rejected had the committee been in
possession of all the facts. True, the committee held lengthy hearings and listened to witnesses who came primed to support projects
for their localities. These enthusiasts, of course, were subject to
questioning, but in the main, the questions failed to develop a strong
case against the projects under consideration.

Besides, these hearings were conducted under the guidance of
interested Senators and Representatives who were adepts in avoiding statements calculated to reveal the doubtful or impracticable
character of projects under debate.

The unofficial waterway improvement associations, officered by
shrewd men who devoted all their time to studying the problems
of waterway "improvements," played a conspicuous part in these
hearings. They acted as counsel for the plaintiffs. Their briefs and
strategy of procedure were planned with skill. Their business was
to promote waterway developments. They derived their support
from two general sources—firstly, from those who expected
legitimately to profit from the commercial use of the completed
projects, and, secondly, from dredging contractors and dealers involved in furnishing materials and machinery used in the construction of these "improvements." Other support came from those in
position to benefit from construction expenditures rather than
from the results in general community and commercial development.

At the outset of his apprenticeship, Burton recognized that there
was need for more information concerning the financial support
of these organizations which were devoting their energies to increasing the expenditures of the Federal Government for waterway
projects. In this opinion he did not stand alone. A number of House
members inclined to independent thought and action shared this
view and gave him valuable aid in securing information regarding

the contributions of individuals and companies who would get their returns directly from construction expenditures rather than from the general benefit resulting from completed projects.

Representative James A. Frear, of Wisconsin, was conspicuous among those members who held the conviction that waterway improvement associations, receiving the contributions of contractors and dealers in construction materials, machinery, and equipment, appearing before the committee and the Congress as advocates of waterway improvements, were not entitled to have their statements accepted as unprejudiced expressions of popular demand. He gave Burton consistent aid. In an interview with the writer, Mr. Frear said:

"To my mind, Burton's protest against items in the various Rivers and Harbors Bills was always based on incontrovertible facts. We were in accord on the principle that no organization receiving contributions from those who would directly profit from the construction rather than from the general public benefits of an improvement could come before the committee or the House with clean hands when assuming to urge improvements in the name of the public good.

"When large expenditures on any watercourse failed to develop a reasonable volume of commerce, he was sufficiently openminded to admit the fact and to oppose further waste of public funds.

"Mr. Burton's silence in going along with his party on a party measure which did not meet his unqualified approval was the accepted course of good men on both sides of the House aisle. On many occasions, however, he displayed vigorous independence, not to say something akin to insurgency.

"He worked obediently in the party harness up to the point where his convictions of right were overcrowded. Then he stood out manfully and gave the House and the country the benefit of his information, his careful conclusions, and his high ideals.

"Time and again, after the House became acquainted with his intellectual power and honesty, he was able to defeat measures or to compel satisfactory compromises in spite of the pressure of the party machine."

It was not long before Burton was recognized by the men around the long oval table as a living encyclopedia of information on every phase of waterway legislation and construction and their commercial results. If he said that a stream under consideration for improvement carried a certain volume of water and traversed a region containing a certain population, his figures were accepted.

Shortly, members of the committee came to respect his deductions from facts when he made them known in response to questions. If he gave his opinion that the "improvement" of this or that creek would not develop a commerce of a total value equal to the interest of the proposed investment, they were satisfied that the project would have to be justified purely on political grounds, if at all.

Considering his convictions respecting political honesty and the scrupulousness with which public funds should be administered, Burton, as an apprentice, was in a tough spot on this committee, to which was committed the logrolling jobs of the entire House.

He was plodding along unobtrusively, feeling that in all probability years would pass before he would be entitled, by promotion under the seniority rule, to sit at the head of the big table, when Chairman Warren B. Hooker suddenly announced that he was resigning from the committee and from the House to accept a more profitable position outside of Washington.

Representative Henry Allen Cooper, of Wisconsin, was the Republican next in line for succession to the chairmanship. Mr. Cooper was greatly respected, but his Republican associates on the committee were inclined to regard him as too much given to insurrectionary impulses and too temperamental to make an acceptable chairman. That position demanded the tact and steadiness of a diplomat.

They took their troubles to Speaker Reed and told him that the best man for the chairmanship was Theodore Burton, whose promotion would involve jumping him over the head of Mr. Cooper. In effect, Speaker Reed told them:

"No, gentlemen, you cannot pass this buck to the Speaker, who is supposed to respect the seniority rule of promotion. If the Speaker established a precedent of this sort, he would open the door to a stampede of applications for promotions to chairmanships by the leapfrog method.

"However, the Speaker recognizes that Mr. Burton has singular qualifications for the chairmanship of your committee. You have my permission to settle your own dilemma in your own way."

Now occurred one of the greatest surprises of Theodore Burton's life—his election by his committee associates to the chairmanship, on December 7, 1898.

The gods presiding over the destinies of our national lawmakers must have smiled when they assigned Theodore Burton, the political purist, to rule over the committee which "cleared" the major part of the political trades of the entire membership of Congress. For Burton, who would never accept a railroad pass, and whose expense account on official business was as clean as a knitting needle, to sit at the head of the political "pay-off" board in the House, appeared a masterpiece of human misplacement. The fates had certainly played a scurvy trick on this White Knight.

Representative Cooper promptly resigned his membership on the committee and broke his intimate friendship with Burton. They were estranged for a number of years, but eventually, the embittered member from Wisconsin resumed cordial relations with his old friend.

Of course, this unique promotion was decidedly flattering to Burton. Perhaps he did not appreciate the tactical advantage which this move gave his committee colleagues in their relationship to him as chairman. He owed his preferment directly to them and not to the Speaker. So, in a certain sense, they had him "in their bag."

Circumstances connected with the fate of the first Rivers and Harbors Bill framed under his chairmanship indicate that the men who had made him chairman did not lose sight of their advantage and did not permit him to exercise the authority and independence which he later achieved. In the Fifty-fifth Congress he fell far short of "dominating" the committee as he did in later years when he held the chairmanship by the Speaker's appointment.

Consequently, the first bill reflected his influence far less than did any other before he left the House to become a member of the Senate. While he was able to keep out of the bill the authorization of certain projects which he regarded as indefensible, he was unable to defeat many others which he considered as experimental and highly speculative. This bill, in short, was far more the committee's than his own. It carried a total expenditure which was unprecedented at that time and which he believed was excessive. On the other hand, it was the best he had been able to do under the circumstances. As a matter of party policy, he believed that it invited attack in the second McKinley campaign which was approaching.

Meantime, President McKinley and his political advisers began to "view with alarm" its total of about sixty million dollars, in those days regarded as a huge expenditure. This bill was "talked to death" in the Senate, on January 4, 1901, by Tom Carter, of Montana, a Republican, who was a close friend of Chairman Burton's.

At the time it was understood that this was done on the direct suggestion of President McKinley. Was Burton crushed because his first Rivers and Harbors Bill was defeated by a Republican Senator in a filibuster instigated by a Republican President from his own state? Not in the least! His smile was genial and perhaps a little cryptic, suggesting the possibility that he considered the members of his committee, rather than himself, as the recipients of discipline.

Another circumstantial consideration supports the theory that Chairman Burton welcomed the defeat of his bill. He had been for years President McKinley's personal friend and faithful political supporter and from the President's first day in the White House he had been frequently summoned there for intimate conferences. President McKinley was a man of great personal kindliness and consideration. It was impossible to believe that he would have inflicted upon his old-time Ohio friend anything in the nature of a humiliation. Quite to the contrary, it was assumed that Burton must have been taken into McKinley's confidence and must have assured the President that the defeat of the bill would not be accepted by him as humiliating.

Burton's industry as a digger for facts in the field of waterway improvements was illustrated by his classmate and intimate friend at Oberlin, E. A. Paddock, President of the Inter-Mountain Institute in Idaho.

"I always called on Theodore when in Washington," related this old friend. "On one such occasion he was chuckling over a recent occurrence. Shortly before, delegates had come up from the South to appear before the Rivers and Harbors Committee from which they wished to obtain an appropriation of several million dollars for dredging a small river in their locality. In a brief preliminary interview they painted a glowing picture of the commerce which this stream would carry when Uncle Sam had improved its navigability. The spokesman for the delegation did not get very far with his story before Burton interrupted him with the statement: 'Gentlemen, it will be impossible for the committee to give you a hearing immediately. If you will appear one week from today we will be glad to listen to your story.'

"He then smilingly confessed to me that, before the day appointed for the hearing, he had visited the region of the proposed improvement and had made all the investigation necessary to establish the fact that the project was unwarranted and even absurd. It was apparent that he enjoyed the astonishment and confusion of the boosters at their own admission of the information which his questions revealed. This was a favorite trick of his and he played it often."

The diligence with which Burton acquired his firsthand knowledge of the rivers and harbors of his country is illustrated by another anecdote related to the writer by S. E. Siegfried, a post office inspector at Cleveland.

"During the year 1901," said Mr. Siegfried, "I was in newspaper work in Tacoma, Washington, where I met Mr. Burton for the first time. He was then Chairman of the Rivers and Harbors Committee, members of which were visiting Tacoma to secure firsthand information relative to various harbor projects requiring large appropriations. Having been assigned to cover the investigations of this committee, I stole down to the water front before six o'clock in the morning to refresh my impressions of the harbor and the general lay of the land. To my surprise, I found Mr. Burton on the ground, notebook in hand, making copious notes as he paused at one spot and another.

"He extracted from me immediately all the information I possessed regarding the harbor and the extent of its shipping. This was only the beginning, however. He 'pumped' every man that we encountered, from the humblest roustabout or sailor to the harbor master. Only when absolutely necessary did he reveal his identity to those with whom he talked. Otherwise, his attitude was that of a traveler intensely interested in the Puget Sound country and its commerce.

"Mr. Burton missed all the parties and pleasure jaunts enjoyed by the other members of the committee, but he enjoyed stealing a march on them. When the first formal committee hearing was held he astounded every one present by the extent of his information.

"His knowledge of the technical details of the entire harbor-and-shipping subject was the sensation of the committee's visit to the city. It was talked of for months afterward by the leaders in civic and business affairs. It was years before I met Mr. Burton again—this time in Cleveland. His memory of our day together on the

Tacoma water front was far more comprehensive than my own and he recalled several incidents that had faded from my recollection. In particular he chuckled over several incidents of the hearing in which he had been able to correct information given by certain citizens who were supposed to be authorities on the subjects. about which they were enlightening the committee.

"How his mind could have grasped and retained so many technical details and figures was astounding to me—as to all others who were privileged to see him in action."

One of the first revolutionary steps taken by Chairman Burton to shift Rivers and Harbors legislation from a political logrolling basis to one of sound business was to open the bill to free debate. Before then the policy had been to jam the measure through the House under unanimous consent, a procedure which virtually precluded the offering of amendments. While this change had its perils and invited inconvenience and delay, he believed that it would result in authorization of a more wholesome character and force the defects of weak projects out into the open.

This proved to be a far more revolutionary step than was at first realized by his colleagues. For example, in 1907, with Burton's knowledge and approval, the writer, in a *Saturday Evening Post* article, included the statement that, up to that time, it had resulted in the submission of five hundred amendments to Rivers and Harbors bills—and debates and discussions which rapidly educated the American people in the abuses of the great national pork barrel. In the same article, the writer told the following anecdote.

On one occasion an amendment to the Rivers and Harbors Appropriation Bill was introduced, setting aside a large amount for the construction of an "ice harbor" for the protection of vessels against the ravages of ice. Burton disposed of this, after he had made a few figures on a slip of paper, by demonstrating that it would be cheaper to burn every vessel harboring at that point and replace it with a new one each spring for several years than to build the "improvements" sought.

After this practice of free debate became an established feature of passing a Rivers and Harbors Bill few, if any, amendments were adopted which Chairman Burton opposed. He enjoyed thrusting the stiletto of sarcasm into an amendment which some incautious member of the House was rash enough to advocate. On one occasion a member offered an amendment authorizing a large expenditure for the building of reservoirs to control the waters of a certain lake and stressed the consideration that this "improvement" was in the interest of national navigation. Burton smilingly replied that he thought the member was a little confused as to the type of navigation involved. As the lake which it was proposed to protect was six thousand feet above sea level and had never been navigated by any craft excepting a birchbark canoe, he was constrained to suggest that the term "higher navigation" was far more appropriate than "national navigation."

All of these thrusts brought volleys of laughter from the members of the House and made front-page copy for the Washington newspaper correspondents. As a result, the country learned that it was difficult to put anything over on the Chairman of the Rivers and Harbors Committee.

Occasionally Burton explained to the House that, although he was not convinced that a certain authorization to be found in the bill was warranted, it had been left to the decision of the House. His own judgment was against the authorization. On the other hand, opinion in the committee was for it and he had allowed it to go into the bill on the understanding that he would explain the grounds of his dissent to the House.

On at least one occasion of this character the House decided with the committee and overruled Burton's objections. This was in the matter of an appropriation of a half-million dollars to complete the Illinois and Mississippi Canal, popularly called the Hennepin Canal. Since the adoption of this project in 1891 about seven million dollars had been spent upon it. Burton believed that it should never have been adopted and that it would not develop a commerce that would justify the expenditure.

In 1905, when a tremendous pressure was brought to bear upon the committee to appropriate enough to finish the project, he did a thorough job of explaining to the committee that he regarded the investment already put into this canal as wasted and that, in his opinion, it would be better to abandon the project than to put a half million more into it. This, however, was a matter on which feeling was strong; virtually the entire Illinois delegation in Congress demanded the completion of the project. Burton did not, he indicated, propose to be accused of czarist methods. If the House of Representatives insisted upon making this mistake, in spite of his warnings, he would give it that privilege.

The House voted the appropriation and the canal was completed. As a commerce-bearing waterway it has been a decided failure.

It has often been asserted that Burton's domination of his committee was absolute. This statement is too sweeping. Chairman Burton faced the unavoidable necessity of presenting to the House, every other year, a Rivers and Harbors Bill. In order to accomplish this difficult task, compromises were unavoidable. Probably he had to do a little logrolling himself, in order to report a bill which was, in his opinion, the best possible under the circumstances.

In the Civil War period, the men of the Middle West believed that the capitalists of the East who controlled the railroads which were tapping the Mississippi Valley and pushing on into the prairie states immediately beyond were in a conspiracy to prevent the development of the "cheap transportation" possibilities of the Ohio River. The Midwesterners felt that not until that great natural waterway from the East to the Mississippi was opened up to accommodate heavy traffic would their rich farming empire come into its own. This was a favorite topic of conversation in the camps of the Union army of the Western front, largely recruited from the farming population served by the Ohio and the Mississippi rivers.[*]

At that time, however, the high-speed complex of today's citizen was unknown. It did not then occur to the farmers west of the Alleghenies or to their sons that after the Government had spent millions in its development, they would themselves neglect to patronize this great provision for cheap freight transportation, this powerful and beneficent competitor of the oppressive railroads. But in a retrospective statement to the Senate, in 1914, Burton admitted that "a diminished use of inland waterways has resulted from greater speed in handling traffic by rail."

In 1925 Tom Marshall, of Indiana, who seldom failed to give the human factor due consideration, wrote:

> As in his public affairs, so in his private life the American rarely prepares himself for the future. He is wholly unwilling to have anything transmitted to him by water that he can get by rail. It irks him to wait the slow process of freighting when there is an express car coming to his town, and if somebody will soon discover how to deliver by aeroplane, that is the way he will obtain what he

[*] See *Sherman, Fighting Prophet* by Lloyd Lewis. New York, 1932.

wants. *He never wants it until he wants it, and when he wants it, he wants it at once.* The farmer does not look over his machinery in the winter time to ascertain what it needs in the way of repair, but waits until a week or ten days before he needs it and then telegraphs for the repair parts to be sent by express.

The whole history of waterway improvement is this: that traffic lessens as improvement increases. The better the waterways become for transportation of products, the less are they used. Now this, of course, was to some extent brought about by the condition of the old Interstate Commerce Act which authorized railroads to meet water competition. And so, as rapidly as the rivers were dredged for transportation, the railways cut the rates and destroyed the river traffic as much as possible. I know of one point on the Ohio where it was cheaper to ship supplies by the railroad and haul them by motor truck from the nearest station to the town, a distance of twenty miles, than it was originally to send them direct to that town by the river.*

Scrutiny of Burton's expressions and acts in the earlier years of his chairmanship of the Rivers and Harbors Committee indicates that, up to the close of the first decade of the twentieth century, he held to the belief that, by sufficient caution, patience, and industry, it would be possible for him to shift national waterway expenditures from a game of political logrolling to a business basis and, eventually, to give his country several great systems of water transportation justified by a profitable commerce. This became his ambition and he followed it with idealism—but with open-eyed recognition of its tremendous obstacles and difficulties. He once focused his view of the waters of the United States in the following sentence:

"We ought to treat water as an entirety: navigation, water power, purification of water, prevention of floods—and there is nothing better that this House can do than to frame some system under which they shall be treated, not merely in reference to navigation, as a separate unit, but to bring all together as an asset of this people as important as the land."

A part of his constructive scheme was to reduce to specific statement his conclusions as to the classes of waterway improvements which offered the most dependable promise of commercial justification. His classification of the streams lending themselves to legiti-

* Thomas R. Marshall, *Recollections of Thomas R. Marshall.* Indianapolis, 1925.

mate improvement as traffic-carrying waterways is illuminating. It reads:

First, rivers which afford access to cities in centers of consumption located at no great distance from the sea, upon which the haul by river can be combined with the movement by sea. Of this class are the Delaware, reaching from the city of Philadelphia to the sea; the Patapsco, between Baltimore and the Chesapeake Bay; the Mississippi, between New Orleans and the Gulf of Mexico; the Columbia and the Willamette, between Portland and the Pacific Ocean.

Second, rivers of considerable size upon which large cities or industrial centers are located and which can be made the means of transportation between producer and consumer in the shipment of heavy and coarse freights, such as coal, iron ore, or building material. In this class may be included the Ohio and the Hudson with its canal connection with the Great Lakes.

Third, short rivers in busy industrial sections, where the consumer and producer are located near to each other. The best illustration of a river of this class is the Monongahela in Pennsylvania. This tonnage consists almost entirely of coal carried from mines on or near to the river to mills or furnaces at or near Pittsburgh.

Fourth, minor streams at or near great cities or thickly populated areas. There are a number of these streams tributary to the waters around New York City, to the Delaware below Philadelphia, and to the Chesapeake Bay. In the case of these streams a market for the products of the locality tributary to the river in question is not far away and freight can profitably be carried in boats of shallow draft.

In an article in the *Associated Sunday Magazines*, a publication then syndicated to leading newspapers of the country, Senator Burton indulged in a long backward look over his course in connection with waterway legislation:

One of the worst errors in our river and harbor policy has been the failure to finish great trunk lines, if we may call main rivers such, and giving too much and earlier attention to the branches. . . .

The Ohio is a great artery of commerce. Improvements have been made costing tens of millions of dollars for branch streams like the Big Sandy, the Kentucky, the Green, the Wabash, and even the Cumberland and the Tennessee. As a result there is a more uniform and at times a greater depth of water in the Kentucky and Kanawha Rivers than in the Ohio where they empty into it; that is, taking into account all seasons of the year, and manifestly all calculations must be made with a view to the minimum depth. There are six feet in the pools in those rivers, and in the Ohio where they flow into it at times not more than three or four feet. A boat could come down the Kanawha or the Kentucky laden with freight and yet not be able to get into the Ohio.

Again he stressed the wanton waste of piecemeal appropriations, the practice of making small allotments for projects that would involve many times the amount given to complete. He had always opposed it and in this instance offered specific examples of its wastefulness:

In 1885 work was begun upon the construction of a harbor or refuge at Sandy Bay, Massachusetts. *Another fifty years will be required to complete this project at the rate of progress already made upon it.* Similar methods are illustrated in the case of the breakwater at Bar Harbor, Maine, where the work has been *under construction for twenty-five years,* and five more years will probably be needed for its completion. . . .

In cases where the Board of Army Engineers strongly urge an appropriation of $300,000 for work upon a contract, Congress will most frequently allow only one-third of that amount or even less. The reason for this is that with a certain sum allowed for river and harbor improvements and each member of Congress demanding a purse for his district it is necessary to parcel it out in small allotments. . . .

Millions of dollars, he declared, had been spent on improvements that from the viewpoint of commerce development had been ridiculous failures. For example, the improvement of the Arkansas River, involving an expenditure of more than three millions. The resulting commercial benefits? Exclusive of saw-logs, lumber, and staves—requiring no channel improvement for their movement—the river carried thirteen thousand tons of miscellaneous merchandise in the preceding year. Including interest at three per cent on the total investment, the movement of this miscellaneous freight cost the government ninety-five dollars a ton.

The Mississippi, "Father of Waters," is an eloquent if somber preacher on the text of waterway improvement disappointments. On this subject Burton wrote:

On that section of the Mississippi River between the mouth of the Missouri and the mouth of the Ohio, there is a stretch of some 200 miles, on which is situated the city of St. Louis. The original project contemplated an expenditure in that locality of $16,000,000. After $12,000,000 had been expended . . . another board made an official estimate and declared it would cost $4,000,000 more than was originally estimated. Now after $16,894,000 have been spent it is estimated that $17,250,000 more will be required to complete the work.

And yet in the old days in the early '80's, *when the depth was from four and a half to five feet, there was ten times as much traffic received and shipped by river from St. Louis as there is today.* . . .

He declared that this example of steadily diminishing traffic on a great river with an ample channel was blindly ignored; that in 1897 a Senate committee, assisted by expert engineers, made a thorough examination of the Missouri River project and reported unanimously that further expenditures on it would be "a reckless waste of money." This stopped appropriations for it for some time but in a few years, "political pressure and local insistence" started a new onslaught with an appropriation of a million dollars in 1910, to which was added four and a half million a little later.

According to the engineers, the annual cost of maintaining the channel between Kansas City and St. Louis would be half a million dollars, "approximately the cost of maintaining the harbors of Boston, New York, Baltimore, Norfolk, and Charleston with the magnificent commerce of those ports."

The proposed expenditure of more than twenty-two millions for the improvement of the upper Missouri River with the admitted expectation that its benefits would be almost wholly confined to restraining railroad freight rates moved him to observe:

There can be no doubt that the tendency of these improvements is to lower railroad rates. . . . *Yet this theory is primarily and essentially vicious,* and I cannot subscribe to it. It seeks to accomplish by indirection, *and that, too, at enormous cost,* what we ought to do directly. What can and should be done by a single stroke of the legislative pen or by the ruling of the Interstate Commerce Commission or a state railroad commission, we ought not to spend millions of dollars to accomplish indirectly.

This theory of creating potential waterway competition in order to reduce railroad rates rests upon the *intolerable and transparent fallacy that the railroads of the United States constitute an intrenched power and are beyond the reach of our laws and our courts.*

Once he declared:

> Our appeal for the modification of railroad rates should be addressed to the courts and to the Interstate Commerce Commission, and not to the treasury and the River and Harbor bills.
>
> We should enact laws to compel the railroads to co-operate with waterway companies, so that boat lines may assume their natural function as supplemental means of transportation to our rail lines. The normal function of internal waterway transportation is to relieve railroads of bulk raw materials and other low-grade freights, while the railroads should carry the more valuable and lucrative products, which in their nature require prompt delivery.

Probably there is not a better example of the statesmanship which characterized the course of Theodore Burton in connection with Rivers and Harbors legislation than that which has preserved the beauty of Niagara Falls from spoliation by commercial enterprise. This was a task of peculiar delicacy and difficulties because control of this great national scenic asset was shared by another nation and also because power companies had already pre-empted a position from which dislodgment was difficult or impossible. Thus, a precedent of great influence had been established which afforded a basis for further encroachments.

The power interests were strongly entrenched at Niagara Falls and naturally were alert to increase their use of this vast reservoir of cheap power by every possible means. No great foresight was required to see that this pressure of commercial ambition was inevitable. The vision of Chairman Burton was in seeing that, like Niagara itself, it would gradually wear away one opposing obstacle after another until this world-famous spectacle would become a power site rather than one of the greatest scenic attractions in the United States.

The measures which he instigated in the Fifty-ninth Congress (1905–1907) to put a stop to this transformation represented a fight of sentiment against commercial utility considerations—always a difficult position to maintain. Although he was a confirmed bachelor, he realized that thousands of bridal couples who had held hands while gazing at the grandeur of Niagara would be grateful to him for saving this great scenic and sentimental shrine from despoliation. The hearings conducted were the most extensive made by the Rivers and Harbors Committee. The broad foundation of information which Burton laid was characteristic of his tactics. As a result of this thorough preparation, his bill was passed and received the signature of the President.

One feature of it especially illustrates the statesmanship of Theodore Burton. In the bill he incorporated certain treaty provisions, which were promptly negotiated with the Canadian government. If this had not been done, undoubtedly the power companies would have attacked the constitutionality of the bill in the courts, perhaps successfully. But the treaty provisions prevented the companies from going into the courts and protected the measure from assault for all time to come. Through the years every person who enjoys the majestic beauty of Niagara Falls will owe a debt of gratitude to Theodore Burton for saving this unique natural scenic spectacle from depletion and defacement by the great power companies. It was a distinguished bachelor's most gallant gesture to the marriage shrine.

CHAPTER 8

An Unhappy Politician

FROM HIS FIRST TERM in the House to his last day in the Senate, Theodore Burton was in continuous revolt against the patronage system, resenting the theory of public service which it involved.

Mark Hanna took as much delight in dividing the spoils of party and personal victory as in carving a Thanksgiving turkey at his family table. To Theodore Burton this implied participation in a custom repugnant to his ideals. So far as his constituents were concerned, he did his best to conceal his feelings on this irritating subject, but was not always successful.

When Theodore Burton was "a freeman" in 1918, after he had retired from public life, he spoke informally before an audience mainly composed of Ohio friends and acquaintances. In this talk he declared:

"It is my experience that those patronage seekers that are most importunate and troublesome are not those who have rendered a man political service. Very frequently they are not from his own constituency. They come to Washington seeking an office. They do not seem to care what it is. Men come down there thinking themselves competent to be guide, philosopher, and friend of the President and all his Cabinet."

When the Civil Service Bill came before the House, on January 7, 1898, he seized the opportunity to tell the country what he thought about the subject of patronage. He said:

"For one, I am willing to vote for a bill forbidding any Representative on this floor from making any recommendation for any position in any of the Executive Departments of the Government. And I would do it . . . because it would relieve us of a burden that at times is too grievous to be borne. Every member here must choose between efficient service as a Representative of the people and the giving of so large a share of his time to solicitation for offices as to render his work inefficient and unsatisfactory."

He appealed to his colleagues to turn aside from denunciation of the Civil Service system to constructive criticism.

"I would not," he remarked, "overlook the hypocrisy of some of the advocates of the system, or ignore the palpable dishonesty of some who have had to do with its enforcement. I believe in changes—changes in detail and administration rather than in principle."

Then this "practical idealist" offered these specific suggestions:

> Let it be provided, first, that confidential subordinates, private secretaries and deputies, particularly those for whom the superior officer is liable upon his bond, shall be excluded from the classified service. . . .
>
> Second. Let there be an examination of those brought into the service by Executive Order, without examination, many of whom were appointed as a reward for political services with only incidental regard to fitness. . . . Such a change would have for its object, not the multiplying of available positions, but the establishment of just rules in making selections and the securing of men of better qualifications.
>
> Third. A better system of making promotions. The heads of Departments and Bureaus have, in many instances, given over this whole matter to their subordinates. . . . If the merit system is a good one, and men are admitted in the first instance by competitive examination, why not promote them by competitive examinations also, or by an efficiency record carefully and justly kept? . . .
>
> Fourth. Make our examinations more practical, and, where an examination is not a feasible test, omit it entirely. . . . Not long ago my attention was called to the examination of an applicant for a position as a plumber. There was a great deal about grammar and geography and other subjects, but not one word about plumbing or any other trade. . . .
>
> Another suggestion: Where a position is to be filled for which there is no eligible list, do not incur the tedious delay of framing examination questions, giving notice, and providing for an examination, and thus postpone a selection until the time has come when the work ought to be finished. I know of an instance in which a

draftsman was needed in an engineer's office, and the whole work had to be postponed, though plenty of competent men were at hand. . . .

These are terse formulae for genuine civil service. In addition, later in his speech Burton gave this analysis of the whole patronage system:

> I now wish to pass to some errors . . . of those who oppose the merit system and argue for its abandonment and the adoption of the spoils system.
>
> First. They say a man in public life can appoint his friends; he can reward the workers. Never was there a greater delusion! Who is to determine who the workers are?
>
> Can a Representative here, who has a friend in the humble walks of life who has done him great service but for whom he is told there is no position in the Government service—can he find a place for him? Can he run the gantlet and pass by the other influences which must be consulted and be sure that he shall secure positions for those whom he would wish to appoint? Is it not the common experience of every one of you that those whose claims are advocated most strenuously are those whom you can not recognize as having rendered the most valuable assistance?
>
> And what is more, how are you going to provide for the whole number? Under the old system there were at least twenty applicants for every available position, and, as you multiply the number of available places, the number of applicants increases in even greater proportion. There are 178,000 in the Government service. How many [political] workers were there in 1896? A myriad uprose and supported President McKinley and the Republican Party. When it came to election day a multitude of freemen went to the polls, in comparison with which the hosts of Xerxes were but as a gathering of home guards. Seven million one hundred and five thousand voters cast their ballots for McKinley. Come, ye dispensers of patronage, how are you going to provide places for all these workers? . . .
>
> Another claim is that it builds up a political party. There never was a worse fallacy! It destroys a party. Every practical politician recognizes that after a successful campaign the open opposition or lukewarmness of the disappointed ones is an element of danger.

Burton pleaded for a law to protect Representatives and Senators in Congress from the importunities of office seekers. Then he suggested: "Visit the White House and see the greed for federal patronage. Some months ago I went up there with a friend who is somewhat of a cosmopolitan and who merely wished to meet the President of the United States. There was a great throng there. After waiting a considerable time, he bluntly said: 'Oh, come along; we can't wait here. People will think we are part of this mob of Senators and Representatives hunting places for their constituents.' "

His closing was brief but Burtonesque:

"It is said that on the tomb of Sulla, in the Campus Martius, there was an inscription, written by himself, which read: 'I am Sulla the Fortunate, who never failed to reward a friend or punish an enemy.' A boast worthy of a modern spoilsman! Modern statesmanship has a higher ideal. It is to build up a great nation; to furnish the justest and most efficient government for all American citizens. . . ."

This speech may have embarrassed some of his constituents who were suffering from an inflamed appetite for office, but it provoked wide approval from the press, particularly in Ohio. It was evidently impromptu. Burton simply boiled over, seizing this opportunity to record his abhorrence of the spoils system, his detestation of the entire scheme of political patronage, and his conviction that it is a party liability, not a party asset.

More than once he refused to conform to the dictation of the Cleveland Republican ring, with a courageous declaration that he would leave public life rather than return to the national capital as a creature of the Hanna machine. In fact, he put this declaration of independence into practical effect in 1902 when he became a candidate for a seat in the Fifty-seventh Congress on the express stipulation that he should conduct his Congressional campaign himself, independent of the Hanna machine or the general Republican organization in Cuyahoga County. On the other hand, at the time when the "Cleveland Shipping Master" had finished his successful conduct of the McKinley campaign, and had been appointed to the Senate by Governor Bushnell in 1897, Burton rendered to Hanna a loyalty that involved at least a temporary sacrifice of such a tempting political advancement for himself.

In 1907, Representative Burton again talked on Civil Service. The high cost of government had become burdensome to the American people. Waste in any form—public or private—was repugnant to Burton. Many of his political associates regarded him as personally "tight" and a crank on the ethics of public expenditures. But more than one of these criticisms concluded with the observation: "However, I'd like to know that Burton would administer my estate when I'm gone. I'd know that my family would get every nickel of it."

He was one of the severest critics of Tammany Hall in the House. Certain Democrats had been mixing praise of Tammany with criticism of Republican extravagance and with a defense of the spoils system as superior to the "hypocritical civil service makeshift." To this Burton replied:

"It would be exceedingly inconsiderate of me to strike a discordant note in this chorus of praise for Tammany Hall. I will not do so. I will only say that the men of this or any country and the events of this or any country are like monuments, good or bad, which cannot be affected by our praise or blame. If, for government and public service, Tammany Hall is the ideal of any gentleman, or of any party, let it remain so, with Boss Tweed as a central figure, and with all others who have been a part of that organization."

Later, referring to defects in the Civil Service system, Burton said:

"Those who are at the head of it [Civil Service] should have just as free a hand in discharging as in appointing, but the appointments should be made from a classified list by competitive examinations. Appointees soon fall into a groove and become mere amanuenses, their one desire being fewer hours and higher salary. The system there will never be perfect unless there is a freer hand in discharging than there is at present." Burton then declared that it would be a great gain for the service if the more important positions could be filled by promotions from the ranks, instead of from the outside.

Possibly the suspicion that he was not an infallible judge of character increased Senator Burton's distaste for dealing with matters of patronage. He made more than one serious mistake in bestowing political preferments. This accounted for the sympathetic response to which his colleagues were stirred by his remarks on the Civil Service Bill and the patronage problem in general. They had also made mistakes.

CHAPTER 9

"The Temptation" of 1897

PERHAPS THE GREATEST TEST of Burton's party regularity
came in 1897, immediately following the election of William
McKinley as President. Hanna had been in high command of
the McKinley campaign and apparently convinced the majority of
Republicans in Ohio that he had done a masterful job and was
entitled to any reward he might ask.

His attitude, if not his words, proclaimed that he had made
McKinley President, though the results probably would have been
the same had any other competent campaign manager been in
charge of McKinley's interests.

In an article by David Rankin Barbee, in the Washington *Post*
of February 22, 1931, Senator Henry Clay Hansbrough is quoted
as saying: "McKinley's nomination was a foregone conclusion even
before Hanna began his fight for him. Hanna made a big job of it,
whereas it was an easy one. . . . It was our strategy, then, to
nominate a conservative man with a winning personality. . . .
McKinley would have been the selection if Hanna had not organized a campaign for him. The McKinley Bill gave him a great
reputation throughout the country. He had a lovable personality
and no enemies. His defeat for Congress, after putting that bill
through, had a strong and pleasant reaction in his favor. This was
climaxed by his election as Governor and by his reelection."

According to Senator Hansbrough, Hanna had a way about him
which irritated his associates in the leadership of the party. "He
could not say no graciously," comments this authority, "and he
could not even decide unimportant things without doing a lot of
fretting."

But when it came to raising money, Mark Hanna was a master.

The Republican campaign fund of 1896 had never been approached in size by that of any party in any preceding national campaign. Mr. Bryan was made to feel the weight of the "cross of gold."

Certainly it is true that Hanna had taught the politicians of Ohio —who were supposed to be letter-perfect in the art of political warfare—the power of money in a campaign. One downstate Republican leader in Ohio sketched the situation in these terms:

"Up to the time when Mark became skipper of the good Republican ship "Buckeye," getting money from the National Committee for use downstate was difficult. . . . But when Captain Hanna took command the lean days of local self-help suddenly ended and it seemed to us as if the funds came to us by the barrel.

"Did those of us who were running for office downstate feel kindly toward Uncle Mark? You know the answer! The boys, running for state and county offices and particularly for the legislature, didn't have to borrow at the bank or mortgage their homes in order to put up a respectable campaign."

In the Republican State Convention held at Toledo, following McKinley's election, the word was passed that Senator John Sherman would be selected by McKinley as his Secretary of State and that Hanna was slated to succeed Sherman in the Senate. Therefore, the convention went on record for this program. Later local Republican conventions in several counties ratified this stand and called upon their members of the legislature to vote for Hanna in the General Assembly. Hanna had enough men in various sections of the state to make these instructions sound like the voice of the entire Republican Party in Ohio. It was, in fact, far from that. It spoke for the machine in the northern part of the state. The Foraker-Bushnell combination did not share it. Foraker was then in the Senate, in the zenith of his influence, and his friend Bushnell was governor, although soon to give way to his already elected successor.

John Sherman, who had not yet resigned the Senatorship to take his seat at the McKinley Cabinet table, let it be known that he did not intend to resign until the new political alignment between the two major Republican factions was more definitely determined. The meeting of the legislature, which then elected the Senators, was only a few months away.

Officers and power were at the disposal of the "home state" President, and opposition to him might be fatal to the interests of those who offered it. On the other hand, it was obvious to Senator Foraker and Governor Bushnell that if, instead of Hanna, some leader in the northern part of the state, who commanded the confidence of the entire party and also of the President, could be named to succeed Senator Sherman, the southern contingent, headed by Senator Foraker, might be rescued from political starvation at Hanna's hands.

Foraker and Bushnell knew their Hanna and his high and mighty ways. They also knew that there was a deep and strong undercurrent of revolt against him in their wing of the Republican organization. Members of the legislature had already been elected and the Governor had "counted noses" very carefully as to their division regarding votes for Hanna. Incidentally, the Governor, as distributor of state appointive offices, had been in position for many months to strengthen his control of legislative votes.

Then there was the general good of the Republican Party as a whole to be considered. With a Republican President from Ohio going into the White House, great changes in the strategic position of the Republican Party in Ohio—and in the nation as well— were imminent. The two parties were about evenly balanced in this modern "battleground of Presidents" and the body of independent voters, who did not hesitate to switch from one party to another, was larger, perhaps, than in almost any other state. This fluid independent vote operated as a standing threat against party security and continuance in power.

Republican leaders recognized that any movement which promised to heal party sores and develop greater party unity should be encouraged. This would demand compromises between the two factional groups and perhaps result in practically a new Republican setup in the state organization. From the viewpoint of the leaders of the southern group, it was impossible to build a united party under the dominance of Hanna. They felt that to confirm him in this position would result in a quick and disastrous revolt on the part of certain Ohio Republicans. Now was the time, they decided, to prevent this calamity by sending to the United States Senate a man close to President McKinley but not subservient to the Hanna machine.

In their opinion, Congressman Burton had every qualification as a compromise candidate against Hanna who could not only defeat him but could unite the factions of the party and present a solid front to the Democratic opposition. While, in a general way, Burton had been identified with the Hanna machine in the northern section of the state, his distrust of Hanna and his characteristic political tactics were an open secret. Moreover, Burton's integrity and ability were recognized throughout the party.

The leaders of the southern group, with the exception of Boss Cox, admired Congressman Burton, despite the fact that he fought their faction consistently. Besides, he did not believe in unlimited financial competition in politics. "The boys" throughout the state had been momentarily jubilant over having plenty of Hanna money to spend, but leaders of the southern group realized that this was a bad habit to get into. Besides, they knew that there was a string tied to every dollar dispensed by Hanna and that he would pull the string and see to it that an obedient response was forthcoming.

Governor Bushnell summoned Burton from Washington by telephone for a secret conference. He arrived in Columbus on February 7, but it was not until eight days later that news of the trip reached the Cincinnati *Enquirer*, which "scooped" all the newspapers of the state. Under a Columbus date line it published, in its issue of February 25, a dispatch from which the following is extracted:

> The *Enquirer* has authentic information that the United States Senatorship was offered to at least two men by Governor Bushnell before he announced his intention of appointing Mark Hanna. These two men are Congressmen S. A. Northway, of the Nineteenth District, and Theodore E. Burton, of Cleveland. . . .
>
> Burton, while always friendly with McKinley, has never been on good terms with Hanna, who on more than one occasion has crossed his political path in Cuyahoga County, and this fact, coupled with the tempting offer of John Sherman's seat in the Senate, it was thought would cause the Cleveland Congressman to eagerly grab the bait held out to him.
>
> He was promised not only the short term, but also the loyal support of the Foraker-Bushnell crowd for the full term, and details were fully gone into to demonstrate to Burton the ability of the Foraker people to control the next legislature and deliver the goods. Burton, however, could not be made to see it as Bushnell pictured it to him and told the Governor plainly that the only thing for him [Bushnell] to do, in view of the overwhelming sentiment in the party favorable to Hanna, was to appoint the National Chairman. Any other course, urged Burton, will endanger party success

next fall and be political suicide for the Governor. Thereupon Burton peremptorily declined the offer of the Governor's gold brick and Bushnell's announcement five days later of his intention to appoint Hanna is evidence that Burton's statement had some influence at least upon him.

Possibly Burton was not actually tempted by this offer of a Senatorship—but he might well have been. Subsequent developments proved that Governor Bushnell promised nothing that he could not deliver and that his count of the Foraker-Bushnell votes in the legislature was exact to a man. Hanna, with the advantage of a temporary seat in the Senate by appointment by Governor Bushnell, found himself facing a deadlock, which could be broken by one vote. This he finally won, and thereby won the seat in the Senate for the full term and was in a position to reward his friends and punish his enemies.

Shortly before Hanna secured the one lacking vote, the Columbus *World* published an intimation that Burton was "receptive" as a compromise candidate. This brought a letter of denial:

Washington, D.C., Jan. 4, 1898

To the Editor of the *World*:

Your article of recent date, in which you state that it is said I am a candidate for Senator, in the sense of being a receptive candidate, is entirely without foundation and unjust.

I am not a candidate for the position of Senator in any sense.

The only way out of the present unfortunate tangle is for the Republicans of Ohio to elect Mr. Hanna. . . . Any other course would . . . introduce an element of disorganization which will be destructive of Republican success, and promotive of faction for years to come. . . .

Very respectfully yours,
T. E. Burton

Inevitably all the Republican newspapers of Ohio under Hanna influence and even those which were simply "regular" in their party attachments patted Burton on the back for his steadfast refusal. There was never before or afterward so warm a feeling for him in the Hanna camp as at that moment.

This was the first time Mr. Burton found himself cast for the role of party martyr—but it was not to be the last. Ultimately he became almost letter-perfect in that role. Party leaders made a note to the effect that, while Burton could not be pushed or driven into a position against his interest or conscience, the halo of martyrdom in the name of party loyalty was as alluring to him as a pail of oats to a halter-shy horse in an open pasture. And repeatedly they made him pay dearly for his high sense of political honor.

Burton was naturally disposed to conciliation and reasonableness in his political relations. He was not a good political hater. He did not crave power for its own sake. His ambition was to accomplish important things. A secure seat in the United States Senate appealed to him solely as an opportunity to contribute to the statesmanship of the country.

It should be recognized that his acceptance of the Senatorship at that time probably would have involved a tacit alliance with the Boss Cox crowd of the southern section of the state. This connection was bound to be repugnant to him. He did not like Hanna's brand of politics, but he did not put Hanna in the same class with Boss Cox. One made his money in business and spent much of it in political activities; the other, in Burton's estimation at least, made his money in politics and had no other visible source of wealth.

The mutual attitude of Burton and Hanna continued to be one of armed neutrality. They worked together on legislative matters in Congress when they could, but Burton did not claim a place in the Hanna camp. Instead, he pursued an increasingly independent course and on many matters refused to yield to Senator Hanna's demands.

CHAPTER 10

Starting the Twentieth Century

WHEN TIME TURNED THE LEAF to a new century and wrote "1900" at the top of the page, it opened a crowded and dramatic era of national experience as richly rewarding to Theodore Burton as to his country. His outlook had been broadened to world dimensions by foreign travel and research.

Twenty years before, as a private citizen, he had begun to learn European methods of dealing with current problems. America's "splendid isolation" had suddenly ended in the violent and unwelcome intrusion of the Old World into the New World's dooryard. The Spanish-American War, the acquisition of the Philippine Islands, Cuba, and various other scattered bits of palm-fringed foreign scenery gave this nation, against its wish, a burden of world responsibility which made it no longer possible to observe George Washington's solemn injunction to avoid all foreign entanglements. We found ourselves elaborately involved abroad and at a time when we had a surplus of troubles at home.

President McKinley—who had been forced into the war with Spain by the well-nigh unanimous public sentiment of his people— was alert to the necessity of strengthening relations with South American countries. Trade reciprocity had long been a McKinley dream and here was an opportunity to press its merits. Therefore, a Pan-American Exposition was held at Buffalo in 1901, and President McKinley attended to urge the advantages of a broader application of the principle of trade reciprocity.

His address was warmly received by our neighbors to the south and by his own countrymen, who were eager for a larger trade with the Latin Americans. On the following day, September 6, 1901, at a reception in his honor, President McKinley was assassinated by a fanatical anarchist.

By this tragic occurrence the picturesque Theodore Roosevelt was catapulted into the White House. Senators Tom Platt of New York and Matt Quay of Pennsylvania had thought to banish him from political influence by forced retirement into the innocuous vacuum of the Vice-Presidency. Suddenly they realized that, instead, they had promoted to the head of the nation and the Republican party the most dynamic and unmanageable personality known to our national politicians—the Rough Rider hero of San Juan Hill, an untamed and youthful crusader in politics, who had caught the imagination of the American people to an extent unprecedented in his generation. National politics was suddenly changed. It felt the impact of a vigorous social conscience eager to do battle with the forces of massed wealth which had grown to great power in a long period of national prosperity, expansion, and exploitation.

Roosevelt's first major encounter in this field was in the settlement of the anthracite coal strike of 1902 involving 150,000 miners. A hard-coal famine raised the price of the fuel to a penny a pound in New York City—while railroad sidetracks were crowded with hundreds of cars of that precious commodity.*

Under strong Administration pressure, the mine operators reluctantly agreed to submit their differences to a commission to be named by the President. This proposal came from the miners. The committee's investigations revealed an oppresive labor situation which shocked the country and did much to advance the cause of organized labor.

As an initial application of the new social conscience this bold move was a great success and gave the President an immediate and tremendous popularity. It attracted to him the support of a group of leaders in public affairs who shared his idealism but, unlike him, were experienced in the difficult technique of national legislation and international relations. Among them was Congressman Burton.

Burton had a rich equipment of characteristics well calculated to inspire Roosevelt's admiration—singular steadiness of purpose, patience in pursuit of any objective, an unflinching regard for facts. Other endowments were Burton's wide acquaintance with leaders of European thought and affairs and a philosophic outlook upon life that was singularly serene. It is human nature to admire most in others those qualities with which we are less conspicuously endowed. Probably it could not be said of the twenty-sixth Presi-

* Harry Thurston Peck, *Twenty Years of the Republic*. New York, 1906.

dent that he envied anyone anything—but he would have been justified in envying Burton some of these traits which made the Ohio Congressman so useful to the new Administration.

In the earlier part of Roosevelt's administration he looked to Burton for information and counsel as to few other members of his party then in Congress. During this period, leading newspapers of the country often referred to Burton as "the Pooh-Bah of the Administration" and the New York *Times* christened him "Busy, Brainy Burton—the Administration's Utility Man," always ready to help out with any task which less industrious aides did not care to undertake.

To connect the Atlantic and Pacific by a canal which would save ships thousands of miles of arduous passage around the South American continent would be a great achievement for any President. When the American people grasped the fact that the battleship *Oregon*, in Pacific waters at the outbreak of the Spanish-American war, would have been saved eight thousand miles of dangerous passage around South America had an Isthmian canal been available, they at once determined that the canal must be constructed, virtually without regard to cost. The enormous commercial advantages of such a ship canal were obscured, for the moment, by its naval importance.* Probably no other undertaking of a similar magnitude ever received from Congress and people an approval so united.

Perhaps no other member of Congress was so comprehensively informed on all the problems involved in this vast enterprise as was Burton. He had participated in nearly every discussion of an Isthmian canal project since 1898 and had the history and the details of the world's international ship canals at his tongue's end. It was therefore logical that he should become President Roosevelt's most influential counselor in everything relating to this great undertaking. By common consent, the membership of the House also turned to him for information and instruction. The House was impressed—and properly so—with the magnitude of the task and the necessity for elaborate discussion of all its problems.

Most irritating to President Roosevelt in the early debates were "the eagle screamers" who were obsessed with the idea that the canal, when built with Uncle Sam's money, should be as exclusively a United States water highway as if it ran from New York to San

* Frederic J. Haskin, *The Panama Canal*. Garden City, N. Y., 1913.

Francisco. It devolved upon Burton to enlighten these national "exclusionists." He discharged this responsibility rather neatly in these words:

"If there is any place where the American eagle ought not to sit or to scream, it is on this canal. We cannot do without the American eagle. Without it, a type of very eloquent oratory would languish and die. The American eagle is not a bad bird; he flies aloft, never backward. And he never sits on the fence."

Burton added, however, that it was not always safe to follow this noble but sometimes predatory bird in sensitive diplomatic situations. "To do so," he declared, "would cause us to adopt a policy of boastfulness and of grab, where one of amity and liberality ought to prevail. If the ideas of those who have spoken in favor of an American canal and of a policy of exclusiveness were to prevail, I fear that in years to come we would find somewhere in the desolate wastes of Nicaragua a monument on which would be inscribed:

'This is the route of a proposed but abandoned canal.
The American eagle is vindicated.' "

The question of the complete neutrality of the canal provoked persistent debate. Burton was able to assure his hearers that "our general policy has been in favor of a neutral canal crossing the Isthmus. This policy was accepted without dissent for the first eighty-five years of our national existence." He proved it by quotations from the state papers of almost every President within that period.

Congressional debate preceding the first enactment authorizing the construction of an Isthmian canal was long and drawn out. Congress required patient education as to the route and the type of the canal and a multiplicity of other physical details.

But the greatest proofs of Burton's statesmanship, as the Congressional schoolmaster and umpire of the Isthmian canal project, were given in connection with the international relationships involved. He amazed his colleagues by the comprehensiveness of his knowledge of treaties between the nations of the world.

The Spooner Act, of June 28, 1902, gave the President of the United States general authority to build the great canal. "A broader authority has perhaps never been given to the Executive than by this Act," Burton declared.

However, this authority was weighted with certain conditions. If these could be met, the route of the canal was to be across Panama and the canal was to be of the elevated lock type. While the President was meeting the conditions imposed by Congress, a new flood of debate broke out in favor of a sea-level canal. Congress had given its order to the President to go ahead with the enterprise and then, in effect, had exclaimed: "But wait! We haven't quite decided what kind of canal we wish you to build. We'll talk about it some more."

Theodore Roosevelt found himself almost inarticulate with disgust. The Government's engineers had become so discouraged that they were ready to quit the Isthmus and return home. In a speech to the House, on June 15, 1906, Burton exposed the folly of this vacillation and delay. Line upon line, he analyzed the Spooner Act and demonstrated that it authorized a lock canal at Panama to be built by the United States Government.

The speech was a model of moderation. Smilingly he began with the statement that "the problems relating to an Isthmian canal have caused discussions in Congress as long-continued and as earnest as those pertaining to great questions of political or economic policy," a statement which was unchallenged. But a layman would have been at a loss to have added to the range of questions with which the speaker was interrupted.

One interrogator was worried about the generations to come and the ships that would wish to use the canal centuries hence. Would those ships be of the same size and character as those now plowing the seas? It was important, the Congressman insisted, that these problems of the long-distant future should be duly considered in deciding the type of canal. Patiently Burton remarked: "In making our plans it is well to provide for the centuries to come; but it is also well to provide that we do not reach the next century before we finish the canal!"

Inevitably the question of the neutrality of the canal was raised, by an inland interlocutor, and the genial end man responded: "The only rational control of this canal is by treaty securing neutrality, as in the case of the Suez Canal. The best protection is neutrality. I should prefer not to see a fort or a gun on the whole Isthmus, but have it protected entirely by an agreement between nations." This sentiment provoked great applause.

Probably Congress was never before treated to a more profound discourse upon the subject of earthquakes, ancient and modern. A member from California declared that the experience of his state sustained Congressman Burton's conclusion that the masonry of the dams of the canal would withstand without injury an earthquake as severe as any California had ever experienced.

Strongly Burton urged the necessity for immediate action instead of more debate and the signal to the President to proceed was soon secured.

For Theodore Burton, then Chairman of the House Rivers and Harbors Committee, an important and agreeable event of the first decade of the new century was a trip to Europe, in 1903, in the genial company of two close personal friends, Harvey Goulder and Paul Howland. This trip expanded his grasp of the possibilities of a national waterway system that could be synchronized with all other forms of transportation. Probably he then knew more of the marvelous waterways of Europe than did any other member of the House. But that knowledge was largely derived from studying official reports. On this trip he proposed to indulge himself in a personal examination of the great waterway systems of the Continent to learn at first hand the conditions which made their development of commerce so much greater and more profitable than had thus far been realized by the waterways of his own country. And to make the trip even more profitable, Major Mahan, of the Engineer Corps, also joined the party.

A farm boy headed for a country fair with pockets jingling with coins was never more joyously expectant than Burton as he set out on this trip. He was going up the Rhine, down the Volga, and up the Danube. His experience in mastering the details of water-borne traffic of his own country had taught him that there was no substitute for a firsthand investigation in this field.

In early July of 1903 the friends went to Brussels and to the scene of the Battle of Waterloo, where Burton charmed his fellow travelers with his minute knowledge of the details of Napoleon's historic defeat. Then they moved on to Antwerp, to the great art galleries, where Burton entertained his companions with his critical appreciation of the paintings. This revealed a new Burton to them. Next they visited Amsterdam and Rotterdam and then took a boat up the Rhine to Coblenz.

Catching sight of the name Bingen, in a travel folder, Burton gaily recited the poem "Bingen on the Rhine" which he and his companions had learned in boyhood from the pages of *McGuffey's Reader*. Certainly they must see Bingen! Therefore they took a further daylight trip up the Rhine and on to Frankfurt am Main, Berlin, Bremen, and Hamburg.

At Berlin they boarded a steamer down the Elbe to Copenhagen and thence to Stockholm, from where they went by steamer to Olaf in Finland. The next lap of their journey was by rail to old St. Petersburg. At Rybinsk the Americans began their trip down the Volga through the wild Don Cossack country on a revenue cutter placed at their disposal by the Engineering Department of the old czarist government.

The instant they had embarked upon this water journey of nearly sixteen hundred miles, declared Mr. Howland, the Chairman of the Rivers and Harbors Committee betrayed intense excitement and concentration. With notebook in hand he became keenly observant and conversation was virtually suspended. No feature of the commerce of that Russian Mississippi escaped his eye. He plied the Russians on board with questions and used them as guides and interpreters whenever a landing was made. To his companions the journey was a novel panorama of wild scenic surprises; to Burton it was a moving feast of waterway information. The steamers which they passed were strikingly similar to those of his own Mississippi and Ohio rivers.

Burton was astonished by the great diversification of dialects—more than one hundred fifty—encountered in this trip down the Volga. No detail of the co-ordination of water and railway transportation escaped his attention. Here, as throughout Continental Europe, the railways and the docks and terminal facilities were government-owned or government-controlled. There were few gaps between water transportation and rail transportation, which were operated as one unified system.

The party left the Volga at Samara and went by train to the Sea of Azov, and thence to Sevastopol, Odessa, and Constantinople. At Orşova, Congressman Burton experienced the supreme thrill of this research expedition—his first view of the Iron Gate of the Danube. His greatest expectations were fully realized by this celebrated engineering structure which made the rapids of the turbulent river easily navigable. For four days he studied this great engineering feat. He told his fellow travelers that he had made only a good start at the job of mastering the secrets of this great piece of construction, but that he would return to it later—which he did, in 1909, as Chairman of the National Waterways Commission.

After this expedition Burton was in a stronger position than ever before to work out his dream of waterway improvements. On the extended trip, he paid his own traveling expenses and those of his secretary. The trip was not officially authorized; therefore he would pay for it out of his own pocket. He never confused public and private expenditures.

Burton Writes a Book on Prosperity Cycles

THE FIRST IMPORTANT TASK which the new century brought to Theodore Burton was a self-appointed and incidental one which had great influence upon his standing as an economic statesman. This was the writing, in 1900 and 1901, of a book published by D. Appleton & Co., in 1902, under the title *Financial Crises and Periods of Industrial and Commercial Depression*. Rechristened more crisply in the spirit of today, it would be called *Cycles*. Its author was certainly not the discoverer of the "cycle theory" regarding the periodic recurrence of times of depression and prosperity; John Mills, for example, had advanced that theory years before.

Burton, however, brought the cycle theory up to date and so thoroughly Americanized it that it looked like a brand-new discovery to the typical American businessman. To be able to detect, considerably in advance, the approach of a serious financial disturbance would be a gift from the gods of Finance, a charm against loss from a falling market. No master of business or finance has ever prayed to his gods for a greater favor than that of asking for a dependable signal as to when to take to the financial cyclone cellar and when to emerge.

Congressman Burton was a powerful legislator, highly respected by the leading financiers and businessmen of the country; his book, therefore, was regarded as the offering of a "practical" man and, despite its formidable specific gravity, it has had a great influence. Burton revised it repeatedly, the last time in 1929 and, according to his publishers, D. Appleton & Co., it reached its twenty-first edition in 1932. Its reception by the public in 1902 was "very gratifying" to its author. The solid merits of *Financial Crises* were acclaimed by economists of that day, both at home and abroad, and many of Mr. Burton's colleagues in Congress said extremely pleasant things to him about his book—which probably few of them had then read!

Financial Crises, however, was destined to have an odd history. Strong intellectual molars were required for its mastication and relatively few readers possessed that equipment. The clipping bureaus soon ceased to send its author review notices and it began to look as if this solemn study had found a quiet resting place in the mortuary department of dull economic literature. Then the panic year of 1907 appeared.

The year started out gaily and, to the average businessman, the American horn of plenty appeared to have established itself as a permanent institution. Only a few wise old financial observers were disturbed, in January, 1907, by suspicions that a storm threatened. They were careful not to proclaim their fears from the housetops.

Burton did not follow their example—a fact which brought him one of the most disagreeable experiences of his life. At a convention of the Cleveland Credit Men's Association, in the spring of 1907, he frankly told his hearers that they should set their cyclone cellars in order, even though the sunlight of prosperity apparently flooded the land.

Forebodings of an imminent financial panic were felt in February, 1907, when the stock market showed symptoms of heart failure after an orgy of wild speculation, but only the more shrewd observers realized that this was anything more than a momentary faintness.

Although money was tight and hard to command even at high rates, the stock market quickly regained its stride. The public was reassured. In May, however, came another "sinking spell" which passed into financial history as "The Silent Panic." Europe, which then had huge stores of gold and was greedy for the high premium commanded by call money in Wall Street, sent to America a flood of that precious metal. This smothered the panic almost instantly.

The mass of citizens, particularly in the Middle West, were not then aware that an actual financial crisis had been averted. Consequently, for the first time in Burton's life, one of his addresses, delivered before a large business organization in his home city, was received with a chilling lack of applause. He was obviously re-garded as an alarmist. Burton, however, felt sure that his justification would shortly be forthcoming. It was!

By the middle of October, banks and business enterprises of all kinds were failing. Cities were unable to sell their bonds and the market prices of securities of all sorts swept downward. There was a common rush to cover. Bank depositors withdrew their balances in gold and scuttled to hide them in deposit drawers and owners of securities converted them, at great sacrifice, into the same coin and packed the proceeds away in safe personal depositories. The procession of hoarders swelled to a mob.

Suddenly, on October 22, a drama of "frenzied finance" commandeered Wall Street for a stage. Its leading players were the "money kings" of America—envied, admired, and hated by the people—with J. Pierpont Morgan the most commanding figure of them all.

Vast kingdoms of wealth as well as the small savings of humble citizens were at stake. Even the physical liberty of scores of financial freebooters hung in the balance. In the background was a crusading President of the United States who had vowed to break the power of the great "money kings" and teach them respect for law.

But this courageous Rough Rider was suddenly brought to face the fact that to save the people of his country from calamity he must strike a quick and unwilling truce with the one man whom he regarded as the supreme chief of the vandal tribes of organized wealth. These "malefactors of great wealth" were in mortal combat to escape utter extinction and hold their own kingdoms intact—and, if possible, to enlarge them by grabbing the holdings of those falling in the fight. Money madness had never reached a higher dramatic climax than on October 24, 1907.

Banks, trust companies, railroads, and vast commercial and manufacturing enterprises had been collapsing by the score since October 16. The question no longer was whether the projects of the more powerful financiers could be saved, but whether all the banks and great enterprises of the country would crash together. George B. Cortelyou, President Theodore Roosevelt's Secretary of the Treasury, hurried to Wall Street and defined the conditions upon which the Federal Government could properly provide a measure of relief; the banks could be collectively helped—not individually. For once the "money kings" must suspend their feuds, get together and fight shoulder to shoulder under an autocratic leader or nothing would be left worth fighting over. Wall Street interests must choose a general and submit to his commands. One man alone was recognized as having the qualities of leadership that would command obedience from all the warring Wall Street forces. Inevitably Morgan, virtually retired, was recalled to take that high command.

The outstanding crash of October, 1907, was that of the Knickerbocker Trust Company. The trust companies virtually were outside the zone of governmental supervision and control and yet were allowed to receive deposits. They were not national banks and therefore not under the United States Treasury Department and were outside of the New York Clearing House Association. The only direct regulation to which they were subjected was that of the state banking department, and this was loose and casual.

Almost inevitably, a number of the trust companies had fallen into the hands of ambitious, unscrupulous, and daring financiers who, by paying higher interest rates than national banks could afford under their official restrictions, gradually attracted a great volume of deposits. They could lend or invest such funds almost without limit, while national banks in the Clearing House Association were compelled to keep 25 per cent on hand in cash.

The Knickerbocker was a large trust company and was in the hands of a group of operators who knew every trick of the game of financial buccaneering. While it is true that such trust companies were not members of the Clearing House Association, their transactions had to be cleared through member banks. This afforded the New York Clearing House an ultimate, if indirect, means of disciplining them. An edict from it that the member bank through which any trust company cleared its transactions must suspend that service was equivalent to a sentence of summary execution. The depositors having funds in the trust company would swiftly execute the extreme penalty. This was precisely what happened in the case of the Knickerbocker Trust Company. The Clearing House directors refused to help the Knickerbocker, so it crashed—and a group of other great financial institutions along with it. Wall Street was a seething maelstrom for about two weeks.*

Morgan, working in co-operation with President Roosevelt's

* See *Morgan the Magnificent* by John K. Winkler. New York, 1930.

Secretary of the Treasury, had the power to crush even the most powerful financiers in America. He decreed succor for one and ruin for another. Secretary Cortelyou placed United States funds where Morgan believed they would do the most good in preventing the collapse of the entire financial structure of the country. This result was the one common objective.

Morgan had made himself the embodiment of financial might. To millions of his fellow citizens his name was a personalized definition of the "money power."

When the President shot through bared teeth the phrase "malefactors of great wealth," the image of J. Pierpont Morgan sprang instantly to the public mind—not because his methods were more unscrupulous than those of his Wall Street compatriots, but because they were more intelligent and successful.

Undeniably President Roosevelt did his part in speeding the tragic tide of fear that loosed itself upon the financial world in the turbulent autumn of 1907. His intentions were noble but his methods were extreme. He overplayed his role of the Great Denunciator of financial wickedness and failed to realize the peculiar sensitiveness of Money—particularly money deposited in banks—and the temperamental swiftness of its reaction to threatened disturbance of any sort.

A magazine editor, a reform orator, a muckraking writer might safely go to almost any length of denunciation of the "money powers"—but not a President! To have a President of the United States belching threats of punishment against the greatest financiers in America was an unprecedented audacity which made Money shrink and quiver.

A panic reaction was inevitable. The very enormity of the abuses against which Roosevelt stormed had created so perilous a situation that the demand of the moment was for Presidential restraint, for speaking softly and momentarily secreting the "big stick."

Roosevelt therefore endured the humiliation of joining hands with Morgan in order to save the country from financial collapse. True, he gave Mr. Morgan his left hand and kept it as closely covered as possible, but this Morgan, whose hand he held, was the same wicked "malefactor of great wealth" upon whom he had visited personal humiliation at the Gridiron Club dinner a few months before.

Mr. Morgan suddenly found himself being canonized by popular acclaim into a Wall Street saint, a valiant deliverer from financial destruction. For the time being, the word of Morgan was law.

What a superb cast of players this money drama commanded! There were heroes and villains of assorted sizes and talents; Baker, James Stillman, Gary, Henry C. Frick, and Ryan—Harriman, Morse, Charles T. Barney, F. Augustus Heintze, and a score of other Wall Street stars. It was the most intense drama of finance ever staged in America.

The curtain went down upon a glorified Morgan, a saved country—and a smiling author of *Financial Crises* who saw his predictions realized and his "cycle" formula justified.

This panic of 1907 transformed Theodore Burton from an "alarmist" to a financial prophet of the first rank. Those who had heard his speech or read reports of it in the newspapers decided that Burton was about the wisest of financial wizards and that they would do well to study his forbidding book. After five years, it suddenly became popular in high financial circles.

Among those who had read it some months before the panic struck was a certain New York businessman of considerable wealth who arrived at the decision that a major panic was certainly due according to the Burtonian theory. Being a man of action, he promptly converted all of his holdings into cash, which was safely deposited.

When, in the light of Burton's "Guide to Fortune," this man concluded that the fury of the panic had spent itself, he quickly reinvested his money in shares of the strongest companies in the country at prices which seemed absurdly low. His brightest hopes for his investments were realized and he became a multimillionaire.

Mark Sullivan, in an article devoted to "Burton's Slump Theory," which appeared in the Washington Sunday *Star* of October 25, 1931, declared that this capitalist attributed the possession of most of his fortune to application of the principles set forth in Senator Burton's book. Said Sullivan: "It is the best book ever written on this subject."

Mr. Sullivan also referred to Senator Burton as a shining example, in the accumulation of his own fortune, of the soundness of the conclusions contained in his book. After noting that thirty of the seventy-eight years of Burton's life were spent as a Representative and a Senator in Congress—with relatively little income aside from his official salary and the returns on his modest investments—Mr. Sullivan says:

"To the last degree he was scrupulous, prudent, cautious. He accumulated his fortune chiefly through practical application, as an investor, of the economic and financial knowledge he embodied in this book. He was mainly an investor of the savings bank and first mortage and 'gilt edged security' type. . . . I doubt if he ever borrowed a dollar for speculation or for any other purpose.

"The secret of Burton's fortune was mainly that he knew the signs of coming depression and at such times he turned his investments into cash; similarly he knew the signs of the end of the depression and at such times, when securities were abnormally low, he reinvested."

From *Financial Crises* Mr. Sullivan reproduced the following quotation from John Mills:

"After each panic or crisis the first three years will witness diminished trade, lack of employment, falling prices, a lowering rate of interest and very considerable distress. Then there will be three years of active trade, slowly rising prices, fair employment, improving credit. Then will come three years of unduly excited trade, in which speculation will be rife, prices will rapidly rise and an unusual number of new enterprises will be begun. The tenth year will be one of crisis, followed again by three years of depression."

Mr. Sullivan characterized as "ripe wisdom" the following excerpt from the Burton book:

"The turning point is marked by no sudden shock like that which characterized the crisis. It comes gradually and quietly and shows the working of recuperative forces which are sure to triumph.

"In progressive countries the existence of a tendency to periodicity of crises, with the regular recurrence of a series of events consisting successively of crises, depressions, improvement, expansion and a new crisis is as well established as any tendency in the history of industry and trade. To ignore this fact would prevent an accurate analysis of understanding of the subject. The mistake lies in fixing a definite duration for the successive events of the cycle, and in failing to sufficiently recognize exceptional conditions of time, place, and social or economic development."

Mr. Sullivan's characterization of Senator Burton is discriminating:

"The author of this book was a plain man and a great man. Burton was far as possible from being a money maker in the ordinary sense of the word; yet, starting with nothing, he died [in 1929] worth upward of half a million dollars."

Thus Theodore Burton started the new century by almost casually producing a book which developed a vitality and influence altogether beyond his modest expectation. It was an outstanding demonstration of the clarity of his thinking.

Locking Horns With Hanna

THE TURN OF THE CENTURY brought Mark Hanna and Theodore Burton into violent political collision. For a time, the continuance of Burton's political career hung in the balance. About the only trait these men shared in common was that of stubbornness. In nearly every other particular they were opposites.

Mr. Hanna had both a passion and a practical need for running things politically. He was even then the Business Colossus of Cleveland. Until 1896 he had held no political office and apparently had not aspired to any; he had gone into politics simply to protect and expand his growing business interests, and he seldom missed a trick.

His nature was magnificently acquisitive; he was, in the current phrase, into everything—ships on the Great Lakes, street railways, steel mills, banks, coal mines, and almost every other form of large-scale enterprise. From his viewpoint as a captain of industry, the only path of safety lay in controlling the politicians and office-holders. It was cheaper and safer politically to control them than to fight them. Incidentally, in those early days, he found great pleasure in being the political power behind the throne. It was his favorite sport and Senator Hanna was not handicapped by a sensitive social conscience, as were Newton D. Baker and Theodore Burton.

On the other hand, Representative Burton had become a power in Congress and Cleveland was proud of him. Moreover, as Chairman of the Rivers and Harbors Committee, he was in position to get anything for Cleveland in the way of appropriations for its harbor improvement that his conscience would permit him to accept. This conscience, however, sometimes had a way of inter-fering. In fact, on one occasion, his committee was agreeable to an appropriation of two million dollars for further work on the Cleveland harbor which Chairman Burton refused on the ground that other projects were in greater need of funds.

Undoubtedly, Senator Hanna also saw that Burton was develop-ing a disagreeable degree of independence and was increasingly resentful of control by the Hanna machine. Probably it was evi-dent to the Senator that Burton's steady increase in standing with the citizens of Cleveland and of northern Ohio might eventually threaten his own position as the big Republican Boss. And so, at the outset of the campaign of 1902, Hanna undertook to teach the bumptious Congressman Burton who was master in Cleveland politics.

Burton stubbornly determined not to be subservient. He did not fully trust the Senator in a political sense and he disliked Hanna's methods. Therefore, when Senator Hanna elected his own men to run the Republican campaign in Cleveland and Cuyahoga County without regard to the wishes of candidates who did not take their orders from him, Congressman Burton served notice that the Chair-man of the Republican County Committee must be as satisfactory to him as to the Senator. For a time it appeared that Hanna had de-cided to yield to this demand. The Cleveland *Leader* of May 22 contained the statement:

"All factions have practically agreed on the election of Paul Howland as Chairman of the next County Committee."

Soon, however, Hanna showed his hand and elected his man Abel to the chairmanship. His resentment aroused, Burton an-nounced that he would retire from Congress rather than allow the Hanna machine to conduct his campaign.

Burton to retire from Congress? Impossible! That would be a calamity not only for Cleveland but for the nation. Editorials in influential newspapers throughout the country reminded the poli-ticians of Cleveland that Burton had changed the operations of the Rivers and Harbors Committee from the undisguised distribution of Congressional "pork" to a great constructive program for de-veloping the waterway commerce of the country; that his absence from the House would involve the loss of a legislator of singular intelligence, industry, honesty, and independence.

An editorial in the Boston *Herald* commented:

It will be cause for national regret if the Hon. Theodore E. Burton . . . retires from the national House of Representatives. It is a noteworthy fact that the Western Reserve of Ohio has sent to the Congress of the United States an exceptional number of exceedingly able men. . . . In the Western Reserve, conscience has counted for something, while there are sections of Ohio where, apparently, money and organization have been the two chief factors in winning political triumphs. . . .

Evidently Senator Hanna at first believed Burton was bluffing. Therefore he allowed things to drift for a time in the hope that the Congressman would back down. Eventually Hanna met the situation by a compromise arrangement which divided the County Central Committee into two groups, one headed by Paul Howland to manage Burton's campaign and that of the Republican ticket in Burton's district, the other group to conduct the campaign in the remainder of Cuyahoga County. This encounter with Senator Hanna greatly increased Burton's power in Ohio politics and pointed the way to his ultimate entry into the Senate of the United States.

The verdict that Hanna had "made McKinley President" was generally accepted and it required courage for any Republican politician of Ohio to refuse to bend the knee to this Ohio boss. But Burton defied Hanna on several issues—for example, on the choice of materials to be used in building the Cleveland Post Office and on the granting of a ship subsidy to build up a merchant marine—Hanna's pet legislative hobby.

The Cleveland Post Office fight was the more dramatic of the two. It started in 1889, when Burton and Hanna worked together in securing an appropriation of three million dollars for the construction of the Cleveland Federal Building. The bill was signed by President McKinley on March 3, 1899. To judge from contemporary newspaper accounts, Burton's constituents credited him with doing most of the work in securing this appropriation.

Hanna promptly announced that the building would be constructed of Ohio sandstone and erected by the labor of Ohio workmen. This was good politics. Burton, on the other hand, contended that the Cleveland Post Office should not be made a football of politics and should be constructed of nothing less enduring and beautiful than granite. To support his contention he presented petitions from thousands of influential citizens. Hanna was infuriated.

He would teach Burton that it was not safe to buck Mark Hanna! Early in 1904, however, Senator Hanna died.

When the Post Office Bill came up for final consideration in the House, on February 27, 1905, Charles W. F. Dick of Akron had succeeded Hanna as Senator, President McKinley had been slain by an assassin's bullet, and Vice-President Theodore Roosevelt had become President. But personal and party loyalty to the dead Senator was stronger, perhaps, than if he were present in the flesh to see the fight through. Mark Hanna had said that the Cleveland Post Office should be built of sandstone and sandstone it should be! Among those who took up the battle for him was "Uncle Joe" Cannon, of Illinois, who had been elected Speaker in the preceding Congress. Burton, however, stuck to his convictions.

The crux of the post office matter came with the final reading of the bill in the House about a year after the original appropriation had been made. Burton had been assured that he was to be heard on the subject of "Granite vs. Sandstone" and during this speech he would offer his amendment, before the final reading of the bill.

In the ordinary course of procedure several hours would elapse before he would be given this opportunity and he therefore left the floor to look after some other business. His secretary, Joseph H. McGann, meanwhile, casually went up to the gallery to note how the bill was progressing. Suddenly he became aware that there was a change in the usual procedure and that even then the bill was being read, just previous to putting it to a vote. There was no chance for Burton to offer his amendment!

"Instantly, I sprang to my feet," recounted Mr. McGann to the writer, "almost bowling over a doorkeeper in my haste. I did not know where Mr. Burton had gone but decided he was probably in the Senate end of the Capitol. I went to Senator Hale's office first and by great good fortune there was Mr. Burton. Apparently sandstone had triumphed so far as the Cleveland Post Office was concerned. Mr. Burton was greatly agitated and hurriedly returned to the House."

The reading of the entire Public Building Bill had to be finished before he could make his plea for a rehearing on the Cleveland item. Then the fireworks began.

"The situation is one," said Burton heatedly, "which in my recollection has never happened in this House before. . . . A contract has been made in which there is an option between granite and sandstone, an option still open and not yet exercised. . . ."

It was really a contest between Speaker Cannon and Congressman Burton. Cannon knew how to use the power of the Speakership and he had the co-operation of a group of skilled parliamentarians on the floor. They were fighting for the vindiction of the sandstone complex of their dead friend, Senator Hanna, and perhaps for certain satisfactions for Uncle Joe. Burton gave a brilliant demonstration of his own ability as a parliamentarian. Not a single parliamentary thrust of that debate but was instantly parried! Moreover, in this controversy as in many others, Burton had the assistance of many members of the Democratic party.

Every possible trick was tried—even an attempt to stave off the vote on the bill until a considerable number of Democrats should tire of the fight and leave the floor. But Burton and his aides forestalled this by posting messengers at each door to prevent any loyal supporter from leaving until the battle was over. At length Burton's amendment carried. The Cleveland Post Office became a monument of granite to his character.

Burton's opposition to Hanna's efforts to secure a liberal ship subsidy also revealed his fighting blood. Hanna was set on becoming a patron saint of a far-flung American merchant marine promoting American trade in every part and port of the earth. His faith that government aid would realize this dream was complete. Burton was convinced that a ship subsidy would prove futile as a means of developing a strong American merchant marine; therefore he would not support it. Hanna had tried to secure the passage of a subsidy measure in a previous session and its defeat was credited to Burton's opposition.

"I am opposed to the ship subsidy bill just as I was last winter," Congressman Burton declared in November, 1901. "In the first place I do not believe in its principle. I do not believe it would be permanently effective in building up our merchant marine or that benefits would accrue in the way of reduced freight rates for our agricultural and other products." Repeatedly and consistently he argued that "a ship subsidy under any conditions is sinister, dangerous and obnoxious." *

Proponents of the bill claimed that few American ships were able to operate in the merchant marine service because of the protective

* Congressional Record, 61st Cong., 2nd sess. (Apr. 7, 1910), vol. 45, part 1.

tariff which prevented our vessels from securing profitable return cargoes. To this Burton declared that the disadvantage was small in comparison with other considerations. It was not, in Burton's opinion, a matter of tariff influence one way or the other. The question of our lack of a strong merchant marine, he pointed out, was "complicated with other problems—railroad rates, port dues, tariff regulations of other nations, banking facilities, preferences and affiliations of the people with whom we deal. It was not a loss that a subsidy is going to restore or a trade that a subsidy can build up."

He asserted that the real reason for the decadence of our merchant marine lay in the fact that the tastes and tendencies of the American people had shifted to another direction; "they have forgotten the sea, in a new and absorbing interest in the land, a situation in which a ship bill would be helpless to accomplish anything."

Burton could have bought political good will from Hanna by easing his opposition to the ship subsidy; but the Puritan-in-politics declined to compromise his convictions.

It is not difficult to imagine Hanna wondering why Burton couldn't meet him halfway on a matter which involved no moral issue, but merely a difference in judgment as to how a certain piece of legislation would work out. To Mark Hanna, this man Burton was a misfit in politics. To him, Burton's "squeamishness" was a perpetual puzzle and offense.

In his campaign for re-election to the Senate, in 1903, Hanna hoisted the pennant of "a ship subsidy or defeat." He was advised that it would be good policy to pipe down on that issue, as Burton had repeatedly demonstrated that he could defeat a ship subsidy measure—ergo, why could he not defeat a ship subsidy candidate? But the hardy old "Shipping Master" bluntly told Ohio voters that if they were against a ship subsidy they should vote against him as he would devote his full powers to passing such a measure if returned to the Senate. The fact that he was re-elected by a flattering majority gave him probably the greatest thrill of his career. However, Hanna's dream was never to be realized.

CHAPTER 13

Rough Riding With "T.R."—1904

RELATIONS BETWEEN the two Theodores—Roosevelt and Burton—were close until one day, early in 1904, when Burton carelessly let himself in for a stretch of rough riding with his militant chief. As Burton entered the House on February 22 the Administration Naval Bill was under discussion. Its provisions appeared to him extravagant and suggestive of an ambition for world power on the high seas not in keeping with the traditions of the Union and certainly not with his own convictions.

Here was a subject to which he had devoted years of study. He felt impelled to express his convictions and did so on the spur of the moment. He did not pause to consider how his words might be received by the former Assistant Secretary of the Navy who had become President of the United States just in time to take over a collection of orphaned islands of assorted sizes, together with the job of building the world's greatest ship canal connecting the Atlantic and Pacific oceans.

"I am opposed to the naval program exemplified in this bill," declared Burton. "It involves great extravagance." The bill, he observed, carried an amount almost seven times as great as that expended in 1886 and nearly as large as that required to carry the entire civil list of the country. He asserted that this great navy was not, in his opinion, justified by the state of affairs in the world and that a combination of all the European powers against the United States would furnish the only sound justification for it; that such a combination not only did not exist but was as unlikely as any situation which could be suggested.

"England," he observed, "is always cited as the type of nation with a great navy; but this is justified by the needs of English commerce and is in no sense a threat to America." He branded the suggestion that Germany might attack us as ridiculous and asked: "What nation of Europe would desire to lose our friendship and good will?" The Monroe Doctrine had been urged as a valid reason for enlarging the navy; but Burton declared that this claim was unsound because the Monroe Doctrine did not involve injustice to other nations. "We cannot be an example for war," he asserted. "We should set an example for peace."

On the following morning President Roosevelt took his pen in hand and gave this industrious Congressman from Ohio something to think about. The Roosevelt letter read in part:

Feb. 25, 1904

My dear Mr. Burton:

I respect your character and ability so highly and have believed so in your power for good, and therefore, as a corollary, in your power for evil if it is misused; and I am so confident in your good judgment, that I write you a word in reference to your speech on the navy. As you can imagine, this speech was a genuine shock to me. . . .

Let me point out very briefly what I regard as fundamental in the position of those who now wish to stop our building up of the navy, and who nevertheless belong to the Republican party. The one unbelievable crime is to put one's self in a position in which strength and courage are needed, and then to show lack of strength and courage.

This is precisely the crime committed by those who advocate or have acquiesced in the acquisition of the Philippines, the establishment of naval stations in Cuba, and the taking of Porto Rico and Hawaii, and the assertion of the Monroe Doctrine, and who nevertheless decline to advocate the building of a navy such as will alone warrant our attitude in any one, not to say all, of these matters.

It is perfectly allowable, although I think rather ignoble, to take the attitude that this country is to occupy a position in the New World analogous to that of China in the Old World, to stay entirely within her borders, not to endeavor to assert the Monroe Doctrine, incidentally to leave the Philippines, to abandon the care of the Panama Canal, to give up Hawaii and Porto Rico, etc., and therefore to abandon the navy. It is also allowable, and as I think, in the highest degree farsighted and honorable, to insist that the attitude of the Republican party in all these matters during the last eight years has been the wise and proper attitude, and to insist therefore that the navy shall be kept up, and built up as required by the needs of such an attitude. But any attempt to combine the two attitudes is fraught with the certainty of hopelessness and ignominious disaster to the nation.

To be rich, aggressive and yet helpless in war is to invite destruction. If anything that the Republican party has done during the past eight years is all wrong; if we ought not to have annexed Hawaii, or taken the Philippines, or established a kind of protectorate over Cuba, or started to build the Panama Canal, then let us reverse these policies and give up building a navy; but to my mind it is to inflict the greatest wrong on the generations who come after us, if we persevere in these policies and do not back them up by building up a navy. . . .

If we are to have a naval station in the Philippines, if we are to have a fleet in Asiatic waters, or to exert the slightest influence in eastern Asia—where our people hope to find a market—then it is of the highest importance that we have a naval station at Subig Bay. If we are not to have that station, and are not to have a navy, we should be manly enough to say that we intend to abandon the Philippines at once, not to try to keep a naval station there, and not to try to exercise that influence in foreign affairs which comes only to the just man armed who wishes to keep the peace. China is now the sport and plaything of stronger powers because she has constantly acted on her belief of despising and making little of military strength afloat or ashore, and is therefore powerless to keep order within or repel aggression from without.

The little powers of Europe, although in many cases they lead honorable and self-respecting national lives, are powerless to accomplish any great good in foreign affairs, simply and solely because they lack the element of force behind their good wishes.

We, on the other hand, have been able to do so much for the Hague Tribunal and for the cause of international arbitration; we have been able to keep the peace in the waters south of us, to put an end to bloody misrule and bloody civil strife in Cuba, in the Philippines, and at Panama, and we are able to exercise a pacific influence in China because, and only because, together with the purpose to be just, and to keep the peace, we possess a navy which makes it evident that we will not tamely submit to injustice, or tamely acquiesce in breaking the peace.

This letter is for you personally. I write it because I respect you and like you.

Faithfully yours,
Theodore Roosevelt

If Burton's reply to the President's disciplinary letter appears apologetic, let it be remembered that he was writing to the President of the United States and to his party chief. Burton, however, could not and would not back down on the main point at issue, as his answering letter shows:

Feb. 24, 1904

My dear Mr. President:

I cannot do otherwise than thank you for your very friendly letter of yesterday, though I hardly appreciated how strongly you favored the increase of the navy. My sole regret for having spoken on Monday was a fear which came to me more after the remarks were made than before, to the effect that you might be injured by what I said. . . .

At the same time, I have been an enthusiast for peaceful settlement of international controversies since before the time when I entered Congress and I shall undoubtedly retain the same opinions after I leave Congress. It is with me a matter of principle. I cannot yield . . . it is impossible for me to agree with the sentiments expressed in your letter about the necessity of a larger Navy, though I recognize the cogency of the arguments which you have made. . . .

I never was more certain of the result of any election than I am that you will be triumphantly renominated and elected. . . . However, I should be glad to think, and really do think, that you care more about accomplishing great results in the great office which you fill than about the election, and on this account dislike to go contrary to your wish with reference to the great naval program. As regards the outlying [naval] stations, I am not disposed to advocate striking them out, or to support anything which looks like an early abandonment of the Philippines, whatever our future policy may be with reference to them.

It is not probable I shall take further part in the debate excepting to advocate a limit upon the further construction of warships, unless other attacks should be made upon me. In conclusion, I cannot too strongly state my regret that I should, in any degree, feel compelled to depart from your leadership in pending public questions, and my heartfelt thanks for the very cordial expression of friendship and goodwill contained in your letter.

Very sincerely yours,
Theodore E. Burton

How little influence President Roosevelt's reproof had is illustrated by the memorable speech which the peace-minded Congressman from Ohio delivered in the House on May 4, 1906. It made a profound impression. One of the ablest Washington correspondents of that time, Mr. Snell Smith, who represented the Cincinnati *Enquirer*, gives the writer this stirring picture of the scene following the delivery of the speech, into which the usually calm and reserved Burton put unaccustomed emotion.

"I witnessed the scene from the press gallery," says Mr. Smith. "It was the most remarkable personal tribute I have ever seen the House accord to one of its members. Immediately after he had concluded, the rules were suspended and all members of the House then present arose, filed past Mr. Burton, shook his hand and congratulated him on his distinguished address. The remarkable feature of this demonstration was its unanimity. I watched it closely and can vouch for the fact that there was not a member present that day who did not personally congratulate Burton.

"Burton's speech is well worthy of a place in a biography of him, for its theme is still alive and vital and will be for many years to come. It is still the classic document on an American navy sufficient —but no more than sufficient—to maintain and promote peace with other nations."

This time President Roosevelt did not take the trouble to write an affectionately reproving letter to Burton. Evidently he regarded his Ohio aide-de-camp as altogether hopeless on this subject.

Burton opened with the disarming statement:

"In opposing our naval policy, it is not my desire to criticize the members of the Committee on Naval Affairs. They have labored long and successfully for the reduction of expenses. They have brought in a measure which promises a check upon the ambitious and extravagant naval program which has found so many advocates during the last four or five years. If they have been at fault in recommending an excessive amount for the construction of battleships, a principal reason has been their opinion that . . . they were responding to the will of the majority of the American people."

He asserted that he was moved by "a hope to promote the cause of peace and diminish the careless disregard of the calamities of war. I give but passing notice to several valid objections to the present naval program, to its great expense, which has so increased that in the last four years it has exceeded by fifty million dollars that of the four years of the Civil War. . . . Although we are said not to be a military people, the cost of the Naval and Military Establishments, with that of the pension list, a legacy of war, now approximates two-thirds of all the expenses of the United States Government."

With great positiveness he asserted: "We already have a navy so formidable that it is far in advance of any reasonable or prospective needs," and he added that probably nearly all of our fighting ships would "rust away without having fired a shot except for target practice."

Burton said he did not hold the position "of the idealist who believes that wars are past"; there would be further collisions between nations and continued necessity for the protecting of American citizens abroad against injustice and violence. "The world has not yet reached the Golden Age of Peace—and yet every tendency is in that direction." Why? Here he gave his ideas on the reasons why wars were bound to decline in frequency: The increasing attention of civilized nations to the pursuits of industry and commerce would operate powerfully to push war further into the indefinite future. Business, the new world power, could be depended upon to offer increasing resistance to the costly interruptions of war.

The power of swiftly increasing intelligence, however, was the greatest and most irresistible enemy of war. It was steadily changing the inertia of conservative opinion; the people everywhere were learning to think about the problems of government and this was forcing governments to follow the march of public opinion.

"With the growth of the human intellect," he declared, "with the absorption of men in intellectual pursuits, and with the increased influence of moral forces, war seems more and more appalling. Nations no longer exist for the sovereign; sovereigns must exist for the nation. The State may be supreme, but the individual is more and more, year by year, and generation by generation. 'Nations,' it has been said, 'are now conquered not by armies but by ideas.'

"But for the inertia which pertains to great political reforms war would have already disappeared."

Burton aroused his audience to applause by a clear and candid statement of his naval attitude which scarcely could be misunderstood by any of his hearers—or by President Roosevelt. It left no opening for big-navy enthusiasts to charge him with being an extreme and impractical pacifist who would imperil his country by denying it reasonable preparedness. More than all else, he desired a secure international peace but he recognized the practical necessities of ample protection against aggression by other nations. The high point in his speech, in the opinion of most of his auditors, was this:

"All recognize that the establishment of courts of justice to decide controversies between individuals is a great landmark in the progress of civilization. Another step just as inevitable is the establishment of similar courts as between nations. The world can not afford to maintain these military armaments. Their decrease and abandonment will not come in a year, but it will come. I would say nothing today against a navy which, man for man and gun for gun, is one of the best in the world, or, as I hope it may be, the best in the world. I would say nothing against a state of preparedness. What I do say is that to maintain this [proposed] great navy is not in accordance with our best ideals, nor is it in accordance with our best interest, material or otherwise."

Burton declared that history would decree "the chiefest glory" of Theodore Roosevelt, as man and President, to be the success of his good offices in bringing the war between Japan and Russia to a close when, without his negotiations, the conflict might have continued for months longer.

The progress of arbitration in the settlement of important differences between nations is commonly unappreciated by the public and even by men in public life. With this fact in mind Burton remarked:

"Just as there has been very great progress in doing away with war, so there has been equal progress in the peaceful settlement of dispute, especially in the last 90 years. From 1815 to 1900 more than two hundred controversies between nations were settled by arbitration. Since 1900 there have been forty more, and each successive bulletin adds to the list. In these the United States was a party in a very considerable share. These arbitrations have settled the most irritating questions, not only questions of boundary, of indignities to citizens, of property and personal rights, but all the great range of questions which in the olden times were incitements to war."

If Burton cherished any hope that his speech, so generously acclaimed by the House, would defeat the passage of the Administration Naval Bill, he was doomed to disappointment. The "one battleship" amendment which he offered was defeated, as in all probability he knew it would be. But he had given his colleagues and the nation something to think about on the burdens of over-sized navies, the natural decline of war as a result of progressing civilization, and a wider acceptance of the principle of settling international as well as individual disputes by resort to law rather than bloodshed.

CHAPTER 14

"Jacta Est Alea"—"Let 'Er Go Gallagher"

UNDOUBTEDLY THE STRANGEST INTERLUDE in the political career of Theodore Burton was his contest with Tom Johnson, in 1907, for the mayoralty of Cleveland. Burton was already recognized as one of the big men in Congress. The people of the country could not understand his entering the race for a local city office rich in possibilities of disaster and unhappiness and their curiosity was keenly aroused.

The Burton-Johnson municipal contest ranks as one of the most celebrated mayoralty campaigns ever conducted in an American city. It had many features which made it unique and commanded generous attention from the nation's press.

Tom Johnson had become a national political figure and the leaders of the Republican Party regarded him as one of the most dangerous men in the country—not because of defects of character but because of the economic theories to which he was devoted. It is almost equally certain that many of the older and more conservative leaders of the Democratic Party, to which he tacitly belonged, shared this opinion.

He was picturesque, brilliant, and human, quick and resourceful in debate, a rough-and-ready campaigner who spoke the language of the "dinner-pail brigade" and was looked upon by the polyglot mass of workingmen in the industrial city of Cleveland as their hero and defender against the powers of great wealth and the greed of public utilities.

In addition to his determination to put the street railways and other public utilities of Cleveland into the hands of the people through municipal ownership, next to Henry George, Tom Johnson was the chief apostle of the followers of the single-tax doctrine in the United States.

Had he hailed from almost any state other than Ohio, his political extermination would not have seemed so urgent a necessity to the national leaders of the Republican Party and to the watchdogs of Big Business and vested interests in all parties. There was no telling, these men reasoned, how far this popular leader might go in state and national politics if he were not given a decisive beating.

Up to that time, Ohio had furnished the nation with four Presidents and the shrewdest students of politics were agreed that her importance as a pivotal state in national elections was bound to increase rather than diminish. While the Western Reserve Commonwealth had not, since the birth of the Republican Party, furnished a successful Democratic candidate for the Presidency, Republican leaders feared that sometime it might do so.

This campaign between the scholarly, serious, reserved Burton and Tom Johnson, the agile and adroit hero of the wageworkers, was highly dramatic. Johnson went into the battle with a fighting joy he had never known before. This time he had something to talk about that he could get across to the boys from the mills.

In his campaigns for Congress he had been hampered by the necessity of trying to interest his hearers in the theories of single tax, but had found this doctrine above the heads of most of his listeners. Now he had something that his humblest hearers could understand: his charge that the workers were being "done" out of exorbitant fares by a greedy traction monopoly. That was simple. So was the argument that this monopoly naturally belonged to the people of Cleveland and that under municipal ownership they would share in its profits.

Who should know more about this than Johnson, who had made a fortune in the traction business? His hearers were eager to take his word on anything relating to street-car finance and operation. The fact that he had been in the game himself did not bother them for an instant; he was on their side now.

Then, too, this remarkable campaigner had a genius for getting laughs from his audiences. He was ready in the repartee of the stump and often, by the twist of a phrase or the turn of a word, diverted his hearers from the points scored by his serious, not to say solemn, opponent.

In these tactics he had the help of a young man of abilities far exceeding his own—Newton D. Baker, who became President Wilson's Secretary of War and later took rank as one of the ablest lawyers of the country. Baker not only had a better education than Johnson but had a sharper wit and a nimbler mind.

The first words uttered by Congressman Burton in this campaign played into the hands of those two skillful stump speakers. Burton spoke before an audience gathered to hear from his own lips the statement that he had decided to respond to the call, which had been expressed in petitions bearing more than fifteen thousand names and in two thousand or more letters, and that, if he were elected, he would desert his agreeable tasks in Congress to free his beloved city of Cleveland from the demagogic rule of Tom Johnson.

Burton's audience was largely composed of workingmen, and it is safe to assume that it did not contain more than a score of men familiar enough with Latin to translate his initial phrase:

"*Jacta est alea!*" (The die is cast.)

"The instant I heard this phrase," one of Burton's campaign leaders remarked to the author a few days later, "I realized what fun Tom Johnson and Newton Baker would have with it. Nothing could have been more typically Burtonesque than to start a campaign speech to a mixed audience with a Latin quotation. I was not mistaken in thinking that Tom Johnson, with the help of Newton Baker, would play ball with this phrase. He caught it instantly and came back with the declaration:

" '*Jacta est alea.* I'm not a Latin scholar, like my distinguished opponent, but my answer to that challenge is: *Let 'er go Gallagher —we're off!*' Burton's Latin phrase ran like a refrain through the whole campaign. From the viewpoint of a scholar it was apt and graceful, but the way Tom Johnson and Newton Baker played upon it made it appear ludicrous. It gave them the chance to get the whole city laughing at Burton, which served their purpose quite as well as answering his solid arguments."

No one disliked being laughed at more than Theodore Burton— and this campaign was a cumulative crescendo of laughter at his expense.

Burton entered the contest solely because he was convinced it was his duty to the Republican Party. Johnson's economic ideas were repugnant to him—but so was the office of mayor! He had no taste for local politics or administrative office of any kind. His bent was wholly in the direction of national lawmaking.

Up to that time, about the only complaint brought against him was that he had been too busy being a statesman to give proper attention to "home matters." This criticism had been brought to his attention on many occasions by men who had worked hard to elect him to Congress—and it rankled. Again, his sense of party regularity and of loyalty to its leaders was strong.

A local newspaper summed up the situation as follows:

> After Hanna died it was the natural supposition that his mantle would fall on Myron T. Herrick. The mantle fell, but it didn't fit— it was far too big for Herrick. . . . Then the Republican "outs," who saw no chance of getting "in" so long as Tom L. Johnson cared to control the destinies of the Democratic party, raised a cry for Burton to take the local leadership. The professional politicians were seconded by honest Republicans who were sincere in their belief that Johnson should be driven from power. . . . Tom Johnson must be defeated, Burton was told, and again and again he was reminded that he owed it to his party to "redeem" Cleveland. At last Burton yielded and . . . consented to make the race. . . .

It was hotly debated whether the demand that Burton sacrifice his place in Congress was first pressed upon him by President Roosevelt and William Howard Taft, then Secretary of War, or by local leaders. Among Burton's personal friends and political associates in Cleveland were men of wealth having large interests in the traction company and other public utility corporations. From the viewpoint of Tom Johnson and his followers, these friends had simply hoodwinked Congressman Burton into an attempt to pull their financial chestnuts out of the fire. Then, too, Burton was himself a man of substance, a conservative, a friend of Capital and of capitalists. He had always held that the wages of workers must suffer when capital could not be profitably employed in enterprises, and that the security of capital involved, in a general way at least, the security of employment. Also Burton had little or no faith in municipal ownership of public utilities and believed that private ownership insured better management.

The character of the local pressure brought to bear upon Burton by his personal, political, and financial friends is sufficiently suggested by a letter from Myron T. Herrick:

October 2, 1907
My dear Burton:

After talking with the friends named to you, I have prepared and enclose to you herewith a rough outline of about the position that I feel a man would be justified in taking in presenting this matter to the public at the present time. This may or may not be of assistance to you in forming your opinion. The more I study the situation, the more forcibly it is impressed upon me that the arguments must be such that the man who runs may read. It would be very easy to present a proposition to the public going Johnson one better in his appeal to the rabble; but the fact remains that here is a corporation fighting for its life—and the problem now seems to be one of salvage, all hope of profit having been abandoned, and a proposition may be put so unfavorable to this company that it would prefer to take its chances in a continued battle with Johnson as long as it can continue to collect the present rate of fare, rather than to face certain bankruptcy in the near future. As I view the situation from a financial standpoint, I cannot conceive how anyone seeking an investment could be satisfied to purchase any securities based on a franchise such as the Big Consolidated has eventually agreed to accept. . . .

The Big Consolidated is this morning selling seven tickets for a quarter. I believe this will be very helpful to the situation. Things seem to be going on rather well. I have endeavored to keep in touch with the trend of affairs. I believe that the East End will be practically unanimous. I learned today of a group of eighteen neighbors on Bell Avenue, of whom sixteen voted for Johnson at the last mayoralty election, but a poll made of them in the last few days shows that seventeen of the eighteen will vote for you this fall. This, of course, is in the East End. The real contest is to be in other quarters, as we both appreciate.

Very truly yours,
M.T.H.

This "personal and confidential" letter from a man of Herrick's business standing—the head of one of Cleveland's foremost financial institutions and an authority upon sound investments—must have had a profound influence upon Burton. His law practice mainly had been built upon the administration of estates and the successful investment of their funds in profitable securities. He knew the elements of unsoundness in a security and could shrewdly calculate the influence upon its investment value of competitive and restrictive conditions.

That he considered the statements submitted by Mr. Herrick with the eye of a conscientious administrator of funds belonging to widows and orphans cannot be questioned. If this constituted a capitalistic view of the situation, he was ready to accept the indictment.

This statement is not intended to imply that Tom Johnson was not equally sincere in taking the position that the traction consolidation was too grasping. He, also, had the courage of his convictions.

Leading politicians held that both President Theodore Roosevelt and William Howard Taft, of Cincinnati, were secretly anxious to eliminate Congressman Burton from a position of leadership in Ohio because, so they held, President Roosevelt was then determined to have Secretary Taft succeed him as President and thought that, if Burton eliminated himself as a Presidential possibility from the Ohio scene, this course would be easier, especially since there was every likelihood that the next Presidential nominee of the Republican Party would be picked from the Buckeye State.

At any rate, the following correspondence took place:

Cleveland, Ohio,
August 28, 1907.

Hon. Wm. Loeb, Private Secretary,
Oyster Bay, Long Island, N.Y.
My dear Mr. Loeb:

There is a matter about which I wish you would speak to the President and obtain his opinion; also I should like your own thought upon the question. An almost overwhelming pressure is brought to bear upon me to become a candidate for Mayor of the city of Cleveland at the election next November.

It is argued:

First: That a crisis has been reached in the affairs of the City, and that its future will be seriously injured if Tom L. Johnson is re-elected.

Second: That under the influence of a powerful ring dominated by him, which includes some three thousand officeholders, and has great power in other particulars, Cleveland will become, instead of a Republican city, strongly Democratic; and that thus the situation assumes not merely local importance but state and national.

Third: That while I could win as against him, the success of any other candidate is problematical.

To this is added the argument that the best and most substantial element of the city has always stood by me in election contests, and that I now owe to them all the sacrifice that would be involved in becoming a candidate for Mayor. . . .

I cannot yet come to the conclusion that I ought to consider it, though I fear that circumstances may so shape themselves that I shall be compelled to do so.

I should greatly prize a free and confidential opinion on this subject.

Very respectfully yours,
T. E. Burton

President Roosevelt replied directly:

Oyster Bay, N.Y.
Aug. 30, 1907.

My dear Burton:

You put a hard question in your letter to Mr. Loeb. There are certain qualities of leadership which you possess which could not be supplied by any one else in the House, and you have a mastery of certain subjects such as no other man in the House can hope to obtain. For you to leave the House, therefore, would mean that in certain lines of leadership there would be a loss that cannot be made up. I would therefore be tempted to protest against your leaving if it were not for my profound conviction that it is exceedingly desirable that you should win out as Mayor of Cleveland.

In view of the fact that our democratic system undergoes its most severe strain in the government of our cities, I feel that it is of the utmost importance to have a man of your experience, power and character, of your long training, theoretical and practical, in public life, take such a position as that of the Mayoralty of Cleveland. Accordingly, if you ask my advice, I should say make the fight.

With all good wishes, believe me,

Faithfully yours,
Theodore Roosevelt

As for Mr. Taft, no correspondence has been found by the writer relative to this matter.

Mr. Taft was a shrewd politician and saw before him, with President Roosevelt's co-operation, an opportunity to secure the Presidential nomination. It is logical to suppose that he would be glad to see any possible interference from Burton eliminated. Miss Grace C. Burton, who served her uncle as a confidential secretary, states that urgent pressure, in personal talks and by other means, was exerted by Secretary Taft to induce Burton to make the mayoralty fight against Johnson and thereby help "to keep Ohio in the Republican fold."

It should be remembered that at this time the break between Roosevelt and Taft had not occurred. Roosevelt had succeeded to the office of President upon the death of McKinley on September 14, 1901, thus serving for the greater part of the term for which McKinley had been elected. Then, in 1904, he was elected President "on his own." In 1908, he determined not to be a candidate to succeed himself, obviously because of the belief that the voters would hold that he had already served two terms in the White House and that two were enough.

In the opinion of many observers of national politics in that period, President Roosevelt then planned to become a candidate for President in 1912 and this plan entered into the selection of Taft as the Republican candidate in 1908.

Not a few of the old-time leaders of the Republican Party assert that President Roosevelt's insistence that Burton should become a candidate for Mayor of Cleveland in order to "wipe Tom Johnson off the political map" was as much to eliminate Burton as a possible Presidential candidate in 1912 as to "finish off Johnson."

There are those who believe that when President Roosevelt selected Taft as his successor there was at least a tacit understanding between them that Taft would be satisfied with one term in the White House and at its close would stand aside for the man who had dictated his nomination.

The point here raised is that if, in 1908, an understanding did exist between Roosevelt and Taft, that the latter would not become a candidate to succeed himself in 1912, it would lend color to the theory that Roosevelt might have had an ulterior purpose in pushing Burton into the Cleveland mayoralty campaign.

Although Theodore Burton made an earnest, vigorous, and valiant fight against Tom Johnson, it is doubtful that at any time he was confident that he would win. And it is almost equally doubtful that he really wished to win.

Interesting light is thrown upon this hot political fight by Joseph H. McGann, then attached to Mr. Burton's personal staff:

"It is difficult to realize the intensity of that campaign. Interest in it was nation-wide and in Cleveland it was at white-heat. The big feature of the contest was the running newspaper debate between Mr. Burton and Tom Johnson. This entailed a prodigious amount of work every day, and the major part of it, of course, fell upon Mr. Burton.

"At the outset of the campaign there was much talk about a series of joint debates between Johnson and Burton, but Mr. Burton's friends realized that he would be placed at a disadvantage in this form of debate by Johnson's peculiar abilities as a rough-and-ready stump speaker. Therefore, Burton was persuaded to insist that their joint debate should be conducted in the press instead of from the stump. The outstanding impression which this experience left upon me was a realization of Mr. Burton's almost unbelievable capacity for intense and sustained mental exertion over a long stretch of time. It was a terrible grind for all of us and especially for him; we considered ourselves in luck if we were able to leave headquarters at 3 o'clock in the morning. Almost invariably we were back on the job at 9 o'clock."

Thomas Monks, one of "Burton's Young Men"—in later years a Vice-President of the Guardian Trust Company of Cleveland—was a candidate for city auditor on the municipal ticket with Mr. Burton in 1907. Says he of that stirring campaign:

"Our political headquarters were in the old Colonial Hotel. Mr. Burton would come in from his speaking tour about midnight and we would all work until about four or four-thirty in the morning. First, he would carefully check the reports brought in from the various wards and give directions for the next day's work. Then he would turn to the newspaper debate with Tom Johnson.

"Mr. Burton's capacity for work was almost unbelievable. He could wear out the younger men who were his captains and lieutenants. In the early morning, when everything on the slate had been disposed of, he would generally remark: 'Boys, I think I'll walk home; it will be good for me as I get no physical exercise.' As the distance from the Colonial Hotel to his home was nearly five miles, some one of us invariably asked the privilege of taking the walk with him—and were well repaid by his conversation on these long walks.

"On election day, with Mr. Burton, we made a flying circuit of the polling places of the city to see how the vote was going. He was particularly interested in the seventeenth ward, largely populated by foreigners. He got out of the automobile at one voting precinct, where there was a big crowd, and was about to make inquiries regarding the vote when a man shouted: 'Hurrah for Tom Johnson— to hell with Burton!'

" 'My! My!' exclaimed Mr. Burton. 'Let's get out of here.' With this he turned his back upon the scene and got into the automobile as quickly as possible. This was one of many incidents of the campaign which revealed how distasteful the whole thing was to him.

"On election night we all gathered in Lang & Cassidy's office in the Williamson Building to receive the returns. It was rather a funereal task and comparatively early in the evening we knew that we were licked. Then I said to Mr. Burton with more sincerity than he thought: 'This is all for the best—you'll see!' Mr. Burton then gave us the first smile of the evening and remarked: 'Tom, I think the strain of the campaign has told on you.'

"The day when he was elected Senator at Columbus, on November 3, 1908, nearly all of his old secretaries and many of his most intimate friends were gathered about him. He was as happy as a boy with a new pair of boots. Turning to Ed Turner, then Prosecutor of Franklin County and later Attorney General of Ohio, Senator Burton related what I had said to him the night of the mayoralty election and remarked: 'Of course I couldn't see it then; but wasn't Monks right?'

"He had demonstrated, by going into the Tom Johnson campaign, his willingness to sacrifice himself for local and party interests and that sacrifice had just been rewarded by his election to the United States Senate."

This campaign furnished the quiet, dignified Burton with excitement and adventures other than those incident to oratorical roughhouse. One night's campaigning trip, for example, came close to bringing him serious physical injury, if not death.

He had taken a fancy to a young letter carrier in the post office, Frank E. Kulas, who had the reputation of being not only alert and reliable but an uncommonly skillful automobile driver. He felt secure with this young man at the wheel and at the outset of the campaign selected him as his driver.

One night information was received at headquarters that no speaker had appeared at a Republican rally in Tood Street. This was in a district of workingmen's homes and Mr. Burton decided that it would not do for the audience to be disappointed and that he himself would speak there. He took with him a local speaker who happened to be at headquarters. They had gone a little distance when this speaker insisted that by turning at a certain corner they could make a short cut and save considerable time.

Burton finally told the driver to follow the young man's directions. The driver made the turn and almost instantly found the automobile going down a forty foot embankment, headed straight for the river. Fortunately the bank was hard clay; if it had been of a more yielding soil the consequences almost certainly would have been serious.

The driver instantly called out: "Don't jump! Lie down in the back." The passengers obeyed and in a few seconds found the car mired in wet clay only a few feet from the river. This was perhaps the closest escape from death by accident that Mr. Burton ever had. After that, at least so far as this campaign was concerned, he refused to ride with any driver other than young Kulas. This young man, by the way, never asked for a promotion in the post office service but repeatedly was promoted and for many years was Cleveland's Assistant Postmaster.

The national interest in this campaign is suggested by the fact that the *Saturday Evening Post* sent the author to Cleveland, when the contest was well under way, to write a character study of Congressman Burton. Quotations from that article are made here because they reflect the spirit and atmosphere of that historic municipal campaign. The writer traveled from hall to hall with Congressman Burton, observed him in action, studied his audiences and their reactions and was forced to the conclusion that this political performance had its element of pathos. Burton had the will to win, but neither his heart nor his hopes were in the struggle. The most revealing portions of that contemporary picture of the contest follow:

> There isn't a boy in Cleveland under college age who has hung upon the fringes of political meetings that has ever heard Theodore Burton presented to a local audience without the ring of the phrase: "Our most distinguished citizen."
>
> Mr. Burton, however, is something besides distinguished and irreproachably respectable. He is honest and able. . . .
>
> An element in the situation which goes to make Mr. Burton's conventionalities picturesque is the fact that Tom Johnson—his antagonist in the big mayoralty fight—is a past master in all the arts

of popular leadership. He is big, genial, a dynamo of goodfellow-ship, a Jumbo magnet of personal attraction. Burton is the antith-esis of all these things. He is tall, slender, with the stoop shoulders of a confirmed student. He exudes refinement, and likewise ex-clusiveness. He is helplessly serious, and his underlip curls forward stubbornly. Where Tom Johnson breathes an all-comprehending fellowship with humanity in the rough, Burton's countenance pub-lishes reticence and suspicion.

He is always Theodore Burton to all men—refined, distinguished, scholarly, reticent—and cannot, for an instant, be anything else to anybody. . . .

His actions and his friendships are arrived at by the process of elimination. He analyzes and questions every person and proposi-tion that comes in his way. Probably, no man ever left Theodore Burton's presence, after a first talk with him, feeling that he had found a new friendship, while Tom Johnson has scores, perhaps hundreds, of these off-the-bat friendships.

How is it, then, that this thin, aloof, almost ascetic man, who has not a single art of the "popular politician," and who is above suspicion in the matter of carrying his ends by the use of money, is able to defy all the traditions of popular leadership and command the loyalty of the people? There is only one answer. . . . Sheer character and ability give Theodore Burton his hold upon the people of Cleveland and of Ohio. . . .

Not many years ago an old Oberlin College friend of Mr. Bur-ton's felt himself breaking under the strain of business cares. "Turn them all over to me," said Mr. Burton, "and I'll attend to them until you are fully rested." This was done, to the immense relief of the man to whom Mr. Burton's services, on a professional basis, were entirely out of reach. Things of this sort indicate that, after all, Mr. Burton is quite human.

There is at least one point in which Tom Johnson's opponent is a politician of the first order. He never forgets a face or a name. At the close of a recent campaign speech Mr. Burton was shaking hands with those of the audience who lingered for a little personal contact.

"I don't suppose you know me, sir," said a little man.

"Oh! yes," interrupted Mr. Burton, "I was introduced to you eight years ago, in Ravenna Hall, at the close of a political meeting, and I'm glad to see you again, Mr. Kysela. Are you still in the cigar business?"

Mr. Burton has the support of the cigar dealer and all of the friends he can influence.

The public outside of Ohio naturally raises the question: "Why does the distinguished Mr. Burton quit a big, congenial, and states-manlike job in Congress, where he can boss the expenditure of millions of dollars and also help Mr. Roosevelt navigate Adminis-tration measures through the House, to come back to Cleveland to mix up in a political roughhouse over the mayoralty?"

And the outside public has so often answered its own question after this manner:

"It must be that he is trying to make a short cut to the United States Senate."

The business men of Cleveland—and those of them, too, who are not in the least infatuated with the reticent and distinguished Mr. Burton—say that this is a mistake; that all Mr. Burton has to do in order to land in the Senate is to stay quietly where he is and keep on being scholarly, distinguished, and honest until Senator Dick's term expires; that he is not after Senator Foraker's seat, and that this is a real case of rallying to the Macedonian cry.

Whether Mr. Burton will oust the Uplift administration seems to depend in large measure upon the possibility of bringing out the "silent" middle-class vote which the figures seem to show has kept in hiding for several years. To the end of getting out this vote Mr. Burton has for several weeks been holding a circuit of good, old-fashioned political "cottage prayer-meetings"—a method of political warfare which he has found decidedly effective. He is able to address some six or eight of these doorstep gatherings in a single evening, shake the hands of the brethren and the neighbors, and give them a heart-to-heart talk on the Tom Johnson dynasty.

According to one of his young men, the defeat of Johnson seemed imminent at the outset of the campaign. "There is no doubt in my mind," says this informant, "that had the election been held one week from the day on which Mr. Burton was nominated he would have been overwhelmingly elected. His defeat, however, was due to the feeling inspired by the newspapers and the Democratic cam-paigners that he had been imposed upon by the public utility in-terests of Cleveland and that his election would amount to an endorsement of the old street railway regime."

The mayoralty campaign, which was exploited in the newspapers from the Atlantic to the Pacific, revealed Burton in a new light to thousands of Ohioans. The attention his campaign attracted from the press of the country gave them a new realization of his stand-ing and ability as a national statesman.

While the campaign was on, it was suggested to the writer that many of those who admired Burton most helped to defeat him in this fight because they believed that his sacrifice would be a poor bargain for Cleveland and for Ohio, the nation, and the national Republican Party. These men thought his defeat of Tom Johnson, if accomplished, would not compensate for the loss of his services in Congress. He had not resigned his seat and defeat would automatically return him to it. That, they reasoned, was where he belonged.

In his campaign for Congress, after his first term, he invariably had the support of the *Plain Dealer*, avowedly Democratic, and the most influential daily paper of Cleveland. In the mayoralty campaign the attitude of that journal was virtually this: Burton belongs in Congress; his services there are invaluable to Cleveland as well as to the nation; as a mayor he would be a misfit and a failure; save him from himself and his bad advisors by defeating him.

In some of his campaigns for the House Burton had no Democratic opponent. Cleveland wanted Burton in Congress and did not want him in the mayor's office. It gave a decisive verdict that the City Hall was no place for him.

That he was momentarily chagrined by the failure of his adventure into municipal politics is certain. His only consolation was that he had given the leaders of his party proof of his party loyalty; by the same token, he had demonstrated to a certain critical contingent of his home following that he had an interest in home affairs and that he did not hold himself above doing battle for local interests.

No testimony regarding the popular reaction to Congressman Burton's sacrifice for the sake of party can be more authoritative than that of Maurice Maschke, the chief political strategist of the Burton forces, who said:

"Some have felt that his candidacy for Mayor of Cleveland against Tom Johnson, in 1907, was a great political mistake. Of course, he was defeated, but I am inclined to think that it strengthened his position in the party in the State of Ohio. There were many Republicans who had previously felt that Mr. Burton was much more interested in national and international matters than in local matters and that he was rather removed from interest in home politics.

"Always, thereafter, Republicans of this county felt sure that

Theodore Burton was interested in them because he deliberately sacrificed himself for the party in the anti-Johnson fight."

Burton returned to his duties in Congress a greatly disillusioned and downcast man, wondering whether he had been so conclusively repudiated by his own people that it was obligatory upon him to resign his seat and retire from public life.

But, back in the congenial atmosphere of Washington, his colleagues took him in hand and labored diligently to convince him that his course in Congress had not been an issue in the campaign and that he would inflict a needless loss upon his party and the public by retiring.

They assured him that the real interests of the country in waterway development, in banking and finance, in foreign relations, and in many other fields required him to remain at his post.

This treatment of his wounded pride was healing and the restoration was completed by a perusal of press comments which his alert secretaries and clerks kept before him from day to day. The local Republican papers throughout Ohio gave him particular consolation. He read them eagerly, systematically. Clearly he was made to feel that his party standing in the state was more instead of less secure than before.

Another factor entered the situation to make him forget the unhappy Cleveland campaign. This was the nomination, at the behest of President Roosevelt, of William Howard Taft, then Secretary of War, as the Republican candidate for President—an event which was dealt with in Washington months before it became an accomplished fact. Congressman Burton was called into frequent White House conferences and became an intimate advisor of the Secretary of War who was destined to become the next President of the United States.

This new relationship was both absorbing and agreeable to Burton, who formed a genuine liking for the jovial Mr. Taft, whose abilities he greatly respected. It also added to his prestige in his home state. The election of Taft to the Presidency would be most important to Ohio Republicans.

Theodore Burton found himself a high favorite at the Republican court, deferred to by the people of his state and regarded as one who might ask almost anything of the new ruler with no risk of being denied.

So the preliminary and final Taft campaigns saw Congressman

Burton in fine fettle, with completely restored self-respect, with renewed ambition, and a new faith in the kind intentions of destiny toward "Cleveland's most distinguished citizen."

Early in 1908 he scanned the political skies with smiling satisfaction; they promised him a place in the sun which he had long coveted—a seat in the United States Senate. This had been denied him in 1904 when Representative Charles W. F. Dick was elected to succeed Senator Hanna.

The power of the Anti-Saloon League had been behind Dick, a far more agile opportunist than Burton, and Dick was elected. But now Burton held a strategic position in the factional setup in Ohio. The old favorites of the Cox machine in the southern end of the state were allied with William Howard Taft of Cincinnati, whose every act had proclaimed him for Burton, who, in 1904, had declared open war upon "Boss" Cox and his organization.

Now why shouldn't the factions get together and restore the moral standing of the party by electing to the Senate a man who was immune to criticism on the score of integrity and ability?

Of course he might be difficult to handle when it came to "practical matters" of state politics—but why not take it for granted that he could be brought into line when an emergency arose?

Those citizens of Ohio not having a professional interest in politics responded eagerly to the possibility of having Burton as Senator. At that time, United States Senators in Ohio were elected by the General Assembly, not by popular ballot. The people, however, made their sentiments known, both to their Representatives in the General Assembly and to Burton himself. He received letters from every section of the state and from hundreds of its most substantial citizens expressing satisfaction at the prospect that he might become a candidate for the senatorship. The Republican press of Ohio also was generally favorable to his candidacy.

When all these indications were most propitious Burton announced that he would be a candidate for the seat in the Senate then occupied by Joseph B. Foraker, who appeared, at the moment, to be the only rival against whom he would have to contend. This announcement brought him pledges of support from every camp of Republicans in the state.

Among those who enlisted under his banner were many factional leaders, particularly in the southern part of the state, with whom he had previously held meager fellowship. He received them all gladly, promised little, and smiled much. He did, however, accept their declarations of loyalty and support.

Thus he created a state-wide obligation to new and old recruits under his banner which he took more seriously to heart, in all probability, than many of them supposed. He did not fail to recognize the fact that he had assumed responsibilities of party leadership in Ohio and that it was as much a matter of good sportsmanship for him as for those who allied themselves with his organization to stand fast by their mutual understanding.

CHAPTER 15

At Last—a Senator!

NOTHING COULD BETTER illustrate the extent to which Theodore Burton held himself subject to the good of the party than his course in the first Taft campaign, a dizzy merry-go-round of Ohio politics.

In August, 1908, members of the National Monetary Commission assigned to investigate the monetary systems of Europe arrived in London and found Representative Burton, a member of the commission, awaiting them. Knowing European sources of information which would be most useful to the commissioners, he had taken an earlier passage, made arrangements for Chairman Aldrich and his colleagues, and was ready to return to America.

As this was shortly before Secretary Taft's nomination as the Republican Presidential candidate, with the election of a United States Senator from Ohio in the foreground, the nature of the business demanding Burton's presence in Ohio was obvious. He had scarcely taken the boat back to America when Senators Aldrich and Hale went into a two-man huddle, forgot European finances for the moment and focused their attention on the Ohio political situation.

Neither of these powerful Senators was over-enthusiastic regarding President Roosevelt or his policies. They regarded it as inevitable that Secretary of War Taft would receive the nomination for President at the Republican Convention called to meet in Chicago on June 16. President Roosevelt already had declared that he would not be a candidate to succeed himself and that he proposed to exert all of his power to nominate and elect Mr. Taft. Burton had been selected to make the Taft nomination speech; also, he proposed to seek the Senatorship.

Immediately after Burton had sailed for home, Senator Aldrich sent a trusted messenger in his wake, one who was charged that his mission must be so secretly accomplished as to escape the attention of the press. In New York, this messenger took the first train to Cincinnati and went at once to the home of Secretary Taft.

Their conference was brief. When it was over, the messenger boarded a train for Cleveland, going at once to the apartment of Theodore Burton, where he faced the most difficult and embarrassing part of his responsibility. This was to inform Burton that Senators Aldrich and Hale and the Presidential nominee of his party united in asking him, "for the good of the party," to put aside his ambition to be elected Senator and agree that he would not oppose the re-election of Senator Foraker.

The messenger was aware that, in the preceding Senatorial contest, Congressman Burton had been disappointed in his failure to receive the nomination which went to Charles W. F. Dick. This defeat, the messenger well knew, had been particularly disappointing to Burton because, at that time, he had asserted his leadership in the state of Republicans arrayed against Boss Cox and the Cincinnati group of politicians of which Senator Foraker was a member. Burton's courageous fight had provoked a response which gave him every reason to expect that, in the election of 1908, his leadership would be vindicated by his election as Senator Foraker's successor.

It is not difficult to imagine the delicacy of the position in which the messenger found himself—to present to Burton the request of the probable nominee of his party for President and of the two most powerful Republican leaders in the nation that he sacrifice his Senatorial ambition and step aside to permit the return to the Senate of the very man who was the most conspicuous beneficiary of the Cincinnati machine which Burton had attacked.

"Mr. Burton took the blow like a man," related the messenger, "without an argument or a whimper. After a moment of thoughtful silence, he requested me to go back to Mr. Taft and assure him that the request would be honored. He stipulated, however, that this withdrawal from the Senatorial race should not be announced until some time after the delegates to the Republican National Convention had been chosen. Such an announcement, he urged, was likely to upset party plans and lead to the selection of some delegates who could not be depended upon to stand by Taft in the convention.

The easy-going candidate for the Presidential nomination thought this an unnecessary precaution, but Burton was insistent.

"Taft had entire confidence that Burton, the leader of the Cleveland forces, would step aside when the time came. Besides, Senators Aldrich and Hale had asked for a heavy sacrifice from Burton and it would be poor policy to be too demanding as to details. Senator Foraker would offer no opposition for he knew that he was slated by Aldrich and Hale to succeed himself in the Senate and he trusted Burton to keep his promise to these Republican dictators. Before this interview, my admiration for Mr. Burton was strong, but it was immensely increased by his fine sporting conduct on that occasion."

At once the messenger returned to Cincinnati and reported to Taft the details of his talk with Burton. Evidently the report was highly acceptable to Secretary Taft. The next move on the part of the messenger was to call upon Senator Foraker and obtain his assurance that he would be a candidate to succeed himself—a task somewhat in the nature of bearing flowers to a bride.

Meantime a furious storm had developed from an incident which had occurred in Texas two years before. It involved an act of army discipline visited upon a battalion of Negro troops at Brownsville, Texas, which subjected President Roosevelt to severe criticism.

This sensational incident, which occurred on the night of August 13, 1906, when Mr. Taft was Secretary of War and was already President Roosevelt's choice as his successor, instantly assumed political importance, particularly in view of the fact that Senator Foraker of Ohio at that time generally was regarded as a formidable candidate for the Republican Presidential nomination. Any occurrence tending to strengthen Foraker's chances of success in this ambition would, of course, interfere with President Roosevelt's plans to name Taft as his successor.

An honorable record as a soldier in the Civil War was then a cardinal asset for any candidate for high office, and Senator Foraker possessed this qualification. He had entered the Union ranks in 1862, as an enlisted private, and had distinguished himself for bravery. This vote-getting qualification could not be ignored by his opponents for party honors.

The transfer of the Negro troops from the North to the military post on the outskirts of Brownsville aroused a storm of resentment. Senator Culberson, of Texas, urged the War Department to send them elsewhere, as trouble and violence were almost certain to occur if they were allowed to remain. Had easy-going Mr. Taft, then Secretary of War, taken prompt and tactful action, the most regrettable incident of the Theodore Roosevelt Administration would have been avoided; but Taft apparently ignored Senator Culberson's protest.

On the night of August 13, 1906, Senator Culberson's direst predictions were realized. Apparently, having failed to secure the transfer of the troops, a certain element of white residents of Brownsville had determined to provoke trouble with them which would lead to their removal as a matter of military discipline.

In his memoirs, *Notes of a Busy Life*, Senator Foraker made this statement:

> During the two weeks intervening between the arrival of the battalion at Brownsville and the shooting affray, there were two or three altercations between citizens and members of Company C. In each case it was shown that the soldiers were not at fault; that the citizens provoked the quarrel and the soldiers did not even resist, but rather only evaded and escaped.
>
> No member of either Company B or Company D had any trouble of any kind with anybody. The police officers testified their conduct was better than that of the white soldiers who had preceded them.

As to the famous "affray" itself, it is sufficient to say that soldiers from the fort "shot up the town" and in the course of this demonstration one man was killed and two were wounded.

Senator Foraker's account contains the following summary:

> The first official report made by Major A. P. Blocksom, Division Inspector General, was based on the unsworn statements of a number of citizens. According to these statements, shots were heard in the vicinity of the Fort a few minutes before midnight, August 13. As stated by some of the citizens, the first shots were fired inside the Fort. . . . These statements were given to support the charge that the firing was by a squad of soldiers who leaped over the walls of the Fort and went in a body up one of the streets of Brownsville a short distance; then returned to the Fort, having fired some 200 or 300 shots, killing one man and wounding two others.
>
> Although the night was dark, citizens claimed that, looking out from the windows of their houses, they were able to recognize the marauders as Negro soldiers. . . .

Twelve of the soldiers were arrested on suspicion but after a thorough investigation by a Grand Jury were released and allowed to rejoin their battalion. . . . A military investigation then was conducted by General E. A. Darlington, Inspector General of the Army, who reported that there was not any reasonable doubt that the soldiers did the firing but that the men so uniformly and persistently denied guilt, they appeared to be banded together to "suppress the truth" and he "could not procure any evidence thereof."

He recommended that, as an example to the whole army, the entire battalion should be found guilty of the shooting and of the concealment of facts connected therewith and should be discharged without honor. This accordingly was ordered by the President, November 5, 1906.

Senator Foraker, an able lawyer, naturally considered the evidence taken by the military tribunals, their findings, and the mandate of President Roosevelt from a legal viewpoint. Studied in this light, he said, "The testimony on which the President acted I saw at once was flimsy, unreliable, insufficient, and untruthful; that the soldiers belonging to these three companies had been condemned and punished en masse and not as individuals; that the guilty had not been separated from the innocent; that all denials of guilt had been treated as 'a conspiracy of silence'; that many of the soldiers had served three and four enlistments, and some of them more— a number of them were nearing the length of continuous service that entitled them to retire on three-fourths pay and with other valuable property rights and privileges"; that at Fort Niobrara, Nebraska, from which they had been transferred to Brownsville, "they had sustained a good reputation as peaceable, docile, law-abiding, dutiful, well-drilled, well-disciplined, faithful and efficient soldiers."

As he had been a soldier himself, it was natural that this apparent injustice to soldiers should stir Senator Foraker's blood. He confessed that in the beginning he too held the popular opinion, based upon newspaper reports, that the men were guilty. But a careful examination of the case changed his mind.

Consequently, at the next session of Congress, the following December, Senator Foraker offered a resolution which was promptly passed, requiring the Secretary of War to submit to the Senate all of the information and documents in his possession bearing upon this incident.

The debate in the Senate on "the Brownsville affray" became the sensation of the hour. On November 19, 1906, the bitter resentment of President Roosevelt was revealed in a stinging message to the Senate, in which he declared that "Major Blocksom's report is most careful, is based upon the testimony of scores of eyewitnesses." To this statement Senator Foraker replied: "The President could not have counted the eyewitnesses. We have them all here in the papers sent to us. . . . Instead of 'scores of eyewitnesses' who have testified to this transaction, there are only eight men at most. . . . Therefore, I say the President has been imposed upon."

This historic debate continued intermittently until the twenty-second of January when Senator Foraker's resolution authorizing a Senatorial investigation was passed. Commenting on the character and tone of his arguments is the following passage in Senator Foraker's memoirs:

> The keynote of my contention was that the men had been condemned without a hearing and that this was contrary to the spirit of our institutions; that it was our duty to undo that wrong by giving them a chance to face their accusers.
>
> The debate grew constantly more and more strenuous, but it will be found that . . . I confined myself to legitimate arguments and carefully avoided saying anything unnecessarily that should have wounded the dignity or the sensibilities of the President. *I was all the while hoping that, with the truth established . . . the President would in manly fashion undo the wrong he had done.*

From the opening of this case in the Senate to the departure of Senators Aldrich and Hale and the other members of the National Monetary Commission for London Senator Foraker pursued his investigation persistently. However, President Roosevelt gave no sign of any change of mind, but insisted that his acts and orders as Commander of the Armies and Navies of the United States were not subject to review by the Senate.

The controversy had reached this stage when Senator Aldrich, the real "General Manager" of the Republican Party, decided that it would be a salutary step in the interest of the party to insure Mr. Foraker's return to the Senate, thus administering a sly rebuke to the unyielding course of President Roosevelt.

Suddenly, this controversy flamed up afresh under circumstances which increased its bitterness. At the annual dinner of the Gridiron Club, in January, 1908, both President Roosevelt and Senator

Foraker were guests. Traditionally, at this unique yearly assemblage of newspapermen no reporters are present and no public report of the proceedings is ever made.

On the testimony of one who was present in 1908 it appears that President Roosevelt, when called upon to speak, made biting allusions to matters of recent controversy between himself and Senator Foraker. The atmosphere of the gathering invited great liberty of speech and President Roosevelt is said to have made free use of that privilege.

Of course Senator Foraker was also immediately called upon by Toastmaster Samuel G. Blythe, who says that his response was restrained but courageous and unflinching. Immediately after he concluded he was handed a card from Senator Albert J. Beveridge which read:

"Dear Senator: I am against you, but I never so admired you as at this instant. You are game and you are masterful. You were altogether thoroughbred tonight."

The Gridiron affair made it instantly clear that President Roosevelt did not intend to alter his attitude respecting the Brownsville matter. The practical result of his Gridiron speech was to serve notice that he was out to punish Senator Foraker.

A large part of the United States Senate was present at the dinner, together with many of the country's most influential political and financial leaders. Scores of them have since recalled that dinner as the most dramatic and exciting they were ever privileged to attend. Unmistakably, it was a declaration of war between President Roosevelt and Senator Foraker, and listeners were quick to consider its possible effects upon national and Ohio politics.*

The ultimate outcome of Senator Foraker's challenge of the justice of the Presidential order and of the Senatorial investigation which resulted is best stated in his own words, written several years later.

> It is now [July, 1915] nine years, almost, since that fateful night. After the lapse of this long period of time, not one single particle

---

* James Ford Rhodes, the distinguished historian, after stating that he had carefully read the three chapters of Senator Foraker's *Notes of a Busy Life* dealing with the "Brownsville affray," declares, "I am not convinced that he has made out his case" and adds: "Military matters in any case require prompt decision and the despotic quality naturally inheres in any executive action. But a calm review of the whole matter cannot fail to convince the impartial observer that the President was right and acted on the best evidence, both legal and human, that was obtainable."

of testimony has ever yet been produced to identify any man who was a member of that battalion with the affray; and I feel that I hazard nothing in saying that not one particle of testimony to such an effect ever will be produced.*

Theodore Roosevelt somewhat redeemed this wrong eight years later, according to the Senator's wife, Julia Bundy Foraker. In her delightful book, *I Would Live It Again*, she records that on June 28, 1916, Mr. Roosevelt wrote Mr. Foraker as follows:

OYSTER BAY
LONG ISLAND, N. Y.

June 28, 1916

My dear Senator:

I have just finished your two volumes which I have read with great interest. Of course, there are certain portions as to which you and I will continue to differ, but if I ever get the chance to speak publicly, I shall elaborate what I said in speaking of you in the libel suit.

Not only do I admire your entire courage and straightforwardness . . . but I also grew steadily more and more to realize your absolute Americanism, and your capacity for generosity and disinterestedness. . . .

There is no use in raking up the past now, but there were some things told me against you or in reference to you which (when I consider what I know of informants) would have carried no weight with me at the time had I been as well informed as at present. . . .

Faithfully yours,

(SIGNED) Theodore Roosevelt

Joseph B. Foraker, Esq.
Traction Building
Cincinnati, Ohio

When the messenger sent by Senators Aldrich and Hale from London to Cincinnati discharged his secret mission, he left Senator Foraker with the feeling that he was to receive vindication in the form of a mandate from the people of his state to return to the Senate and finish the job of justifying his course in the Brownsville controversy. But he had the less consoling consciousness that President Roosevelt would probably pursue him to the end of his political life. He knew that, should events so shape themselves as to place him in position to become a candidate for the Presidential

---

* Joseph Benson Foraker, *Notes of a Busy Life*, vol. 2. Cincinnati, 1916.

nomination, Roosevelt would exert powerful influence to crush his hopes.

Meantime, Burton nursed the somewhat cold consolation that he had proved himself a good party soldier and had obediently accepted an indefinite postponement of his Senatorial ambitions at the moment when they seemed about to be realized.

Now, in Columbus, Ohio, on the evening of September 17, 1908, William Randolph Hearst dropped a bomb from the sky by reading portions of several leters, filched from their owner, which had been written by John B. Archbold, of the Standard Oil Company. These letters made it appear that Senator Foraker was being paid by the Standard Oil Company to influence national legislation which might affect the interests of that corporation. In the newspapers of the next day Senator Foraker made public this reply:

> I do not know whether the letters given out by Mr. Hearst are true copies or not, but I assume they are, for I was then engaged in the practice of law and employed by the Standard Oil Company as one of its counsels in connection with its affairs in Ohio. . . . The employment had no reference whatever to anything pending in Congress, or to anything in which the Federal Government had the slightest interest. . . . That employment ended before my first term in the Senate expired. I have not represented the company in any way since.

But Mr. Hearst had not yet shot his bolt. In St. Louis, on the evening of September 18, he read the following copy of a letter from Mr. Archbold to Senator Foraker, dated January 27, 1902:

> My dear Senator:
> Responding to your favor of the 25th it gives me pleasure to hand you herewith certificate of deposit $50,000.00, in accordance with our understanding. Your letter states the condition correctly, and I trust that the transaction will be successfully consummated.
> Yours very truly,
> John D. Archbold

In a statement made public in the afternoon papers of September 19, Senator Foraker went into details respecting all of his relations with the Standard Oil Company and particularly the nature of his employment as attorney for it in 1902. In the course of this answer he said:

It will be remembered that the Standard Oil Company was first sued and the decree of dissolution was entered in the Supreme Court, which made it necessary for the company to reorganize. Difficulties arose in carrying out that decree, which delayed their reorganization. . . . It was then that I was employed, not to participate in the litigation, which was in the hands of competent counsel, but to investigate the whole situation . . . with a view to advising the company how, in my opinion, it could . . . reorganize as not to violate any law or any judgments. . . . Nothing connected with this work had any relation to anything whatever pending in Congress or to any matter in which the national government was interested in the slightest degree, nor did anything connected with the employment relate to or conflict with any duty of mine as a Senator. . . . I have never had any relation whatever to the company since.

Explaining the transaction involving the $50,000 certificate of deposit, Senator Foraker stated that he had been approached by a friend to help buy the *Ohio State Journal*. Being unable to contribute himself and wishing to keep the paper in friendly hands, he approached the Standard Oil Company, which was persuaded to advance $50,000. The transaction, however, fell through, the paper went to other purchasers, and Foraker declared the check was returned.

Senator Foraker's comment on the next development of his unhappy situation is decidedly pertinent and revealing. In his memoirs he says:

How the controversy would have ended if it had been left to Mr. Hearst and me alone is of necessity only speculation. But the flood of letters and telegrams that commenced to pour in upon me from every direction, from other states as well as from Ohio, were of the most encouraging character. The flood continued until President Roosevelt gave out an interview of such hostile character, and President Taft assumed such an attitude of hostility, for political reasons, as a matter of policy, rather than because anybody had changed his mind on this subject, that the tide again turned against me.

In his answer to President Roosevelt's attack, Senator Foraker scored heavily by bringing out the fact that he was one of the subcommittee of three which framed the Elkins law, approved on January 19, 1903, which put teeth into the Sherman Antitrust Act and under which all the successful prosecutions of the Standard Oil Company were conducted. Then, on his own initiative, Mr. Foraker made public a letter from Mr. Archbold, bearing the date of May 7, 1906, and reading:

My dear Senator:
In the possibility of an action being brought against us in Ohio, are you in position to accept a retainer from us in connection with such a matter?
Your early response will oblige,

Yours very truly,
John B. Archbold

The answer to this was dated May 9, 1906, and read as follows:

John D. Archbold, Esquire
26 Broadway
New York
My dear Sir:
My duties in the Senate have so multiplied that I found it necessary to retire entirely from the practice of the law. I have not taken new employment for more than two years past. On this account, as well as because of my relations to the public service, I cannot accept a retainer in the contingency named, as I would be very glad to do if it were otherwise.
Assuring you of my proper appreciation for the compliment involved in the inquiry you make, I remain

Very truly yours,
J. B. Foraker

No matter what proof of innocence he had to offer, Foraker had not a chance in the world. Virtually every adult citizen of the Buckeye State was convinced that the Standard Oil Company had wrecked the oil production business in Ohio by means of secret concessions in freight rates. Any officeholder or candidate for office in Ohio at that time who carried upon his garment the smell of "Standard" petroleum, raw or refined, was out of luck. Miss Ida Tarbell and all the army of lesser "muckrakers" had opened the eyes of the public to the fact that no business was safe from the throttling hand of monopoly so long as any competitor could secure secret freight rates lower than they were able to obtain.

The moral of this tale, however, is that President Roosevelt rode with the tide of changed popular sentiment respecting Big Business, monopolies, and special privileges of every kind. Almost literally, he boiled Senator Foraker in oil. All the documentary proofs of innocence that the eloquent and courageous Senator from Cincinnati could present counted for nothing.

The instant the Archbold letters were made public, that weatherwise political skipper of the Republican ship, Senator Aldrich, and his first mate, Senator Hale, of Maine, knew that the craft of their old-time friend and companion, Joseph Benson Foraker, had hit the political rocks and would never be salvaged. Consequently, they released Congressman Theodore Burton from his sacrificial pact with them and gave him a hearty Godspeed in his drive for the position which he had long coveted and which he had once refused as a matter of party loyalty and fairness to Mark Hanna.

Burton had every reason to look forward to the support of both the retiring and the incoming Republican President of the United States. It is true that Senator Foraker was still a candidate for re-election and that former Speaker of the House, General J. Warren Keifer, together with one or two other lesser candidates, were in the offing. They were not, however, in a position to obstruct Burton's own happy course.

Suddenly a new and disquieting pennant appeared over the horizon bearing the insignia of "Brother Charlie" Taft. This caused a surge of astonishment to sweep over the happy countenance of the candidate from Cleveland.

Candidate Burton, in common with the other Republican leaders of the state, was aware that the situation must be as difficult for Secretary Taft as for himself, for this wealthy half brother of the Republican Presidential nominee was known to have been unstinted in his generosity to further the latter's political ambitions. According to current "inside information," Charles P. Taft had spent upward of $800,000 in securing the Republican Presidential nomination for his brother, and the end was not yet in sight. Appetite for political success apparently was contagious in the Taft family and "Brother Charlie" had developed it.

When the Senatorial candidacy of this owner of a string of Ohio newspapers and of a major league ball team was announced, thousands of citizens of Ohio were moved to exclaim: "That certainly puts either Bill Taft or Theodore Burton—perhaps both—in a fix."

Curiosity to see how "Smooth Bill" Taft would ease his way out was intense. This delicate situation in the Taft household had not a gleam of humor for Theodore Burton. It brought all the stubbornness in his nature into action. He was not again tamely to be cheated out of promotion to the Senate.

Burton threw himself into a fierce political fight. Promptly he proceeded to build up an organization of seasoned politicians upon whom he felt he could depend.

His forces in the northern part of the state were under the command of Maurice Maschke, with whose ability and loyalty Burton had long been acquainted. This Harvard graduate had been one of the original group of "Burton's Young Men" who had fought his earlier political battles with him and, at least to a considerable extent, shared his ideals and followed his methods.

At that time it was widely recognized that the Republican Party in Ohio had, in Harry M. Daugherty, of the city of Washington Court House, one of the most resourceful political strategists in Republican ranks. Daugherty was intensely human and "the boys" out in the state quite generally came to regard him as their friend and a big man in the party.

When it became known that Daugherty had enlisted under the Burton banner, the practical politicians of the state recognized that Burton's prospects must be bright. Probably no other supporter of the Cleveland Congressman contributed more to the success of his campaign than did Mr. Daugherty.

The entrance of Charles Taft in the race did not discourage Senator Foraker, despite the fact that they were both residents of Cincinnati, where the Republican machine of Boss Cox had been virtually all-powerful for many years. Senator Foraker was fighting for vindication and he also proposed to "stick it out" to the end. The atmosphere of the contest must have been quite as murky to him as to Burton. Remember, only a few weeks before, William Howard Taft had entered into a triple pact to give Foraker a clear right of way for a return to the Senate and to vindicate his controversy with President Roosevelt regarding the "Brownsville affray." Now Foraker found the wealthy half brother of William Taft a powerful candidate for Foraker's Senate seat—and Burton, another party to the pact, was also a candidate.

In Senator Foraker's *Notes of a Busy Life* is the following statement:

The honorable Champ Clark was right in saying that the Brownsville Affray put me out of the 1908 race for the Presidency, but he was wrong in saying it also put me out of the Senate. It destroyed whatever chance I might otherwise have had for the Presidential nomination, however, not because my course with respect to it was either wrong or unpopular, for the exact opposite was true, but because it made President Roosevelt, then at the height of his popularity and power, openly active and hostile. He was strong enough to nominate William H. Taft. . . . He was not strong enough, however, to defeat me on that account for re-election to the Senate. My defeat was due to another cause.

Then follows the story of the Archbold letters.

Of course, both Burton and Foraker recognized that Charles Taft's generous gifts to the pre-convention campaign of "Brother Bill" must be regarded as a substantial lien upon the good will of any President, regardless of the close blood tie between William Howard Taft and this surprise candidate for the Ohio Senatorship.

Burton was the first of the contestants to get an inkling as to the lines upon which President Taft would proceed. Almost immediately after the Presidential election he was summoned to a conference with the President-elect and made to understand that his acceptance of a certain important Cabinet portfolio would be very agreeable to the new Chief Executive.

In response, Burton assured the President-elect of his appreciation of the implied compliment but indicated that he hoped no such offer would be tendered because he would feel compelled to decline it. His ambitions were legislative, not administrative; he was a candidate for the Ohio Senatorship and believed that he was fitted to render his party, his state, and his country a much more useful service in the Senate than he could in the Cabinet. Then he took a dignified departure and promptly returned to his campaign in Ohio.

He had found nothing in the President's manner to indicate that the refusal of a Cabinet position by the leading Senatorial opponent of "Brother Charlie" was particularly surprising or disappointing to his jovial friend. Perhaps the new President was only going through the motions of meeting his obligations to "Brother Charlie" and possibly he was relieved that his tentative offer of a Cabinet position had been refused.

Its acceptance, of course, would have virtually insured the election of Charles Taft to the Senate. But would it have been an unalloyed satisfaction to the new Chief Executive to have a brother in the United States Senate who might easily be regarded as an "Administration oracle"?

Soon Burton was again summoned to a conference with President Taft and this time was invited to indicate his attitude toward a more desirable and important Cabinet post. His answer was the same as before—"not interested."

According to credible information, this ceremony was repeated two or three times before the Ohio legislature met—and also before President Taft announced the personnel of his Cabinet.

A secretary in Congressman Burton's employ at that time relates this incident:

"It happened to fall to my lot to inform Mr. Burton that President Taft's ranking secretary had telephoned requesting an immediate conference. Mr. Burton hurried out, but returned in a surprisingly short time. As he passed my desk I caught an inviting twinkle in his eyes.

" 'Well, if it's a fair question, sir, what did he offer you this time?' I asked.

"His face lighted with merriment as he leaned close to my ear and, in an undertone, replied, 'Secretary of State!' "

Newspaper statements that the most alluring Cabinet positions within the gift of the President had been dangled before Burton's eyes went unchallenged and apparently they did not cause President Taft any particular embarrassment. Instantly on Burton's election to the Senate, President Taft sent him a cordial message of congratulation. Senator Burton at once became one of the most frequent callers at the White House and the President indicated that he relied greatly upon Burton's counsel and regarded him as an intimate friend.

If Burton, under the circumstances, had accepted a Cabinet post members of his organization would have felt that they had been sold out by their leader; that the man from whom they had expected rewards in the coin of desirable Federal appointments had traded them out of these places to secure a Cabinet position for himself.

Shortly before the legislature assembled, the political skies cleared for Theodore Burton in a manner which seemed almost too good to be true. All of his Republican opponents withdrew, making it possible for him to receive the united support of his party. Commenting on this occurrence, the late Granville Mooney, Speaker of the Ohio House in 1908–1909, made this observation to the writer:

"There was a conference of party leaders at the Chittenden Hotel and Senator Foraker finally agreed to withdraw on condition that his withdrawal should be the first one announced. Then, Charles P. Taft and General J. Warren Keifer withdrew. The whole matter was very skillfully handled."

Thus Burton knew, before a vote was taken, that he would be elected Senator and probably would receive every Republican vote in the Assembly. In the burst of sunshine which fell across his path when the last obstacle to his ambition disappeared, he did a most characteristic act, bringing to Columbus his most beloved relatives to witness the formalities which made him a Senator from Ohio.

With him were his sister, Mrs. Mary Burton Shurtleff, of Oberlin; his brother, Edward Burton, of Lincoln, Illinois; his niece, Grace C. Burton; and his cousins, Miss Jennie M. Grant, of Cleveland, and John C. Grant, of Chicago. Mrs. Shurtleff was thirteen years his senior and, to use his own words, had been a "second mother" to him.

This was the family party—but in the background was an unofficial observer of the ceremonies—the sweetheart of his Oberlin College days. It is said that she gave no sign that the occasion revived memories of a campus engagement. Even the new Senator did not hold himself more firmly to his dignified role throughout the ceremonies than did the woman who might have been his wife had she not decided, years before, that "Oberlin's most distinguished alumnus" was a far greater success as a scholar and statesman than as a lover.

Senator Burton's address to the Assembly was delivered with a warmth unusual for him, and betrayed his happiness in the occasion. His declarations of appreciation for the honor conferred upon him, of his realization of the responsibilities which it entailed, and of his desire not only to help restore harmony in his own party but to represent the whole people of his state, regardless of party affiliations, carried a conviction of sincerity that greatly moved his hearers. His deep, melodious voice, easily heard in every part of the House, had a strong emotional quality; his heart as well as his mind was in his utterances. It was "Burton's big day."

His comments on the tendency toward the centralization of

power in the Federal Government were of a character to satisfy the most ardent Jeffersonian Democrat. He urged that every state should zealously retain its own individuality and declared: "Government is efficient and economical just about in proportion as those for whom improvements are made bear the burden and exercise a watchful eye in the incurring of expenditure and in the prosecution of projects for their benefit."

He declared that it would be his aim "to have some part in those great progressive movements which are the distinguishing characteristics of the time and which are especially manifest in this land of free institutions and boundless wealth." As a final word he said, "It should be the object of all our endeavors to resist the importunities of those who are seeking to make of the government an agency for personal advantage."

The reception which followed this rather naive speech was the high moment of Theodore Burton's life up to that time.

An alluring objective before him as a United States Senator was the privilege of a larger participation in the foreign affairs of the Government. Few members of the House had developed greater influence in foreign affairs, but this was a field belonging in a special sense to Senators.

He was going to have a good time as a United States Senator digging into difficult problems involved in our relations with other world powers. The future looked very bright to Senator Burton that day of his election as he shook hands with hundreds of his Ohio friends and then took his family group to a jolly dinner.

CHAPTER 16

Burton's Great Waterways Dream

URTON'S TRIP TO EUROPE, in 1903, devoted to a private inspection of continental waterways, inspired him with high hopes for realizing his ambition to purge the Rivers and Harbors Committee of its pork-barrel taint and devote it to the great task of upbuilding systems of American waterways that would justify the cost by their commercial use and benefits.

He was familiar with the blindness and indifference of Congressmen and their pork-hungry constituents to the waste, extravagance, and commercial futility of many of the projects which they proposed. On the other hand, he had faith in the tendencies of his fellow men when subjected to education to correct erroneous impressions and practices.

Burton hoped to give his country groups of waterway systems comparable in their usefulness and commercial success to those of Europe. There were great differences between a vast country of relatively thin population and a group of small and densely populated countries in which both rail and water transportation facilities were mainly under government ownership. The European system could be only remotely approximated in the United States. Burton, however, saw that a comprehensive knowledge of European waterway achievement would be of value in educating the United States Congress and public.

One reason for his confidence was the fact that President Roosevelt was aggressively interested in waterways. Shortly after Burton's return from his own private survey of European waterway systems, Roosevelt sent an experienced newspaper man, Judson C. Welliver, to the Old World to investigate the "Relations Between Waterways and Railway Traffic in Europe." Welliver did a distinguished job.

A smaller man might have felt jealousy on the score that the President had rather "beaten him to it" by sending Welliver on this European quest. But not Burton. He realized that his chief was impatient of Congressional delays; therefore he had ignored Congress to secure the benefit of what could be learned from Europe regarding the successful co-ordination of water and rail transportation.

A little later, in 1907, Burton was to receive another cheering proof that in President Roosevelt he had a militant ally for the promotion of his great waterway plans. The President decided that the waterway needs and possibilities of the West were not adequately understood and that something should be done to remedy this deficiency. Again he decided to side-step Congress and get the information without bothering the lawmakers for funds or authorization. Out of hand, on March 14, 1907, he created, by Presidential mandate, the Inland Waterways Commission and appointed as its members the following Representatives, Senators, and Federal officials: Hon. Theodore E. Burton, Chairman; Senator Francis G. Newlands, Senator William Warner, Hon. John H. Bankhead, General Alexander Mackenzie, Mr. W. J. McGee, Mr. F. H. Newell, Mr. Gifford Pinchot, Hon. Herbert Knox Smith.

The necessity of appealing to Congress for an appropriation to defray the expenses of the investigation was avoided by placing existing government facilities at the command of the commission, the members of which were already receiving government pay.

As various individual members of the commission were given the duty of investigations and reports covering the general localities of their residence, the spread of the investigation was greatly extended without material increase of expense. In this manner virtually the whole West was covered.

Nearly all of the experts involved in the investigation were engineers attached to the War Department. Altogether the details of this sweeping investigation were cleverly manipulated to confine its expense to existing governmental establishments and facilities. Chairman Burton was delighted with the results of the work.

At the outset, Burton formulated a manual of tactics to outwit Congressional logrollers and force them to help put Rivers and Harbors improvements upon a higher plane.

He proposed to build up, by a gradual process of accretion, a system of committee and House rules of procedure which, automatically, would discourage highhanded raids upon the national treasury in the name of waterway improvements. Also, he included in this protected bulwark precedents calculated eventually to acquire the force and authority of specific rules. For example, the precedent was established that no project would receive the serious consideration of the Rivers and Harbors Committee which had not first been approved, after careful investigation, by a board of army engineers assigned to the service of the committee and acting as a project clearing house, with the responsibility of creating standards and co-ordinating all waterway activities. Under previous practice army engineers had acted individually. One would investigate a project carrying an appropriation of perhaps $500,000 and would recommend it, while another engineer would take up one far more worthy, costing perhaps $200,000, and reject it.

Another objective was to obtain a plain declaration of the total cost of a project and the time necessary to complete it. This was aimed at the practice of sneaking in a project ultimately to cost perhaps several million dollars under an insignificant initial appropriation of, say, $100,000.

An equally important part of Burton's plan was to assemble authentic information on waterways which had actually developed a profitable volume of water-borne commerce, as contrasted with unsound projects which had resulted in disappointment and failure. This arsenal of factual information should cover every "improved" waterway in the world. There must remain no excuse for any member of Congress to champion an unsound project for lack of evidence of its unsoundness. Burton realized that Congress would always contain at least some men who would not permit an obviously unsound project to be slipped through without challenge when evidence to disprove its practicability was at hand.

In a word, Burton proposed to make it increasingly difficult for any pork-grabber to get away with his spoils without plainly showing his hand. All this would involve an almost incredible amount of labor on Burton's part, but he was eager to throw himself into it with full force.

He did not, however, delude himself with the expectation of complete and immediate success. He knew that the most he could hope for in immediate results would be a material reduction of obviously questionable items.

The Illinois delegation in Congress had met with many disappointments at the hands of Burton as Chairman of the Rivers and Harbors Committee and considered him decidedly unsporting about certain waterway projects for which they desired generous appropriations.

This situation had become most embarrassing to "Uncle Joe" Cannon. At least by implication, his home state colleagues were asking: "What's the good of having a Speaker of the House from Illinois if he can't get us a fair share of Federal appropriations for waterway improvements? He should know that our constituents are on our necks and riding us hard. They want a Chicago-to-the-Gulf waterway and a lot of other projects. Burton is making a big fuss about diverting water from Lake Michigan and, meantime, is busy diverting appropriations to the Ohio River."

This theme of Burton's favoritism to Ohio and his "unfairness" to Illinois had been industriously developed by the Illinois members and others interested in the Chicago-to-the-Gulf waterway project, until it became a thorn in the Speaker's side.

Speaker Cannon had sought to solve the difficulty by what seemed to him refined diplomatic tactics. He had known for some time that Burton desired, above all else, to head a research commission empowered to collect the most comprehensive fund of waterways information ever assembled. Shrewd "Uncle Joe" had returned evasive and dilatory answers to such a proposal whenever it was suggested, hoping that the desire for this commission would do more than any act of party discipline to soften the attitude of Chairman Burton toward Illinois waterway demands. It was a subtle temptation—but somehow it failed to work.

Then, quite unexpectedly the Speaker relented and decided to do the handsome thing by the stiff-necked Chairman of the Rivers and Harbors Committee. He was given his coveted commission, with fifty thousand dollars for its operation, as a reward for "distinguished service." Undoubtedly the canny Speaker decided that this surprise maneuver might win the hard-bitten Burton to a more generous attitude toward the waterway demands of Illinois. But Burton had a disconcerting tendency to keep matters of this kind carefully separated.

The National Waterways Commission was created by the Rivers and Harbors Act of March 3, 1909, by the Speaker's permission. Now Burton was equipped to realize his ambition to collect the greatest assemblage of waterway information ever brought together in the world; to capture all the vital facts of waterway transportation wherever man had dug canals, cleared streams, built locks, improved harbors, and constructed freight terminals.

The devotion with which he attacked this task is indicated by the following:

QUESTIONS TO BE CONSIDERED BY SUBCOMMITTEES OF THE NATIONAL WATERWAYS COMMISSION

1. Relation between waterway and railway transportation, including terminals and transfers, competition, intercorporate relationships, and joint tariffs.

2. Canals, including advisability and desirability of canals for deep-draft vessels. Distinction between short canals connecting large bodies of water, such as the Soo or Panama, and long artificial waterways like the Erie Canal and the canals of the Ohio Valley.

3. Method of making appropriations, including the proportional shares to be expended each year. Proper steps to be taken before the adoption of projects for improvement.

4. Appropriate division between appropriations by the Federal Government, on the one hand, and by States, minor political divisions, and individuals on the other.

5. Relation of waterway improvements to bank protection, flood and drought prevention, and irrigation.

6. Policy relating to harbors, including the ownership and control of wharves and docks.

7. Relation of waterway improvements to water power.

8. Methods in the improvement of rivers, including the construction of locks and dams.

9. Comparison of European and other foreign waterways with those of the United States, including questions of navigability, land and floating equipment, and tows; the question of the cooperation of rail and water lines, and a comparison of European and American transportation rates, both by land and by water.

10. Reasons for decline in inland waterway transportation.

11. Effect of forestation, as well as the influence of cultivation, increase of population, and growth of modern improvements upon the volume of streams, uniformity of flow, floods, etc.

12. The most desirable size and type of boats or barges, including methods of propulsion.

These questions were prepared by Burton who also wrote the following questions to be answered by United States consuls.

1. In what manner is the cost of river and harbor improvements provided?

2. In case improvements are made in harbors, to what extent does the government or other agency making the improvements also construct, as part of the improvement, docks, wharves, or terminals for freight?

3. What is the navigable depth, at mean low water, of the leading harbors and the range of tide in the same?

4. What is the navigable length and the channel depths and widths at mean low water of the principal rivers and canals?

5. Can you state the increase, respectively, in recent years of freight carried by railways and inland waterways, and what is the proportion carried by each at this time?

6. (a) What are the comparative rates for the carriage of freight by railway and by inland waterways?

(b) State, if practicable, with illustration, what the influence of the improved waterway has been upon the freight charges for land carriage.

7. What is the apparent tendency as regards further development of inland waterways by canalization of rivers and the construction of canals?

8. What is the approximate amount of money expended to date in the respective countries for the improvement, construction, maintenance, and repair of rivers, harbors, and canals?

9. Are there statistics given by public documents, or otherwise, stating the tonnage handled in or on the different ports, rivers, and canals, and the value of such tonnage?

10. (a) What is the length and depth at mean low water of each canal, (b) the number of locks and dams in each canal or canalized river, (c) the available length, the available width, and the depth on sills of each lock, (d) the kind of material used in construction, (e) and the approximate cost of each structure?

11. What is the nature of the engineering work carried on at each particular improvement?

The questions to consuls were followed by others—and eventually by the National Waterways Commission in person.

While Burton had every reason to expect that the commission would be continued indefinitely until the big task was completed, its actual authorization was to March 4, 1911. Knowing the uncertainties of politics, he determined to take no chances but to crowd into the authorized two years all the research results possible. The original members of the commission were Theodore E. Burton, of

Ohio, Chairman; Jacob H. Gallinger, of New Hampshire, Vice-Chairman; Samuel H. Piles, of Washington, Wm. Alden Smith, of Michigan, F. M. Simmons, of North Carolina, James P. Clarke, of Arkansas, William Lorimer, of Illinois, from the Senate; D. S. Alexander, of New York, Frederick C. Stevens, of Minnesota, Irving P. Wanger, of Pennsylvania, Stephen M. Sparkman, of Florida, John A. Moon, of Tennessee, from the House of Representatives. The two Secretaries were Woodbury Pulizer and Joseph H. McGann.

Nearly all of these men, in the preceding ten years, had investigated the principal waterways of the United States and some of them had studied the European systems. It was a disappointment to Senator Burton that Judson C. Welliver, whose report on the "Relations Between Waterways and Railway Traffic in Europe"—made for President Roosevelt at executive expense—could not accept an appointment as a secretary of the commission.

The experts and attachés of the commission originally included: Rear-Admiral C. S. Sperry, Navy Department, Col. W. H. Bixby, retired, Engineer Corps, United States Army, Maj. F. A. Mahan, retired, Engineer Corps, United States Army, Prof. Frank H. Dixon, Dartmouth College, and E. C. Merchant, Columbia University.

Tuesday, August 9, 1909, when the *Kronprinzessin Cecilie* left New York harbor for Germany, was a gala day in the calendar of Senator Burton. He was off on his great quest in high spirits.

The commission first explored the canal system of the Berlin district, then passed down the Moldau from Prague to the Elbe. Then came the passage down the Danube to Orşova. Burton recalled to the members of the party that in 1903 he had first visited Orşova, Budapest, and the "Iron Gate" of the Danube on a private expedition and had promised himself that sometime he would return to make a thorough investigation of this amazing waterway for his government, with engineers and experts in attendance.

While the party was given elaborate entertainment in Vienna, Burton applied himself unsparingly to the real business of the trip; in prosecuting the investigation he was tireless. Officials of European governments were grilled with searching questions which omitted nothing that promised to contribute to the completeness of his understanding of European waterways.

In Bavaria, Ludwig's Canal and Strassburg harbor and canal were examined and the party explored the Main River and the Rhine. At various stops they were welcomed by burgomasters. Burton amazed his hosts with his knowledge of their own waterways and railroads and his grasp of the entire European transportation system.

Days were spent in Holland and Belgium studying the harbor and canals at Amsterdam and Rotterdam and the channel from Rotterdam to the Rhine. The canals of Belgium were especially interesting. In France trips were made up the Seine and all about the Paris and Le Havre districts. The canal systems of England were next carefully inspected—particularly those of London, Manchester, and Liverpool.

The staff members of the various United States consular offices—and all of them were visited—quickly discovered that the Chairman of the Rivers and Harbors Commission had not exhausted his repertoire of questions in his preliminary inquiries mailed from Washington and also that he had assimilated their answers.

It was his habit to make brief notes himself, dictating them later. The closeness of his observation and his capacity for grasping the vital details of the transportation which he was observing may be illustrated by a section selected from his notes written in Hungary. In part it reads:

> Up to 2 o'clock we saw 3 tows moving upstream and 1 downstream.
>
> The revetment work is styled "bank fences." The expense of longitudinal dikes and of the revetment of the banks is met by the General Government. Only the high dikes or levees are built by the proprietors of the land on the two sides. The levees are 1½ meters higher than the known high water.
>
> There is no invariable number of barges in a tow; 3 is a frequent number, but there are sometimes 5 or 6.
>
> At Györ there were 6 barges moored near the wharf. In this and in other places there is a small wharf boat that rises and falls with the water, located next to the landings, for the purpose of loading and unloading.
>
> At Györ we passed a steamer with 3 barges headed upstream. This is the fourth headed upstream. At 2:57 met the fifth upstream-bound barge.
>
> In the section below Györ the width is about 420 meters.
>
> At 3:02 met a small steamer with 1 barge loaded with rock.

> At 3:20, at Komárom, passed a steamer with 1 barge bound down, the second in this direction.
>
> There is an active competition with the railways. The companies do not really realize any profit from passenger traffic, but are obliged by the government to maintain it. There is considerable local traffic between nearby towns.

Burton's notes reveal that he was greatly impressed with the extent to which the expense of the development of European waterways was shared by local units of government—provinces and municipalities—which, by the same token, participated in their maintenance and control. This brought the waterways closer to the needs and interests of the people than they were in the United States; the local community had a direct interest in them and an equally direct voice in their control. This principle applied in the United States would contribute much to the elimination of prevailing abuses of Federal generosity.

Still another major European feature to which Burton gave attention was that of terminals providing physical unification of rail and water commerce. Here was a weak link in the existing American system. But his notes reveal that great improvements at home were possible in stopping terminal gaps devised by railroads to cripple the effectiveness of water competition.

On the ship which brought the party back to New York Chairman Burton worked incessantly, digesting and codifying the mass of information which he had collected. He was genial and happy and, in the words of one of the secretaries, "oozed satisfaction at every pore." He was bringing back to America the ammunition with which to riddle the entrenched system of the political distribution of waterway improvements and develop great practical and profitable systems of water-borne commerce.

The next expedition of the commission, in November, examined the Mississippi River from St. Paul to New Orleans. Everywhere the Chairman looked for practical opportunities of applying the lessons he had learned in the Old World. A considerable group of the members inspected the Missouri River from Kansas City to its mouth, and the Illinois River from its lower portion to the head of navigation.

For some time this commission was the joy of Burton's heart. Apparently he was untroubled by the thought that he might not be permitted to complete the ambitious research task. But his confidence was destined to suffer a jolt.

Once, at least, he tripped on a technicality and gave members of the Rivers and Harbors Committee—who were angered by his criticism in the Senate—a chance to "get even" with him.

The National Waterways Commission was to expire in two years, or on March 4, 1911. In the River and Harbor Act of February 27, 1911, its term was continued until November 4, 1911. In 1910, however, Senator Burton vigorously opposed the granting of an appropriation of fifteen thousand dollars for expenses of subcommittees of the Rivers and Harbors Committee of the House and the Commerce Committee of the Senate for making special investigating trips. He did so because there was already such a commission—the National Waterways Commission—which had that authority and money appropriated for expenses. This opposition of Burton's to appropriating expenses for another investigating committee, together with the fact that he persistently fought objectionable provisions of the Rivers and Harbors Bill of that year, caused the Senate-House Conference Committee to decide to end the life of the National Waterways Commission.

Mr. Alexander, Chairman of the Committee on Rivers and Harbors, declared: "Burton will not let us have our expense provision; we will kill his commission." Senator Bailey of Texas was the only member of either house who spoke for Burton and pleaded for the extension of the commission when the conference report on the 1911 bill was up in the Senate.

The Master of Waterways had been caught napping on a technicality, had stubbed his toe on a petty fifteen thousand dollar item and had been publicly humiliated. However, the press of the country blazed up in a barrage of protest that amounted to a nation-wide tribute to Burton and his National Waterways Commission. One influential Eastern paper contained the following editorial:

> Senators and representatives in conference on the Rivers and Harbors Bill have done the nation an injury in order to punish Mr. Burton. They have killed the National Waterways Commission because its chairman was bright enough and bold enough to point out the "pork barrel" features of the measure they were about to enact.
>
> The work of the Waterways Commission has only fairly begun. It was established under the last administration to accomplish an

important reform. Now its usefulness is cut short through the spitefulness of those whose toes were stepped on by Chairman Burton. . . .

Rivers and harbors appropriations, in the congressional view of the case, are made not for the encouragement of navigation but for the development of political prestige. Legislators need the money to keep their districts in line. And, of course, as long as it is the people's money that is used Congress has no compunctions. . . .

There should be some way to continue the life of the Burton Commission. The nation needs it.

These editorial expressions are representative of those which appeared in scores of the more independent and conservative newspapers. Burton's humiliation was turned into a virtual ovation.

A cloud of mystery had settled over Burton's sudden change of front regarding Rivers and Harbors bills after he had gone up to the Senate. Colleagues in both houses of Congress had accused him of being inconsistent. Many of them had charged that, now that he no longer sat at the head of the Rivers and Harbors Committee in the House, he was jealous of the hands into which he had passed that scepter of power and was supercritical.

But the solution of this mystery is simple. Before Burton relinquished the chairmanship of the Rivers and Harbors Committee to Dr. De Alva Alexander, the ranking Republican member of the committee, he took pains to sound out the latter's attitude toward the structure of policies and rules of procedure which had been so carefully built up in the preceding years. He left that conference with the assurance that the Burton policies would be followed "to the letter."

When he learned the character of the bill that would be offered to the House by the committee in 1910, he was astounded. It authorized expenditures of more than $260,000,000 and was an almost perfect example of the old logrolling and "dribbling" policy of prosecuting Rivers and Harbors work. Burton immediately wrote a letter of protest to Chairman Alexander and warned him that he would oppose this old-fashioned pork-barrel bill in the Senate.

This 1910 Rivers and Harbors Bill—the largest ever reported up to that time—gave Senator Burton an opportunity to demonstrate that he was broad enough to push aside an opportunity to retaliate upon those who had killed the National Waterways Commission.

In the Senate, on April 15, Burton spoke for three hours and on the following day for an hour and fifty-two minutes opposing many of the provisions of the bill which he considered unsound. On the 19th the bill was considered for amendments. Again Burton spoke, condemning many of the amendments. The bill, however, was passed substantially as offered and was accepted by the Senate.

Immediately upon its passage Burton was summoned to a conference with President Taft, who apparently stood ready to veto the bill if Senator Burton so advised.

After careful deliberation, the Senator, according to my informant, told the President that in his judgment more harm would be done to the progress of Rivers and Harbors improvements of a sound and justifiable character by the veto of the bill than by its executive authorization with all its unsound items. This led to what is known in the history of Rivers and Harbors legislation as President Taft's famous "never again" message. In a word, he signed the bill under protest and attached a message embodying Senator Burton's objection to many of its authorizations and saying that his approval of the bill was a choice between two evils, but that he would "never again" give his approval to a Rivers and Harbors Bill containing such provisions.

As a Senator, Burton criticized the 1910 Rivers and Harbors Bill because it threatened all the work he had done to place waterway legislation upon a constructive business basis. His advice to President Taft which prevented the Chief Executive from vetoing the bill was proof that he was moved by patriotic instead of personal and political motives. He could not bear to see the progress of waterway developments halted for two years in order to afford him a personal triumph over those who had devised the overthrow of the system of waterway legislation that had reformed the pork barrel.

Burton's standard for the final valuation of any project was that its commerce must pay a profit on the investment. Like a wise administrator of a great private corporation investing millions in the expectation of an ultimate reasonable return, he was willing to wait for the enterprise to develop earning power and justify the investment—but it must qualify at the start as a sound risk. He was a hard-boiled investor of Uncle Sam's millions.

Writing in the *Metropolitan Magazine* of August, 1912, Angus McSween, the severest critic of Burton's political course after he became a Senator, summarized his service to the water-borne commerce of the country in these words:

"As a member of the House of Representatives Burton was considered . . . the most courageous, independent and statesmanlike Republican in the body. For years he had been chairman of the Rivers and Harbors Committee and he had transformed the making of the Rivers and Harbors Bill from a log-rolling process . . . into a careful scientific provision for river and harbor improvement from which the commerce of the whole country would derive the greatest possible advantage.

"Burton . . . treated every project he considered solely with respect to its merits, and the Democratic members of the House were as zealous in backing up his efforts as were the right-thinking Republicans.

"In ten years Burton never had a rivers and harbors bill reported by him, from his committee, amended by the House. All kinds of combinations were formed against him by men whose efforts to get increased appropriations he had rejected, but the majority was always with him."

CHAPTER 17

Burton on Banking and Currency

T HERE IS DRAMA in the story of the founding of the Federal Reserve System, the most important piece of monetary legislation enacted by Congress in Senator Burton's lifetime.

The foundations of the System were laid by the National Monetary Commission created in 1908, following the violent panic of 1907. In his book *Financial Crises and Periods of Industrial and Commercial Depression,* published in 1902, Burton had stressed the need of a greater elasticity of our currency.

Up to the time when the Federal Reserve System became operative, on November 16, 1914, the bank reserves of the country were immobile and unavailable for immediately meeting the money exigencies of widely separated and diversified sections of the country when those exigencies were most extreme. Money reserves were centered in the great cities—to a large extent in New York City. Wall Street "call loans" or "brokers' loans" were considered the most fluid of all.

A high official of the Federal Reserve System said to the writer: "In the old days I was a western grain buyer and learned by personal experience the exigencies of the flow and flux of agricultural money to and from New York. At one time I had a considerable surplus of my operating capital in New York, sent there by the local banks of my territory. But when I needed it to buy grain from farmers, it could not be promptly recalled, for Wall Street was in something of a pinch. Therefore I had to borrow money in New York myself when I had plenty of funds there that had been put out on call loans. This taught me the need of a dependable and flexible reserve system to meet emergencies."

President Theodore Roosevelt, in a message to Congress on

December 3, 1907, stressed the immediate need for emergency currency legislation and Speaker Cannon lost no time in appointing a Banking and Currency Committee, with Charles N. Fowler, of New Jersey, as Chairman and Burton as one of the members. Within a month, the committee presented the Fowler Bill "to establish a simple and scientific monetary system founded upon gold." It provided, among other things, for banking currency based on commercial paper. Speaker Cannon, however, considered it too radical; he wanted nothing done to upset the prevailing status. Fowler agreed and urged that no legislation whatever be put through during that session of Congress.*

Burton, however, urged that an immediate emergency currency bill was necessary to prevent another panic like that of 1907.

Meantime, a Senate committee under the chairmanship of Nelson W. Aldrich presented a bill which provided for currency based on government, municipal, and railroad bonds. The railroad-bond feature created a furor and was stricken out.

The House would not accept it and one of its opponents was Burton. He favored the Vreeland Bill, providing a plan by which ten or more banks could associate and be jointly liable for the circulating of their notes. He urged it as an emergency measure "as a safeguard against panics," a means of avoiding inflation and a pathfinder for future legislation.

Meantime, bills by the score flooded the Senate and the House. Apparently every legislator had a panic panacea.

The first session of the Sixtieth Congress was drawing to a close and still no bill had been presented that was acceptable to both houses. In Republican caucuses it was decided to start a course of education based on the Vreeland Bill. Burton, Vreeland, and others held "classes" to familiarize the members with the bill's merits.

Leadership of the drive for emergency currency legislation naturally gravitated to Burton; he was already a recognized authority on panics, currency, and banking and he was the ablest speaker in the Vreeland Bill group. Then, too, his colleagues believed that in formulating an emergency currency measure he could be depended upon to lay the foundations for a sound and permanent currency and banking system. This hope was brilliantly fulfilled, for his emergency legislation provided for the creation of the National Monetary Commission to make world-wide studies

* Congressional Record, 60th Cong., 1st sess. (Jan. 27, 1908), vol. 42, part 2.

of currency and banking systems and formulate one that would progressively meet all requirements of flexibility and security.

In a House speech, on May 14, 1908, Burton said that in any currency reform measure it should be kept in mind that contraction as well as expansion of the currency should be secured; that no system should be accepted that failed to afford security for every bank note in circulation; that the agency which issues paper money must also provide for its redemption; that no corporation or individual should make undue profit from issuance of bills; that new methods should be adopted slowly.

He admitted that, at the moment, no permanent solution of the problem could be reached but said that the Vreeland Bill would serve well as a stopgap. Speaking of this occasion many years later, Vreeland told the writer: "Burton made a powerful speech. He was a wonderful man."

Again, in one of his "educational" speeches, Burton said: "I reiterate . . . that we should have an opportunity to try different kinds of currency because no radical change will be accepted except after trial by gradual steps. There is no settled public opinion. Every other country would allow a bank to issue circulating notes upon its resources either from a great centralized bank or from separate banks. This is the true principle of currency issue, to make the amount outstanding commensurate with the volume of business of the country and the resources of its banks. The time is coming when that general principle is going to be adopted; whether through a central bank, by strong association of banks as in the Vreeland Bill, or by individual banks backed by the responsibility of all."

Eventually a conference was called, with Vreeland, Burton, and others representing the House and Aldrich, Allison, and Hale the Senate. The result, largely through the influence of Burton, was a bill which combined the best features of both the Aldrich and Vreeland bills, with one exception: Aldrich insisted upon inserting a provision whereby national banks could issue notes secured by bonds in time of stress, a provision in which neither Burton nor Fowler believed.

When Burton presented the conference report to the House and admitted that the bill embodied two conflicting theories relating to currency, he said:

"To anyone who is familiar with the sentiment of the country, it must be clearly apparent that no radical change can be made in the currency system at present. . . . No one can with confidence venture a prediction of the method which will be ultimately adopted. Most advanced sentiment among students of finance as well as the great majority of bankers favors circulating notes based upon the resources or assets of banks.

"The country would be more ready to accept this opinion if a plan were proposed which is free from danger and entirely equitable as between banks and the public, but it must be said that no method has yet been set forth in any bill which is free from very valid objections."

Besides this feature, the Aldrich-Vreeland Bill provided for associations of co-operating banks. It passed the House in a hot session.

"You were never so highly honored as today," said the incorrigible John Sharp Williams addressing the Speaker. "This bill ought to be entitled the Cannon-Aldrich Political Emergency Bill. . . . The other day the House declared the Aldrich Bill altogether wicked. . . . The Republican Senate said the Vreeland Bill was altogether iniquitous. . . . But today the great discovery that two iniquities compose a perfect good! . . . This comes in response to the sincere prayer of the Speaker: 'Oh, God, anything! It makes no difference what, even if it be really nothing, just so I can call it something. Anything before the House adjourns! It will not do for the Republican party to go to the country with absolutely nothing!' "

In the Senate the Aldrich-Vreeland Bill met with rough sailing. Burton opposed the revised bond security clause, as did many another soundly informed legislator, but he was willing to conciliate. A measure must be passed, whether ideal or not. But no conciliation was ever possible for Senator La Follette. He was determined to defeat the measure and to that end started a filibuster. A strange occurrence prevented its success.

After he had talked some nineteen hours against this currency act, he retired from the chamber to snatch a brief rest, leaving Gore, the blind Senator from Oklahoma, to hold the floor. Gore had arranged that, when weary, he was to be relieved by Senator Stone, of Missouri. Therefore when Gore had performed his sentry duty he called upon Stone to relieve him. Being blind, he could not see that Senator Stone was momentarily absent from the chamber. The instant Gore sat down Senator Gallinger demanded a roll call.

This broke the filibuster against the Aldrich-Vreeland Bill, which was passed on May 30, 1908, in the last hours of the session.

Senator La Follette explained his hostility to the bill in these words:

"It is my settled belief that this great power [of Wall Street interests] over government legislation can only be overthrown by resisting at every step, seizing upon every important occasion which offers opportunity to uncover the methods of the system . . . built up by privilege, which has taken possession of government and legislation." *

The Aldrich-Vreeland Act was frankly a stopgap measure. Its power to meet real panic conditions never came to test for no crisis appeared within the next few years. But it was ready to be used if needed. Senator Carter Glass, in his book *An Adventure in Constructive Finance,* said that the Act had to be "hastily and radically changed in 1914 on the frantic plea of alarmed bankers, before it could be made operative in that emergency [the World War]."

A most important provision of the Vreeland-Aldrich Act was the creation of a monetary commission. Its work, together with the education which the country received in the debates on the Emergency Currency Act, laid the foundations for much wiser legislation in the form of the Federal Reserve Act, passed in 1913.

Meantime the National Monetary Commission investigated the currency and credit systems of all the countries of the civilized world, collected a vast volume of vital data and then took plenty of time for its digestion and for the preparation of a bill embodying the wisdom gained in this vast research enterprise. The personnel of this commission was of a character to command respect. As originally constituted, on May 30, 1908, its members were:

Senators:

Nelson W. Aldrich	(Rep.)	(R.I.)
William B. Allison	(Rep.)	(Iowa)
Julius C. Burrows	(Rep.)	(Mich.)
Eugene Hale	(Rep.)	(Me.)
Philander C. Knox	(Rep.)	(Pa.)
John W. Daniel	(Dem.)	(Va.)
Henry M. Teller	(Dem.)	(Colo.)
H. D. Money	(Dem.)	(Miss.)
Joseph W. Bailey	(Dem.)	(Tex.)

* Robert M. La Follette, *La Follette's Autobiography.* Madison, 1913.

Representatives:

Edward B. Vreeland	(Rep.)	(N.Y.)
Jesse Overstreet	(Rep.)	(Ind.)
Theodore E. Burton	(Rep.)	(Ohio)
John W. Weeks	(Rep.)	(Mass.)
Robert W. Bonynge	(Rep.)	(Colo.)
Sylvester C. Smith	(Rep.)	(Cal.)
L. P. Padgett	(Dem.)	(Tenn.)
George F. Burgess	(Dem.)	(Tex.)
A. P. Pugo	(Dem.)	(La.)

There were, of course, many changes in membership before the commission made its final report on January 8, 1912.

The Monetary Commission was thought by some to be an organization of yes men. It was said they were permitted to rubber-stamp plans for a great national monetary system dictated by Senator Aldrich in collaboration with experts and bankers—and that was about all!

But it is impossible to believe that Senator Burton could bring himself to play the role of an obedient yes man. He had always been jealous of the integrity of his conclusions and finance was one of his special fields. His influence with Senator Aldrich and his other colleagues must have been important.

The specific purposes of the National Monetary Commission could not be more clearly stated than in this paragraph from its final report:

> We propose to create an institution which can, among other things, conserve the public credit; issue properly secured circulating notes; control movements of gold and foreign exchange; receive and disburse the Treasury balances; insure the cooperation of all banks in the public interest; equalize banking and credit facilities in different sections of the country and insure adequate assistance on reasonable terms to partially developed communities; secure uniform rates of discount; prevent interruption of domestic exchanges; provide means for replenishing cash reserves and for their concentration for use in any direction wherever needed, and establish standards of notes and bills of exchange issued for agricultural or other purposes.

In the summer of 1908, following his appointment as chairman of the commission, Aldrich went abroad with certain of its members and some of his advisers to educate himself in international finance.

The party included H. P. Davison, of Morgan & Co., Professor A. Piatt Andrew, "expert" of the commission, and George M. Reynolds, a prominent Chicago banker. Among the official members of the commission, besides Aldrich and Burton, were Senators Hale and Daniel and Representatives Vreeland, Overstreet, and Padgett.

Chairman Aldrich was fortunate in his choice of the commission's expert. Professor Andrew, of Harvard University, brought to this task a rare combination of personal qualities and an impressive academic equipment. In 1909 and 1910 he was Director of the United States Mint; and in 1910, before the life of the Monetary Commission officially expired, he became the Assistant Secretary of the Treasury. Burton regarded Professor Andrew as singularly equipped for the commission's work.

In London, the commission's hearings were held in a large drawing room of the Hotel Metropole. Referring to this London meeting, Burton said: "For some ten days I was a member of the subcommittee in London and it was very assiduous in its labors. We sat every day from ten-thirty in the morning until seven in the evening and heard the leading bankers of England, who gave us information with frankness."

But Burton, as has been noted earlier, did not long remain in London with the commission. He was needed at home to look after his own political interests.

Aldrich and his special advisers, in the meantime, soon discovered that they were handicapped by the lack of authoritative written material on banking and finance and engaged experts in various fields to write on these subjects. In this way the commission built up an extraordinary library. As the months went by, Aldrich began to take note of that astute German, Paul Warburg, whose views on international banking and American currency were attracting so much attention.

Months passed and as yet no bill was formulated.

Came 1910. It was high time to do something definite; but Aldrich was not yet willing to let the commission wrangle over what form the bill should take. In the fall he sent out invitations for a week of duck shooting at the exclusive Jekyll Island Hunt Club off the coast of Georgia. The guests made an elaborate show of their hunting equipment, knowing that not a gun would be fired and that their real mission was a secret conclave on the bill to be framed by the Monetary Commission.

Besides Aldrich and his secretary, Arthur B. Shelton, those present were A. Piatt Andrew, H. P. Davison, Frank Vanderlip, and Paul Warburg—the men, in the opinion of Aldrich, best equipped to give him a good, hard, intellectual wrestling match. Senator Aldrich was the only official member of the commission participating in this private party. The gathering was shrouded in secrecy. The location of the clubhouse afforded ideal seclusion. Every guest knew that this was no yes-man session—that he was expected to state his own views with the utmost frankness.

An entire week, virtually day and night, was devoted to discussing the financial system of this country and ways to improve it. No stenographic record was kept. All this was primarily for the education of Senator Aldrich. What these men finally threshed out formed the basis for the so-called Aldrich Plan. But Aldrich still was in no hurry to present a finished bill.

In this period the name of Burton did not often occur in connection with the formal work of the commission. However, the writer is assured that Senator Aldrich repeatedly conferred with Burton on the problems before the Monetary Commission. Senator Burton's contribution to the work of the commission, and particularly to the bill for a Federal Reserve System which it formulated, was of an importance out of all proportion to his participation in the public hearings.

In Warburg's book, *The History of the Federal Reserve Act*, there is this interesting sidelight on the meetings of the Monetary Commission and Burton's part in them:

> Senator Burton recalled that Vreeland, Bonynge and Burgess were likely to be the more radical members of the Commission, in respect to their ideas on the guarantees, the securities for currency, and the volume of currency practicable for reform purposes. Inasmuch as Burton had come so recently from the House, and seemed to have especially friendly relations with these three, Aldrich used to turn to him to keep the debate equable. When the three seemed likely to create an impasse, Aldrich would turn to Burton and say, "Well, what do you think about it, Mr. Burton?" Then Mr. Burton would suggest some compromise viewpoint, and matters would smoothly proceed.

The plan, as drafted at Jekyll Island, with additions and subtractions, was finally issued in pamphlet form in January, 1911. It suggested the establishing of a National Reserve Association, a co-operative union of banks. Aldrich sent the bill to Vreeland with a letter saying it was only to be used as a basis for discussion in the commission. The plan met with approval—except for minor differences of opinion—by many influential men and certain important associations such as the Board of Trade Conference.

To educate the public generally, an association for "promoting banking reform" was established, called the Citizens League, with Paul Warburg as chairman. Thousands of dollars were spent to disseminate propaganda. This was intended to be absolutely nonpartisan, but politics soon began to appear.

An important conference was held between the Monetary Commission and the Currency Committee of the American Bankers Association. Then trouble began! In the Aldrich Plan there were to be a board of directors and executive officers consisting of a governor and two deputy governors, to be selected by the President of the United States from a list submitted by the board of directors, subject to removal for cause by the President of the United States. J. B. Forgan, President of the American Bankers Association, and the bankers objected strenuously. It must read, they insisted, "a governor to be selected by the President of the United States from a list submitted by the board of directors and subject to removal for cause by two-thirds of the board of directors." Aldrich finally yielded to the bankers, thus running the risk of allowing the whole plan to drift into politics.

But now the insurgents began to insurge. Anything Aldrich proposed was to them the work of the devil. These sharpshooters had a clear target for criticism in the fact that the proposed bill had been written by a Wall Street banker in collaboration with other banking advisers from the same zone. Aldrich had called in probably the most competent advisers in the country—but the smell of Wall Street saturated their garments and this was enough to set off in full cry the entire insurgent pack. Cummins, of Iowa, finally found a way to down the enemy and "save the country." On April 13, 1911, he presented a resolution "requiring the Monetary Commission to make a final report on or before December 4, 1911," and to dissolve the commission on December 5, 1911.

This was a hard blow. Aldrich, who had retired from the Senate in March of that year, did not think the country was ready to accept a bill, so it was decided to let the matter ride until the next Congress. At that time Aldrich believed that a Republican

President would be elected and the commission would be undisturbed.

In withholding from Congress the report of the Commission and the National Reserve Association Bill which it had prepared until after the Presidential election, Chairman Aldrich exercised what he regarded as rather obvious political strategy. When the election was over and the country went Democratic, both as to the President and the Congress, the Monetary Bill, so laboriously prepared, was brought to the acid test.

In July, when Cummins demanded a report, Burton asked that the bill go over. In August, when Cummins again urged that it be put to a vote, Burton again objected. Cummins, however, persisted. Again peacemaker Burton came to the rescue. "The enactment of such a bill [the Cummins Bill to force the commission to report]," he said, "casts a certain discredit on the Commission, but more important than that, the Commission can't complete its work in time nor by the coming winter." He suggested an amendment to Mr. Cummins' measure providing that salaries of all members of the commission should cease, also that the commission should file a report by January 10—but that the commission should be continued.

On the following day Burton offered another amendment—that the commission should continue until a final report could be made. Then he took the opportunity to instruct the Senate in the history of currency in the United States and to explain his own currency theories. He said he objected to a national bank note currency based on bonds as being too rigid. Bank notes should be issued in response to demands of trade.

A few days later Burton again presented an amendment to which Cummins finally assented. It not only asked for a report by January 8, 1912, but provided for abolishing the commission in May of that year. The Burton measure was finally passed, with March 31 as the date for the commission's expiration. The bill presented in the final report could only be a basis for discussion and this was precisely what Aldrich considered it. It was something on which to build.*

Briefly, these were the main points of the Aldrich Plan:

There was to be a National Reserve Association, to be owned and managed by stockholding banks and authorized to do business with banks only. A more flexible note system was to be created and

* Aldrich died April 16, 1915.

the gradual abandonment of government bonds as a basis for bank notes was stipulated. Short-time notes were to be issued, secured by "lawful money" and by bills having their origin in commercial transactions. Also, there was to be a concentration in one place and under one control of the gold and cash reserves then widely distributed throughout the country. And, as above described, there was the provision upon which the bankers had insisted, that of having the governor of the association selected by the President.*

The main objection to this plan was by those opposed to the so-called central bank idea, although the proponents of the bill tried in vain to convince the country that their plan was not for a central bank, as in England, but for an association of banks, doing business with banks only. The objection was plain party quibbling. The reason advanced for the dread of a central bank was political. It was urged that such a bank might fall into the hands of a Wall Street group. Besides this point against the Aldrich Plan, the fear of undue government or political interference was voiced—a possibility suggested by the method of management.

On the whole, Burton approved this plan but did not think it ideal. In an address on July 12, 1911, before the West Virginia Bankers Association, he said that the Aldrich Plan came nearer to solving the currency problem than any other yet devised. But he did not believe in bond-secured currency, as he had told the House and the Senate many times, because it was too rigid and unelastic a base. He did not approve, on the whole, the provision in the Aldrich Plan for rediscounting commercial paper, but he considered the plan good in the main.

It is related in the book by Carter Glass, *An Adventure in Constructive Finance*, that Wilson, as soon as he was elected in November, had begun to think about currency legislation and had summoned Glass to a conference where he asked him to begin at once on the drafting of a new bill. Glass, as well as Wilson himself, was a student of finance and was sincerely interested in currency reform. He vividly described the trials and vicissitudes of an honest and conscientious legislator trying to get a banking and currency bill passed.

During the following months Burton had many invitations to speak on currency problems. He made the most of the chance to explain the good points of both the Aldrich Plan and the Glass Bill.

* Nathaniel Wright Stephenson, *Nelson W. Aldrich*. New York, 1930.

In the new bill there was not to be a co-operative association of banks with stockholding members, but the country was to be divided into financial "regions"—twelve in all—with one central bank in each. Each of these regional Federal Reserve Banks was to be virtually independent of the others. Every national bank must subscribe to the stock of these Federal Reserve Banks. In the Aldrich Plan membership in the National Reserve Association was optional. Instead of a National Board of Directors, the Glass Bill provided for a Federal Reserve Board chosen somewhat differently from the method provided in the Aldrich Plan. Both Carter Glass and President Wilson were agreed that the banks should have a large share in the control of the new system.

William Jennings Bryan, however, was obdurate in his determination that the Government should control and President Wilson felt compelled to adopt this demand of his Secretary of State. The board, then, was to be chosen as follows: It was to consist of seven members, including the Secretary of the Treasury and the Comptroller of the Currency as ex officio members, and five members appointed by the President of the United States with the consent of the Senate. Burton did not approve this plan of management. He said, "It involves a degree of interference which is not justified." *

As a concession to the bankers, an Advisory Council was provided for, with a certain number of bankers to meet with the board occasionally in an advisory capacity. Another capitulation to Bryan was in the matter of note issuance. Bryan insisted upon "Government notes," while President Wilson, Chairman Glass, and practically every other student of finance felt that only notes issued by banks were possible. Through the astuteness of Wilson, however, the day was saved. Only upon application to the Government by the banks could the notes be issued. This appeased Bryan.**

Burton spoke adversely of this feature of the bill. He said banks "ought to take care of the notes they issue; they should not impose the burden of taking care of them on the Government." However, he approved the provision in the Glass Bill under which paper currency issued to any one regional bank should bear a distinctive mark indicating to which bank it was issued.

* Speech in Richmond, Virginia, American Bankers Association, September 18, 1913.
** Carter Glass, *An Adventure in Constructive Finance*. New York, 1927.

All summer the bill was discussed—condemned and approved by turns—by both Democrats and Republicans. In September it passed the House. Three Democrats and eighty-two Republicans voted against it, forty-eight Republicans being in its favor.

Then the bankers arose to denounce the Glass Bill. They accused it of almost everything undesirable. According to Glass, Vanderlip tried to present a bill that would meet the bankers' cry for a central bank, but in vain. Wilson was for the Glass Bill—and that was that! The opponents of the bill said that if it passed there would be a great constriction of commercial credits. Others said there would be inflation.

Early in December, Burton proposed a bill providing for the organization of a Federal Reserve Bank owned by the people and entirely controlled by the Government. The capital stock was to be $100,000,000, open to popular subscription in shares of $100. This bank was to do business solely with other banks.

"It is not with the hope for present success," said Burton, "that I submit this bill, but it is as an appeal to the future, the best judge of all our actions." He insisted that the pending Glass Bill was based on the wrong principle, that of dividing the country into separate sections, each with a separate bank. Burton's bill was promptly rejected.

It was about this time in the proceedings that Senator Elihu Root made a notable speech against the provision in the Federal Reserve Act that the Government issue notes at the discretion of the Federal Reserve Board, for making advances to Federal Reserve Banks. These were to be obligations of the United States and were "to be redeemed on demand of the Treasury Department of the United States or in gold or lawful money." Senator Root thundered on this provision—the one Bryan insisted President Wilson should insert and which, as inserted in the bill, was regarded as quite harmless. The bill, however, went back to the House conferees and, according to Glass, they made it safe against inflation.

The bill came to a vote in the Senate on December 23, 1913. Three Republicans alone voted for it—Weeks, Norris, and Sterling. La Follette voted each time with Burton against it.

However, the Act of Congress creating the Federal Reserve banking system was a long stride toward a stable currency and banking system and eventually both the Republican and Democratic parties claimed credit for its creation.

The Federal Reserve Act has been, for the most part, a great success. The Federal Reserve Banks opened on November 16, 1914, "just in time to steady the finances of the country" following the beginning of World War I in July.

When Theodore Burton returned to the House of Representatives in 1921, he visited Dr. E. A. Goldenweiser, Director of Research of the Federal Reserve Board, to learn how the system was working out. He was reassured by what he learned and admitted that the system seemed to be working better than he had expected.

This, be it remembered, was in 1921. The vast credit inflation of the years immediately preceding the deluge of 1929 was yet to come. That the Federal Reserve System contributed to this credit inflation will scarcely be denied by any competent observer; but the system as a whole had worked out surprisingly well.

One aim of the framers of the Federal Reserve Act was to prevent the use of reserve funds for speculation on the stock exchange and thus to permit small banks throughout the country to have funds available for commercial transactions when needed. This was not accomplished, as witness the Wall Street speculative debacle of 1929. By a Senate investigation in 1932 it was developed that the Federal Reserve banking system had been used in large measure in stock market transactions. Instead of remaining a commercial banking system, it had become an investment banking system. Out of this discovery came the Glass-Steagall Act which divorced investment banking from commercial banking.

Also, it was made evident that the Federal Reserve Bank of New York City, by reason of its location in the financial capital of America, had acquired influence over the entire system which many of its legislative guardians felt was too dominating. So far as possible, the system had to be prevented from furnishing nourishment for Wall Street—the "big, bad wolf" of financial America! This development had been a natural one by reason of the fact that foreign financial negotiations inevitably centered in New York and in its Federal Reserve Bank, to which the other regional reserve banks sent their fiscal transactions coming under the head of foreign business.

The New York Reserve Bank cleared all business of this character for the other Reserve Banks scattered over the country. The watchdogs of the Federal Reserve System scented the possibilities of danger in this situation. The remedy was simple—a provision in the amendment to the Reserve Act that transactions of this kind must receive prior approval by the Federal Reserve Board.

How deeply the Glass-Owen Currency Act of 1913 is indebted to the Aldrich Plan is a debated question. Senator Glass vehemently denies in his book that anything of the Aldrich Plan was incorporated in his bill. He insists that the two bills are "absolutely opposed," that they "differ in principle, in purpose and in processes." Burton, on the other hand, in one of his many talks at the time, said, "In many of its features the Glass Bill is identical with the plan of the Monetary Commission." And in 1915, in the Senate, Burton said:

"With reference to the currency bill, I want to say here that I was one of the men who had to do with the framing of the Aldrich-Vreeland Bill, in the face of stubborn opposition from the other [Democratic] side, but the time came when 'the stone that the builders had rejected became the head of the corner.' With regard to the Federal Reserve Act, I did not vote in favor of it, but I did say, however, it would better the conditions as they previously existed. There was a commission which worked on the currency and banking problem, of which commission I had the honor to be a member for something like four years, and the accusation of plagiarism can be made with absolute certainty against the framers of the Federal Reserve Act when they look to that report, because its essential recommendations were all embodied and it furnished the basis for the present measure."

A. Piatt Andrew, the official "expert" of the commission and the close adviser of Aldrich, says in a letter to the writer that the essential features of the Aldrich Plan findings were incorporated in the Federal Reserve Act in 1913.

Those who were antagonistic to Aldrich feel that there was no merit in his plan and that he gave nothing toward the framing of the Federal Reserve Act. But Senator Gillett, of Massachusetts, once said to the writer: "In the Federal Reserve Act the Republicans sowed and the Democrats reaped."

CHAPTER 18

Senate Filibuster

THEODORE BURTON'S HISTORIC FILIBUSTER against the Rivers and Harbors Bill, in September, 1914, is the most picturesque episode of his long and distinguished Congressional career. As an exposition of how Congress has spent hundreds of millions of dollars of public funds on doubtful, unsound, and absurd projects it is a masterpiece. It gave Senator Burton front-page position in the leading newspapers for several days in succession.

Burton, long identified in popular thought as the Chairman of the House Rivers and Harbors Committee and, therefore, considered the high priest of the Congressional pork barrel, was out to assault a Rivers and Harbors Bill with intent to kill!

It seems clearly evident, in view of the character of the man as revealed by all his public acts and utterances since he first became associated with waterway legislation, that Burton's one motive in fighting this bill was to defeat its huge expenditures of public funds because he believed them to be wasteful, extravagant, and wholly unjustified.

The preliminary engagement of his celebrated filibuster started shortly after eleven o'clock on Thursday, September 3, 1914. The Rivers and Harbors Bill then came before the Senate as "unfinished business." Burton mildly ventured the opinion that this measure called for a thorough discussion.

This news was received as depressing by the friends of the bill—and the Congressional pork barrel was never without a multitude of friends in both parties in all sections of the country.

The Sixty-second Congress, be it remembered, was overwhelmingly Democratic and the platform upon which this Democratic

Congress and President Wilson had been elected had denounced Republican extravagance and pledged drastic economies in the expenditure of public funds.

However, the bill sent up by that House committee and tenderly nursed by the Senate Committee on Commerce provided directly for an expenditure of more than fifty-three million dollars and indirectly for an additional forty millions—ninety-three millions for the improvement of the country's rivers and harbors.

Inevitably, the opening of World War I brought the problem of spending more than ninety millions of dollars for improvement of our rivers and harbors into sharp relief—especially in view of the possibility that the United States would soon be drawn into war as an active participant. In a word, it was a moment when it was certain that Uncle Sam would have unprecedented need for every available dollar.

There was keen curiosity in the Senate Chamber and on the part of the press regarding Burton's opinions of the European conflict and its consequences to America. But let his own words, uttered in deep, melodious tones which emptied the Senate cloakroom and filled the Chamber, tell the prelude to the filibuster.

> Since the previous discussion on the River and Harbor Bill, which came to a temporary close on the 22nd of July, an unexpected and startling situation has arisen, a great European war, the frightful consequences of which are likely to be beyond the wildest conjecture.
>
> In the first place, the maintenance of enormous armaments, the expenditure by the nations of Europe of two billion dollars a year on armies and navies and compulsory military service have all stimulated the military spirit. It may have been alleged that all this was preparation for defense, but it is perfectly manifest that with so great armies, with such pride in soldierly qualities, the time would come when some cause for irritation would bring on a war. . . .
>
> To this cause may be added the overweening ambition of certain sovereigns, who have not yet come to realize that they are not the State. . . .
>
> I can not discern any note of encouragement in the present situation. I can not agree with those who portray benefits to the United States from a material standpoint. No doubt some forms of agricultural production will command higher prices; probably there will be a stimulus given to certain classes of manufacturing and thus a temporary benefit may be granted to a portion of our popu-

lation, but that will be more than counter-balanced by the general confusion and demoralization in the operation of trade.

Here was the start of a characteristic Burton speech on the beauties of peace and the horrors and wickedness of war. But the mildness of his opening did not soothe any of the Senators who were responsible for the passage of the Rivers and Harbors Bill into the hope that the Senator from Ohio would long hold himself to the theme with which he had begun. They remained vigilantly at their posts as he continued:

> It is . . . our duty as Senators to guard the common weal, to make sure that no cry or urgency or emergency shall cause us to en-act hasty or injudicious legislation. It is especially desirable that our appropriations should be characterized by reasonable economy. . . .
>
> Propositions are pending to raise an extra $100,000,000 by taxation. . . . In the month which has just passed it is stated that there has been a decrease of $11,000,000 in the duties levied upon imports into this country. There is every prospect that diminished revenue from customs will appear in still greater degree in the future. So I do not deny that the question of added revenue ought to be considered by Congress. But I can not agree with one reason given as to why Congress must levy additional taxes, namely, that it is necessary to provide funds for river and harbor appropriations on a larger scale, no doubt, and in larger amounts than ever before.
>
> While no opponent of this bill is here to oppose a river and harbor bill which would be beneficial to the whole country, we do maintain that the bill now pending is the climax of waste and injudicious expenditure. We do demand that all of its provisions be carefully scrutinized; that the general policies upon which it is based be examined, and we do ask that no new projects be under-taken unless they have some degree of urgency or at least promise a benefit commensurate with the probable expense.

Burton had his heavy batteries loaded and ready for action. He once more dwelt upon the evil practices of the "dribble system," which he, as Chairman of the House Rivers and Harbors Committee, had finally been able to stop but which had again crept into rivers and harbors bills after he had become Senator. The particular bill under consideration contained a number of projects of this type and he seized the opportunity to enlighten the public regarding the Congressional return to this unsound practice of lifting a modest slab of side meat from the pork barrel—with a concealed

string attaching it to a succession of future chunks of far greater
value. He continued:

> Now, how are you going to stop the present system? How are
> you going to conform to the opinion, I believe, of every Member
> of the Senate, that the best way to deal with projects of any magni-
> tude is to provide the total amount required for them in the be-
> ginning? Mr. President, I am afraid there is only one way, and that
> is to defeat a river and harbor bill.
>
> I do not say this as any intimation that I think this bill ought
> to be defeated in its entirety, but it should be pruned and purged.
> I recognize, of course, that the measure results from an accumula-
> tion of erroneous methods and policies which have been in vogue
> for some four or five years past, and that you can not in one bill
> reform the whole system. Waterways, like railways, steam and
> electric, and auto trucks and wagons, are all agencies of transporta-
> tion, and if any one of them is unprofitable it should give place to
> another.

Illustrating the popular greed for pork, he cited the fact that the
total unexpended surplus of available funds on hand at the moment
was $14,000,000 more than was spent in 1913 and $19,000,000 in
excess of the expenditures of 1912. In short, the speed of construction lagged behind that of Congress in handing out the money.

Then the former head of the Rivers and Harbors Committee
paused to make a notable admission persistently overlooked by
those who profess inability to understand his change of attitude
toward waterway appropriations after he went up to the Senate.

> I do not claim to be free from blame for projects for which the
> Government of the United States has been appropriating. The
> House committee, when I was chairman, made mistakes. A different
> idea prevailed at that time as to what could be accomplished by
> inland waterway improvement from that which the intelligent
> sentiment of the country now sanctions.

A glance at the shifting positions of America's two major freight-
carrying agencies—her waterways and her railroads—is useful in
understanding these corresponding changes of attitude on the part
of Burton and his followers toward expenditures for developing
waterways.

When he was made Chairman of the Rivers and Harbors Committee, in 1898, railway transportation was an adolescent giant, but

the control of railway rates was unknown except by means of cheap waterway competition or by the threat of it. On the ground that the investment would justify itself by its competitive influence in keeping down excessive railway freight rates, vast sums had been invested by the Government in the improvement of streams carrying a traffic of inconsequential volume.

This "potential competition" became the slogan of the pork-barrel devotees. It was stretched to justify projects absurd from any other viewpoint. Burton, given to straight thinking and direct action, thought that the way to control railway rates was to control them by direct regulation, not by threatened waterway competition. Therefore, when the United States Interstate Commerce Commission was established, he regarded the old doctrine as outlawed and obsolete.

Although the first Interstate Commerce Act was passed in 1887, two years before Mr. Burton entered Congress and twelve years before he became Chairman of the Rivers and Harbors Committee, it did not acquire even a "baby set" of teeth until 1910, the year after he had entered the Senate and made his notable criticism of the Rivers and Harbors Bill then sent up from the House.

In 1890, at the end of Burton's first year in Congress, there had been 163,597 miles of railways in this country; in 1910, there were 240,293 miles. In this decade the volume of freight traffic carried by the railroads increased about 175 per cent. All this indicates the fact that railways, as freight carriers, were meeting the needs of American business and achieving a rapidly increasing popularity.

Therefore the accusation made by those who were in Congress when he was Chairman of the Rivers and Harbors Committee that Burton was "reversing himself," was inconsistent and "intellectually dishonest," seems entirely unjust. Burton went on:

> This bill is the climax of injudicious appropriations. . . . I will mention a minor item in the bill. The Red River below Fulton, Arkansas, to the mouth of the Atchafalaya has a length of about 475 miles. This bill came to the House with no appropriation for that stretch. It had been ridiculed somewhat in the past. I had attacked it myself on the floor of the Senate in 1910. . . . But the Senate has made an appropriation of $100,000 for that stretch of the stream.

> Now, let us see what that appropriation would accomplish. The total traffic for the year ended June 30, 1913, on this portion of the

river was 44,967 tons.* Included in this there were floated logs, which need no improvement, amounting to 42,540 tons, and lumber, 1,100 tons, leaving a balance of miscellaneous freight, made up of grain, hay, etc., of 1,227 tons. For the facilitating of the carriage of that 1,227 tons Congress is asked to appropriate $100,000.

This is an absurdity! . . . It is now proposed that we appropriate $80 for every ton of freight that would be aided by this improvement.

Burton multiplied examples of equally absurd appropriations involved in the bill, to the delight of the newspaper correspondents. He wished, he said, to prepare the Chamber and the public to understand the details of this bill which had been introduced at a time when it was proposed to tax the people a hundred million dollars to make up for a deficit of Federal income because of the influence of the war in Europe.

Not many felt free to take a stand at Burton's side and fight openly with him. This restraint did not follow party lines; it laid a silencing finger upon the lips of Republicans and Democrats alike. A special inhibition, however, seemed to rest upon the Democratic members, so far as criticism was concerned. The gods had given them a long-delayed chance at the fats of office and they were very lean and hungry.

Republicans, too, who saw the openings for telling criticism against the Democrats for their broken economy pledge felt constrained to remember the strictly nonpartisan character of waterway improvement legislation. Therefore Senator Burton's arraignment was virtually a single-handed assault upon the pork-barrel bill.

He did, however, receive conspicuous help from Senator Kenyon, of Iowa—later a judge of the United States Circuit Court of Appeals—who maintained a running fire on the defenders of the measure to the last hour of the debate. Senator Gallinger, of New Hampshire, also took a stand against the bill. These two repeatedly made the point that President Wilson had not, thus far, uttered a word of caution to Democratic Senators against the passage of this huge expenditure.

One effect of Senator Burton's speech of September 3 was that of developing opposition to the bill in Democratic ranks. His able

* Senator Burton's breakdown of this total tonnage figure equals 44,867 tons instead of 44,967 tons as he stated.

Democratic colleague from Ohio, Senator Atlee Pomerene, gave him aid in debate as did also Senator James Hamilton Lewis, of Illinois, the Democratic whip of the Senate, who, together with Senators Pomerene and Bankhead, played an important role in crystallizing Democratic sentiment against the measure.

Probably the most important result achieved by Senator Burton's preliminary attack upon the bill, however, was that of arousing the press to an editorial discussion of the Rivers and Harbors pork barrel. There were thousands of these newspaper editorials and most of them found their way to the desks of Senators and Representatives. Taken as a whole, they were extremely cheering to Senator Burton and his supporters. Inevitably, however, many of the newspaper editorials which frankly condemned the pork barrel as a shameful national institution offered arguments in justification of items in the bill involving waterway "improvements" in their own localities.

Previous to this response from the press of the country, Senator Burton evidently harbored no intention of going through with a last-ditch filibuster, but after reading the press clippings, he became resolved upon that course.

Among the first projects protested by Burton was that of the Trinity River in Texas. "The Trinity," said the Senator, "has been the subject of much pleasantry. It was said that in the last election in Texas the only thing that went dry was the Trinity River; and in the reports made upon this stream engineers who have examined it have expressed doubt whether even by canalization and the construction of thirty-seven locks and dams there will be sufficient water to float even small-sized boats. . . ."

The mention of the Trinity stirred the Texan Senators. Up popped Culberson and asked:

"Will the Senator let me read from the remarks made by him as a member of the House of Representatives on January 9, 1901?

" 'We have not included in the bill any new projects for locks and dams except the Trinity River, in the State of Texas, where we have . . . authorized $750,000, part for general improvements and part for the construction of locks and dams. I [Burton] am frank to say to the committee that on first examining this project I did not think favorably of it, but I gave it a good deal of consideration. The committee called before them the engineers having the improvement in charge, and it seemed to us that an expenditure of this amount was justified.' "

Burton, however, was not at all abashed. He said that he commended to the Senator from Texas the "more accurate information" that had been received since that time and suggested the "desirability of examining that project and ascertaining whether or not the report of the first engineer," upon whom he had relied, was correct. He went on to say that the Trinity River appropriation of that year was based on the engineer's report and that it was not until 1904 that he himself had visited that locality and gone down the river some twenty or thirty miles by boat.

"Mr. President," earnestly asserted Burton, "the stream was so narrow that the boat could hardly go forty rods without bumping into one bank or the other. Never, since I saw the stream, have I favored any other course than making the best disposition we could of a very bad proposition."

This subject kept recurring, however, throughout the debate.

Senator Simmons, of North Carolina, urged that if Senator Burton would specify the items to which he objected, he would be given a vote on them at any time. This clever challenge was not accepted by Senator Burton for two reasons: He knew that an easy and popular way for a member to escape responsibility for voting for a doubtful project was to shift that responsibility to the Senate as a whole and say, "Gentlemen, you decide it," with the inevitable result that no member having at stake a project authorized in the bill would feel free to vote against any other project. Also, Burton was determined that the Rivers and Harbors Bill as a whole should be put on trial, together with the methods and principles upon which it had been formulated. Defeating a few of the most outrageous items in the bill was only one part of his purpose, and relatively a minor part.

There was quickened attention when Senator Burton said:

> I want the vote, whatever it is, to be a fair expression of the individual judgment of the Senate. Do you believe, Senators, in any such river and harbor bill as this? Do you believe in that $2,250,000 for the buying of the Chesapeake and Delaware Canal, that defunct corporation with a defunct and played-out canal, when there is to be expended upon it a further amount up to $8,000,000?
>
> I come to another item here. Do you believe in that appropriation of $4,500,000 for the Cumberland River, for which there is

only $340,000 appropriated in this bill? If this was a matter of your own personal business, would you favor anything of that kind?

I have noticed the course of this river and harbor legislation now for nearly 20 years, and I say a situation has been reached at which it requires radical treatment. It is perhaps the last chance I will have to discuss the river and harbor bill, but I am not going out of the Senate without doing what seems to be my full duty.

With devastating thoroughness and irritating deliberation and good humor, the former Chairman of the Rivers and Harbors Committee exposed one after another of the devices by which Congress proposed to waste millions of the people's money in this bill and had wasted it in preceding bills since he had been in the Senate.

A remarkable feature of this debate, which continued for days, is that no statement of material fact made by Senator Burton was challenged by his opponents. It appears from an examination of the Record that not one of them had the courage to dispute any figure Burton offered—and in the proceedings he seldom consulted a note or memorandum of his own.

Finally, however, the Senators grew restive. Something had to be done to stop this apparently ceaseless flow of argument. Finally John Sharp Williams, of Mississippi, arose and spoke:

> There are still some Senators who think they are the Senate but the Senate can teach them better if the Senate will. . . . The only way under the sun to do it is to pass a resolution in this body to stay in permanent and perpetual session until this bill is passed. Do not give the filibustering Senators from 11 o'clock at night until 11 o'clock the next morning to hunt up new pegs whereupon to hang verbiage or even to rest. Do not let anybody interrupt them. Let them talk until they drop upon their seats. Let them talk until their mouths are so dry that they can not utter another word.*

The Senate had always maintained a certain fiction regarding procedure and courtesy to be followed, among which was the assumption that no member or group of members would openly admit the operation of a filibuster. To do so would be to admit an ungallant disregard for the convenience and rights of colleagues. However, in the course of the debates the charge was made that Burton was attempting to run a filibuster. In reply, on September 18, Senator Smoot said that since June 18, when the bill was re-

* Congressional Record, 63rd Cong., 2nd sess. (Sept. 18, 1914), vol. 51, part 15.

ported, the Senate had been in session 440 hours; that Burton had spoken with interruptions for eighteen hours, Kenyon for fourteen hours, and Gallinger for five hours—a total of thirty-seven hours. Senator Smoot remarked that this was not an unreasonable proportion of time for the opposition to consume in the discussion of so important a measure and that there was no reasonable ground for characterizing the procedure as a filibuster.

But a filibuster it proved to be. At six o'clock on the afternoon of September 18th, Burton began to talk.

"Mr. President," he said, "I am convinced that the methods of the last four years have been radically wrong." And on and on he went, hour after hour, showering the Senate with facts and figures.

Senator Kenyon, Burton's ally, who had become a warm friend during their frequent rides in Rock Creek Park, says, in recalling this dramatic episode:

> The debate ran some time before the friends of the Rivers and Harbors bill realized that Senator Burton was running a filibuster. I had talked from one in the afternoon until six when Senator Burton took the floor . . . At the outset he talked continuously from six in the afternoon until midnight. . . .
>
> I suggested to the Senator that I would take the floor for two hours and give him a little rest; but he liked the fight and told me "I'll talk a little longer—" and he certainly did! Senator Gallinger gave us a little help. Borah was away, but Burton received a wire from him saying, "Hold the fort; I'm coming." . . .
>
> Representative Frear, of Wisconsin, came into the Senate and took a seat near Burton. Then he handed up to the Senator from Ohio a lot of excellent ammunition which consumed considerable time and was read into the records.
>
> The preparations [for conducting this filibuster] were quite elaborate. The walls of the chamber were hung with maps and charts which gave it the appearance of a school room. Senator Burton wore an alpaca house coat, which some of the reporters referred to as a dressing gown, and a pair of easy house slippers. In his hand was a long pointer. He used this in referring to the maps and charts and in so doing he was the picture of the traditional old-time school master.

And this, of course, was exactly the role Burton had assumed—a teacher, long-suffering and unbelievably patient—with the greedy, obstreperous boys of the Senate. At 12:30 in the morning, after Burton had been talking continuously for seven hours, the

Chamber became quiet. Few remained to hear his remarks. A quorum count was taken and the sergeant-at-arms was dispatched in a taxi to hustle in those Senators who had escaped to get a little rest. As soon as the proper number had assembled, Burton went on talking.

One peculiar fact distinguished this historic filibuster from all others. It held closely to the subject under consideration. There was no reading into the record of materials not germane to Rivers and Harbors legislation merely to occupy time and hold the floor.

At five o'clock in the morning Senator Martine, of New Jersey, noticing Burton's fatigue, smuggled in some whiskey in a cup of tea, thinking to give the Senator a much-needed stimulant. Burton, however, waved it aside saying he would stick to water—and went on talking.

At six o'clock Burton temporarily surrendered the floor, thinking he would go to his office for a nap. His fellow Senators, however, were determined to wear him out and thus end this long struggle. They therefore immediately demanded a count of those present and dispatched a deputy sergeant-at-arms to arrest him and bring him back to the Chamber in order to constitute a quorum.

The hours dragged by but Burton talked on. During that time he twice made a motion to have the bill sent back to the committee for revision. The first time his motion was not carried and the second time it was tabled. For twelve hours Burton talked, almost continuously. Then Kenyon intervened and made a motion that the Senate adjourn. This the Senators refused to do and Kenyon therefore took the floor for the next three hours, enabling Burton to rest and eat some breakfast.

In the most strenuous portion of his oratorical marathon Burton had been speaking for several hours and had begun to show exhaustion when Senator James Hamilton Lewis, of Illinois, the Democratic whip of the Senate, brought him a chair and said: "Lean on this, Senator, and spare yourself as much as possible. You will receive every consideration that I can contrive. While members of my party are eager to see this filibuster defeated, we would all regret it deeply if you exerted yourself beyond your strength. No man in this Chamber is held in higher personal affection by his colleagues, without regard to party ties, than you are, sir, and it is by no means certain that all the Democrats here wish to see this bill go through as it is written."

There was more behind this gallant overture from Senator Lewis than any of his colleagues understood. A personal friendship between the two men began in 1897 when Lewis entered the House of Representatives from the State of Washington. The fact that this young Representative had studied law at the Ohio Northern University had interested the Chairman of the Rivers and Harbors Committee and led to an immediate personal acquaintance, unusual between a freshman and a veteran member, who was also a leader in the House.

This was the background of the dramatic filibuster incident so far as these two actors were concerned.

As soon as an interview with President Wilson could be arranged, Senator Lewis presented the picture of the filibuster to him and pointed out that, with a hundred million dollars of a new tax burden to be collected from the American people and with other and perhaps greater burdens imminent, it was an unfortunate time for the Democratic Party to lay itself open to the charge of extravagance in the expenditure of public funds. Together they worked out a plan to cut the fat from the authorization of the Rivers and Harbors Bill and reduce it to a mere skeleton of the original measure.

From the viewpoint of many members of the Senate and House, the word brought by Senator Lewis that the bill must be cut to $20,000,000 was a virtual demand that they commit political hara-kiri. The shrewd Democratic whip of the Senate realized this. It would not be an easy task to enforce the decision that he had secured from President Wilson. Incidentally, his own prestige would suffer if he fumbled this difficult and delicate mission, for which he was, himself, responsible.

While Senator Burton valiantly fought the filibuster battle, hour after hour, on the floor of the Senate, Lewis broke the sad news from the White House to the Democratic Senators. Possibly Senator Burton did not understand precisely what his friend was doing for him, but the surrender came with almost breath-taking suddenness after he had addressed the Senate for twenty-one hours. Burton's help had come, with dramatic unexpectedness, from the "camp of the enemy"; the debt of friendship incurred by the young Democratic member of the House from Washington, back in 1899, had been paid with compound interest.

It was a red-eyed, disheveled group of Senators who filed out of the Chamber, at five-thirty on Saturday, the 19th. Burton himself, after twenty-one hours of almost continuous talk, went immediately to his hotel room where he fell into a deep sleep. Hours went by, again and again the maids tried his door, the telephone rang, messengers arrived, yet nothing disturbed him.

Twenty-four hours later the hotel management, becoming alarmed, had a small Negro boy climb through the partially open transom. The noise evidently disturbed the Senator, for he roused from his long sleep and gazed with astonishment into the frightened eyes of the boy climbing into his room.

Burton had the happy faculty of being able to fall into a deep sleep almost instantly and to awaken quickly, greatly refreshed and invigorated. Perhaps this habit accounted for his endurance during those days of strain. Burton himself, however, in writing to a cousin, Mrs. Ella Grant Wilson, said "it was the Grant blood."

The fight was not quite over, however, though victory was assured. On Monday, spirited attacks were again made on the bill by Senators Burton and Pomerene. But by this time sixteen Democrats had put their heads together and agreed that Bankhead, of Mississippi, who had formerly been a member of the Rivers and Harbors Committee under Burton's chairmanship and had frankly opposed this measure, should put the motion to recommit the bill to the Senate Committee on Commerce. This he was to do with instructions that $20,000,000 be appropriated (instead of $93,000,000) to carry on projects already under way. Bankhead was chosen in order that the record would show that the motion came from Democratic sources and that it was not made at the instigation of Burton.

In running down the flag in surrender, Senator Stone, of Missouri, said:

> When I saw my distinguished friend from Ohio stand here day after day and night after night, talking, talking, talking, as a river flows on forever, to prevent the enactment of this important measure first reported from the Committee on Commerce of which the honorable Senator is a member, I could not but reflect that it was a strange ending of a great career. When I saw him stand at his desk through all the hours of the night, wearying himself and wearying his colleagues, forced by fatigue to walk back and forth in slippers and slouch coat, frequently leaning or sitting on the arm

of his chair, with his voice grown weak and husky, still talking, reading and talking, I could not but be astonished at the performance. . . .

I am not going longer to oppose this $20,000,000 proposition. I am going to quit and take what I can get for I recognize that the filibusterers have licked us.

In a personal way, Senator Burton's "endurance debate" added immensely to his reputation throughout the country. Hundreds of newspapers, Democratic and Republican, editorially commended him for his courage, honesty, and high sense of public duty.

Not a few of these editorial articles suggested that the Republican Party could do much worse than to choose Senator Burton as its Presidential candidate. There can be little doubt that the popular reaction to his filibuster influenced his candidacy for that nomination in 1916.

Commenting on the filibuster and its influence upon Senator Burton's standing, former Senator Bristow said:

"That famous fight increased Senator Burton's standing and influence immensely, in spite of the fact that it resulted in many bitter disappointments to Senators who had worked hard to embody in the bill provisions enabling them to go back to their constituents with fat chunks of pork. These men awoke to the realization that, on all matters which went against his sense of principle and conscience, he would fight and fight hard and that it was the safer policy to avoid a conflict with him.

"Not only was that particular filibuster fully justified, but I will go to the length of saying that, up to the time I left the Senate, I had never known of a filibuster that was not justified from the viewpoint of public interest."

In still another particular was Senator Burton's filibuster of outstanding importance to the country. It made a distinguished contribution to the subject of the right of unlimited debate in the United States Senate—which has been heatedly contested from the First Congress of the United States to the present.

In the Sixty-ninth Congress (1925–1927) in which General Charles G. Dawes took his seat in the Vice-President's chair, he berated the Senate for holding to a decadent rule which permitted one Senator to obstruct the serious business of legislation for the country. To say that this speech was not well received by the body over which Dawes was to preside is a mild statement—but his address served to focus public attention upon the merits and demerits of the Senatorial rights of "unlimited" debate and, incidentally, upon the peculiar function of the Senate as a check upon the House of Representatives—a function deliberately bestowed by the far-sighted founders of the Government.

Those Senators who were members of that body in 1914 must have recalled the Burton filibuster and wondered if General Dawes, former Director of the Budget under the first administration of President Coolidge, had forgotten that the right of unlimited debate had enabled Senator Burton to prevent the expenditure of some seventy-three million dollars for Rivers and Harbors improvements, many of them of doubtful value.

"Again the advantages of unlimited debate in the Senate have been vindicated," commented the Boston *Transcript* of September 24, 1914.

For a time, at least, Senator Burton's successful battle against the Rivers and Harbors Bill put a check upon extravagant pork-barrel legislation. The reformative influence of this filibuster is commonly credited with having lasted more than twelve years. In this connection, however, it is to be remembered that we soon entered World War I, involving expenditures which taxed the resources of the country to the limit and, in large measure, put "public improvements" on the shelf.

Human nature, however, was not changed either by Senator Burton's filibuster or by the war. When he returned to the House, in 1921, he had repeated occasion to oppose Rivers and Harbors provisions and did so. His presence there operated to forestall great excesses and absurd projects.

The real significance of Burton's courageous filibuster would be lost by considering it in its narrower sense as an assault upon a particular bill or upon a certain class of appropriations. It was far more than that; it was a masterful clinic upon diseased legislation in general; a profound exposition of chronic methods of national waste on the part of those responsible for spending the people's money. It revealed with singular clearness Burton's attitude toward the public trust which he was elected to discharge. It showed not only his characteristic abhorrence of waste in general but particularly of waste of funds entrusted to the administration of public servants.

The strain of the month had told on Senator Burton. He was tired and needed a rest. His doctor kept urging him to get away from Washington, to go somewhere, perhaps to the mountains, where he could enjoy the autumn scenery and indulge himself in his favorite sports.

But Burton had no "favorite sports." As Charles A. Webb, Secretary of the House, said,

"The Senator analyzed the situation carefully, as was his habit in everything, and came to the conclusion that he was woefully lacking in means of recreation, such as golf and other sports, so he did the next best thing. He went to the Congressional Library, got out some French and Spanish books and spent his recreative period in Asheville translating them. That was the nearest approach to a sportsman's life that the learned Senator could make."

CHAPTER 19

The Burton Blues

ARLY IN 1914, Senator Burton fell under the spell of a black mood which led him to make the supreme mistake of his political life. In the opinion of many of the shrewdest political leaders of Ohio and the nation, it ultimately cost him the Presidency of the United States. Certainly it put Warren G. Harding in the United States Senate, in a strategic position to be selected, in 1920, as the Presidential candidate of the Republican Party.

Under the shadow of this strange mental complex, Senator Burton violated the fixed habits of a lifetime, took counsel of his fears instead of his friends, and abandoned his characteristic methods of basing his conclusions and acts upon carefully determined facts.

One of the first men to whom Senator Burton confided his inclination to retire from public life was William Tyler Page. The friendship between Burton and Page began in 1889, on almost the first day of Mr. Burton's service as a Representative. It was, therefore, almost inevitable that Senator Burton should discuss with Page his inclination to retire from the Senate.

"Quite early in the spring of 1914," Mr. Page related to the writer, "I met Senator Burton in the corridor coming toward my office. The Senator's face, before he saw me, wore a serious, troubled expression. I thought I knew what was on his mind, for a rumor had reached me through a mutual friend that he was considering the possibility of retiring from public life. Almost immediately, he entered into a frank discussion of this possibility.

" 'We have come upon strange times,' said the Senator. 'There is a new drift in practical politics which is no respecter of persons and takes little account of the service which a candidate for public office has rendered or is able to render. We are now living in a time when politics is in a state of flux and it is extremely disquieting to me.

" 'Then there is the matter of the direct primary, with which I have had no experience. The thought of making a strenuous and state-wide campaign to secure the nomination, followed by another equally severe and extensive effort for election, is distasteful to me.'

"Then he paused for a moment and observed: 'Page, a very shrewd man once remarked that republics are ungrateful. There is more than a little truth in that observation. I am quite decided in the opinion that I shall withdraw from public life.'

"He was extremely low in his mind, in one of his blackest and bluest of moods. Then, too, I knew his sensitiveness, his pride, and his stubbornness. That conversation depressed me greatly. I felt that his retirement from the Senate, at that time, would be a calamity to his party and his country as well as to himself."

When the sudden blow of his announcement that he would retire fell upon his political associates in Ohio, consternation and resentment prevailed among them. They charged him with scrapping, without warning, a state-wide party machine in which their own political fortunes were involved.

One of the strangest phases of Senator Burton's mental state was the fact that he announced his decision not to become a candidate to succeed himself several months before it was necessary to do so in order to comply with the requirements of the election laws or to provide for the readjustment of personal alignments within the party. This was a radical departure from his settled habit in dealing with political problems. His practice in handling matters of patronage and political strategy was to make no decision as long as he had any hope of developing further information of importance.

This time, however, he reversed himself; he made only a casual, halfhearted attempt to learn the attitude of the voters toward his candidacy, repelled or disregarded the advice of friends, and surrendered to a melancholy which few dared attempt to penetrate.

Self-depreciation was not a normal state of mind with Senator Burton. He was far too intelligent to underestimate his own abilities. But, in his historic case of "blues" in 1914, he discounted his standing with the people of his own state and failed to recognize the depth and constancy of their pride in him.

Relatively few of them were deeply concerned with the particular lines of national and international effort with which he was absorbed. They were content to know that Ohio was maintaining its tradition for distinguished statesmanship in the Senate of the United States and that the opinions of the scholarly Burton were respected throughout America and Europe. He looked after the interests of his state vigilantly and capably—therefore, let him run his world-statecraft to suit himself!

But, in this strangely despondent mood he fell into the error of believing that the newspapers reflected the sentiment of the people. He harbored the delusion that the man in the street followed his course in national and international matters with critical eyes and was as eager to quarrel with his views as were the editorial writers of newspapers. This is indicated in the text of his statement of retirement which was released in Washington, on April 8, 1914, and published in the leading Ohio newspapers the following day. It was as follows:

> I am averse to becoming a candidate for re-election to the Senate and shall not be a candidate unless circumstances arise which I do not anticipate will occur. While, on some accounts, I should be glad to continue in Congress, where I have been actively engaged for more than twenty years, I have no importunate desire to return to the Senate.
>
> But more important than this, my chief anxiety is for the success of the Republican Party in the State of Ohio at the coming election. The prospects are extremely favorable. Yet it is possible that someone who has been less involved in the factional dissensions of the last two years would be more favorably regarded. Any personal ambitions of mine should be subordinated to the success of the principles which I have advocated. This conclusion is emphasized by the loyal support which has been given me in many campaigns in the past. Again, my convictions have compelled me to take positions in legislative matters, which, temporarily at least, have been unpopular. . . .
>
> It is my intention to take a more active part in the discussion of present-day problems in Ohio than I have ever taken before. During the years of my service, I have been compelled to remain at Washington most of the time. The extra sessions of Congress each alternate year and the protracted length of all sessions have prevented me from devoting the time which I desired to my native state. I should enjoy the opportunity of advocating certain reforms in seeking to analyze the tendency of the time with entire freedom

and without the handicap of any candidacy for office. Indeed, I have come to be more interested in certain great measures now confronting us than in the holding of any office.

In concluding this statement, I most earnestly appeal to all who have affiliated with the Republican Party in Ohio to ignore personal controversies, to make concessions and unite upon principles which the conscience of the people can approve.

Theodore E. Burton

It is safe to say that the average citizen of Ohio—the man in the street—cared less about Senator Burton's attitude on foreign affairs than he did about the brand of cigars which the Senator smoked. In fact, probably the representative working man would have felt quite a flicker of interest in the information that, for more than twenty-five years, Ohio's scholarly bachelor statesman had been faithful to "The Belle of Cairo" and had consumed thousands of boxes of these five-cent cigars, each bearing the likeness of a gay and sinuous Oriental dancer.

The prevailing estimate was that the Senator was suffering from an attack of cold feet. A more discriminating diagnosis of his malady would have been that he was the victim of a violent attack of political indigestion. He was fed up with politics to the point of nausea and revolt.

Concurrently with the Senator's announcement of his retirement, the Cleveland *Plain Dealer* carried this comment:

> Tired of the turmoil and strife of politics, in which he has been engaged for a quarter of a century, Senator Theodore E. Burton, tonight, in a formal statement, declares he will retire voluntarily from public life. He will not be a candidate for re-nomination or re-election and in his statement sets forth some of the reasons why.
>
> The retirement of Senator Burton came as a surprise to his closest friends. While they knew his aversion to engaging in a bruising political contest, his friends, until late this afternoon, were convinced the statement of tonight would be an announcement of his candidacy for re-election. Aside from the reasons assigned in his statement, it is known that the Senator shrank from the prospect of being hammered and pounded in a bitter political campaign because of enemies within and without the Republican Party.

The next day the same paper carried the following dispatch from its Washington correspondent, Walker S. Buel:

What new complexion of Republican politics here will follow the retirement from public life of Senator Theodore E. Burton? . . . Men of influence and most active in the Cuyahoga County Republican organization have been aligned for years with Senator Burton. To a large extent, control of the organization is considered to lie in their hands. . . .

When the Senator steps aside, will there be a new alignment? Maurice Maschke, Collector of Customs, and A. N. Rodway, Chairman of the Republican county executive committee, formerly collector of internal revenue, received their federal appointments through Senator Burton. . . . Mr. Maschke and Mr. Rodway were considered to a large degree responsible for Mr. Burton's election to the Senate. Their allegiance to the retiring Senator dates even before the State Republican convention at Dayton, in 1906, at which Mr. Burton made his first state political fight. . . .

That was but a preliminary skirmish in the later battle between Senator Foraker and William Howard Taft for President, in which Congressman Burton took the Taft side. After Mr. Taft's election, Congressman Burton became a candidate for Senator, and was indorsed by the Cuyahoga County Republican organization. . . . Will Mr. Maschke, Mr. Rodway, and the other Burton adherents continue to stand together in politics, or will they separate after Senator Burton retires and each go his own political way? . . .

Surprise was expressed by a number of Republicans yesterday over Senator Burton's decision to quit the political stage. Maurice Maschke had this to say about his retirement:

"It seems there is a serious defect in our political system when the country must lose the services of a man of exceptional ability and unquestioned integrity the moment he takes a stand against the political current of the day. When public opinion veers strongly in one direction, some see clearer than the mass, set themselves boldly to stem the current and speak with no uncertain sound in resisting the tyranny of the majority. But under our political system they go out of office surely and quickly." . . .

A notable career in public life will end with Senator Burton's retirement. Both in the House and the Senate the member from Cleveland has been a leader; one to whom his colleagues looked for careful judgment on important questions. . . .

The turn of events leaves the Republicans of Ohio in a peculiar position in reference to the senatorship. Had Mr. Burton remained in the contest there could have been no justification in refusing him a re-nomination. His withdrawal leaves former Senator Foraker the only aspirant for the honor with a long record in conspicuous public office. . . .

It is not to be presumed for a moment that the senatorial nomination will now be conceded to Mr. Foraker. Other candidates of one kind or another will make their appearance, emboldened in their ambition by the present Senator's retirement.

On April 9 the Cleveland *Plain Dealer* carried the following dispatch from Columbus:

Harry M. Daugherty may get into the Republican senatorial race. Tonight it became known that many letters and telegrams from Republicans had reached him, the writers insisting he shift his position of not being a candidate for any office and enter the senatorial race. . . .

Months ago he said he was not a candidate for any office. . . . Friends now insist the withdrawal of Senator Burton has so completely changed the situation that a new deal is required. . . .

Preceding the announcement of the movement for Mr. Daugherty came another. It was to have all candidates now in the field withdraw and let the nomination go to Warren G. Harding, of Marion. It was stated that Senator Foraker resented the idea he ought to get out of the way and that his personal representatives spurned any plan to get together on any man save Mr. Foraker. . . .

The refusal of Mr. Foraker to make way for Mr. Harding raises a political situation that may cause trouble. Mr. Harding for many years was a spokesman for Mr. Foraker, but swung to ex-President Taft, in 1908, in an abrupt manner the Foraker forces have not forgotten. . . .

Those who claim to know stated here today with emphasis that Ambassador Myron T. Herrick will not get into the senatorial race. The telegraph cable companies have done a large business sending cablegrams to Mr. Herrick in the last two days but there will be a declination, his associates are certain.

The influences which led Senator Burton to take the eccentric course that threw the Republicans of Ohio into confusion can readily be traced.

They began, perhaps, back in 1909 when the opposition newspapers in Ohio tried to convince the voters of the state that Burton was about the nimblest and most obedient of the Aldrich yes men. It was a fierce onslaught, but its logic stands in need of challenge.

In April of 1909, President Taft called Congress in special session to enact a tariff revision law. This measure, later known as the Payne-Aldrich Tariff Act, was the target of much abuse. It was claimed that, in the campaign of 1908, the Republican Party had promised a downward revision of the tariff but that this measure as finally framed made practically no reductions in duties, but greatly increased the duties on almost everything, including staple commodities, especially newsprint paper, and textile products. The newspapers, both Democratic and Independent, were vituperative in their attacks upon those who supported the measure and the so-called Independents in the Senate, led by such men as La Follette and Beveridge, pounded the bill day in and day out.

The newspapers opposing Burton kept hammering away at the fact that during these days he simply followed the crowd led by Aldrich. However, an examination of the record reveals that occasionally Senator Burton showed symptoms of courageous opposition to Aldrich's will. Repeatedly, he voted against the decrees of the tariff-making machine and with La Follette, Beveridge, Bristow, and other Republican radicals who sided with the Democrats.

For example, Burton was one of sixteen Republicans who opposed a tariff on hides and voted for their duty-free admission. Again he supported Senator Bristow's amendment lowering the duty on typewriting paper and writing paper. Burton also voted to reduce the duty on rough lumber.

The brilliant Dolliver, of Iowa, was the leader of the Republican rebels against the rule of Senator Aldrich and it was by no means a novelty for him to find Senator Burton temporarily in his group of followers, along with the Democrats, resisting a rate of duty which he regarded as altogether too high. From the Dolliver viewpoint Senator Aldrich was captain of a pirate crew recruited in Wall Street for the purpose of enriching the "money power" at the expense of the masses, particularly the struggling farmers of the Middle West.

It can scarcely be denied that the crusader from Iowa made out a strong case and greatly endeared himself to the Democrats.

During the closing hours of this tariff fight Senator Burton was undecided whether he should support the bill or oppose it on final roll call. He walked the floor debating the course which he ought to pursue and finally decided to vote for the bill largely because he felt that, since he was a Senator from Ohio, his vote against the measure would be heralded as a repudiation of President Taft by a Senator from his own state who had been elected to support the Administration.

The most striking example of undiscriminating condemnation of Burton for "voting with Aldrich" was a cartoon, by Stanley, which appeared in the Cleveland *Press* of September 15, 1909. It pictured Senator Burton and Senator Dick standing on the platform of a railway station bearing the sign "Ohio." In this cartoon Senator Burton's traveling bag bore the legend: "Voted with Aldrich—114; against Aldrich—14." Sitting in the window was an Ohio farmer engaged in trying to work out a cost-of-living puzzle and remarking, "By heck, this is a hard one!" The bulletin board on the front of the station bore the inscription:

> Trains
> Due—now
> Taft
> Explanation
> Special—
> Quite a bit late.

This, however, ignored the fact that Senator Burton had stood out against Aldrich in a number of important items in the tariff schedule. In a measure, at least, Senator La Follette, of Wisconsin, might legitimately have been substituted for Burton in this cartoon—with the change of the legend on the suitcase to read: "Voted with Aldrich—75."

The writer has no inclination to absolve Senator Burton from the onus—if onus it be—of being a regular among Republicans and a "sincere protectionist"—a phrase which Senator Reed Smoot applied to his colleague from Ohio when discussing his tariff views. Smoot told the writer that in 1908 he had engaged in an extended conversation with Burton and was convinced that his adoption of the principle of protection involved a genuine change of conviction.

Nevertheless, the fact that a copy of the cartoon was found among Senator Burton's personal papers indicates that he was harder hit by this shaft of being an Aldrich yes man than he admitted to his most intimate political supporters—or else that he had a greater sense of humor than was commonly supposed.

Hubert Fuller, Burton's chief secretary at that time and for several years preceding, who afterward became a Cleveland lawyer, has painted for this biography an interesting picture of the background of the Senator's depression:

Senator Burton had been in the House of Representatives for many years and had repeatedly been elected without any Democrat being nominated to oppose him. The result was that the Senator had not become hardened to abuse and, on the contrary, was extremely sensitive to it. He told me that he did not object so much to the abuse from a personal standpoint as for the reason that it was particularly painful to his sister, Mrs. Shurtleff, of Oberlin; that Mrs. Shurtleff—being an elder sister and he being the youngest child in the family—had mothered him, carried him in her arms when he was a small child and had been particularly close to him and, therefore, these attacks upon him were extremely distressing to her.

During the Taft Administration he supported the President from a feeling of loyalty to the Administration. . . . In a measure there was visited upon Senator Burton by the newspapers a great deal of that disappointment and criticism of the Taft Administration which found expression in the Bull Moose movement. Senator Burton supported President Taft in the pre-convention fight of 1912, and was bitterly assailed by many papers in Ohio, which had hitherto been Republican but which then came out to support Roosevelt.

For example, when he returned to Cleveland, after the Ohio State Convention in March of 1912, at which the delegates-at-large and alternates to the Chicago convention were instructed to vote for Taft, the Cleveland *Leader* published a cartoon representing Senator Burton leaving the train and being greeted by a committee consisting of Judas Iscariot, Benedict Arnold, and one or two other characters of unhappy repute.

At the Chicago convention in 1912, Senator Burton was prepared, as a spokesman for President Taft, to agree that Taft should not be renominated with the proviso that Roosevelt should not be nominated, but that some candidate should be nominated upon whom both sides could agree. This candidate, it was suggested, should be Arthur Hadley, Governor of Missouri. When this suggestion was conveyed to Roosevelt it was indignantly rejected. He was said to have denounced Hadley as a traitor. Senator Burton campaigned vigorously for Taft but had no hope of his re-election.

When Woodrow Wilson became President he inaugurated a legislative program to provide for a new banking system and also to curb the tendency toward monopoly by the larger business interests of the country. Measures in the Wilson Administration were not framed in committee. Rather they were framed by unofficial advisors of Wilson.

As thus framed they were introduced in the House or Senate by some spokesman and referred to the appropriate committee in which the Democrats had the chairmanship and the majority of the members. No amendments were ever adopted by the committees except with the approval of the President and his advisors. When the bills reached the floor they were adopted by the Democratic majority as written and no Democrat dared oppose them to the extent of even offering an amendment, under penalty of political death. . . .

Senator Burton took an active part in the debates upon these various measures. . . . He offered various amendments and supported them in vigorous speeches. However, the majority was adamant and voted down every amendment offered by the Republican Party.

One evening as the Senator and I were starting on an automobile ride, he expressed his unhappiness at the situation in about the following language: "I am extremely disappointed in my services in the Senate. It is no longer a great deliberative body. Measures are sent down from the White House and orders are given to the Democratic majority to adopt them as presented without the crossing of a 't' or the dotting of an 'i.' Men who openly oppose measures in the cloak room march out to the floor on roll call and vote for their adoption. I wonder what the public would do if it realized the real situation—that the legislative branch of the Government is completely submerged by the Executive and that arguments and logic are of absolutely no avail in the framing of legislation."

I told him that I did not really feel that the public would be much disturbed even if they did realize that this was the fact; that I thought that Woodrow Wilson dominated the Administration and was stronger than the individual Senators; that a reading of American history seemed to disclose the fact that the most popular Presidents had been men like Theodore Roosevelt, who were in constant turmoil with Congress and "ate a Congressman raw every morning for breakfast." Senator Burton said that this would seem to be true, but he could not believe the people would quietly accept the complete submergence of one of the three co-ordinate branches of our Government. In any event, service in the Senate, he repeated, was becoming extremely distasteful to him.

The Republican Party in Ohio, as elsewhere, was badly split and it seemed likely that, in 1914, the "Bull Moose" Party would set up a full ticket unless the Republicans nominated candidates who were acceptable to them. Senator Burton felt that, having been a leader of the Taft fight in Ohio in 1912, he would be particularly distasteful to the Progressives of the state and would be a target for them. He wrote letters to a few close friends in Ohio, asking them to indicate the sentiment of their communities as to his re-election. The replies which he received were not reassuring.

One reply, in particular, came from Ashtabula County, where he was born, and told him that he would not be able to carry that county if nominated. This made a very strong impression upon him. In the meantime, Senator Julius C. Burrows, a veteran Senator from Michigan, had been defeated for renomination by J. Alden Smith. Burrows was an elderly man with a long and distinguished service, and he was crushed by his defeat. Senator Burton told me that Burrows came up to him, put an arm over his shoulder and said: "Do not end your career in defeat. You will be very much happier to withdraw from public life undefeated than to go through a campaign and have to accept the bitterness of loss."

Also, at this time, members of the Congress were being bombarded with thousands of letters, telegrams, and petitions on such controversial issues as the prohibition question and suffrage for women until Senator Burton came to feel that legislation was likely to be the result of pressure and threat rather than deliberation and judgment—that a Senator would vote according to the volume of the harassments he received rather than the exercise of his own judgment.

These things combined to make Senator Burton unhappy in the latter years of his first term in the Senate. He more and more talked about declining to run for renomination.

In the spring of 1914, former Senator Foraker announced his candidacy for election to succeed Burton. Senator Burton felt that, having served one term, he was entitled to renomination without opposition within his own party and that he ought not to be called upon to make a fight for renomination. One or two other men of lesser renown, like Ralph Cole, became candidates. One week-end in the spring of 1914, the Senator told me that he had about decided not to be a candidate for renomination. I urged him again, as I had on other occasions, to run for re-election, and reminded him that, no matter what the real reason was for his determination to retire and no matter how unhappy he might be in the Senate, if he failed to run there would always be those who would accuse him of being afraid of defeat.

I secured the Senator's promise not to make any announcement until the first of the following week and told him that I wanted to draw up an announcement for re-election and submit it to him before he reached his final decision. He told me that I could draw it up but that, while his mind was practically made up, he would hold the question open until the first of the week. I drew up an announcement for renomination, short and vigorous, defying his enemies and inviting them to battle.

On Monday morning the Senator came into the office and as he passed my desk said he had definitely decided not to be a candidate. I then asked him if he would give me two weeks' leave and let me go to Ohio. He wanted to know for what purpose and I replied: "When I come back you will be a candidate and we will have petitions for your candidacy signed from all over the state." He answered: "No, I will not agree to that. If there were any spontaneous demand for me, my friends in Ohio would not need to be invited to circulate petitions. I might consider running if petitions were spontaneously circulated." Thereupon he announced his decision to retire from public life. He then got in touch with Warren Harding and persuaded Harding to become a candidate.

Possibly no man had ever entered the United States Senate with a feeling of more profound satisfaction and assurance than had Theodore E. Burton. His every personal characteristic marked him as predestined for this high position. "A born Senator" was a phrase repeatedly on the lips of his friends.

Yet few Senators have found their service in the "American House of Lords" more disappointing than Burton did. He met with a disillusionment which irritated and often wounded him. He had become accustomed to being treated with almost unprecedented deference in the House. The entire membership often arose to its feet when he was about to deliver an address and he was listened to with rare attentiveness. Any bill which he opposed was in doubt until the vote was taken.

He was, in fact, a House institution—a man of extraordinary power whose leadership rested upon recognition of his intellectual force and honesty.

Accustomed, for years, to this position of power, he was unable, on entering the Senate, to realize that his reputation would not secure for him a consideration not enjoyed by most of the newer members.

He knew, theoretically, that the seniority rule was applied in the Senate as in no other legislative body; but failed to realize that it was inexorable and undiscriminating; that his many years of service at the other end of the long Capitol corridor could not soften its application and that his position in the Senate would be that of a youngster who must take his place at the foot of the class.

He had been the shining example, in the House, of the power which a committee chairman could exercise. Suddenly, on his promotion to the Senate, he was "put in his place," giving way, in some instances, to men of far less legislative experience. Also, as a matter of good Senatorial manners, he was expected to be grateful for being assigned to the tail end of certain committees not especially desirable to him. Of course, time and the death and election defeats of members outranking him would remedy this situation. But this reflection did not do much to soften the irritation which the seniority rule had upon his sensibilities.

He no longer carried the major burden of the work of a great committee on his shoulders. He had no specific single project upon which he could concentrate his prodigious energy. He was like a man of habitual and enormous industry suddenly left without a task equal to his abilities. Senator Henry Clay Hansbrough, of North Dakota, sketched the situation to me in these words:

"I had been a member of the Rivers and Harbors Committee in the House when he sat at the head of the table and made his great reputation. He was a master at that table, kindly and considerate, but master! The fortunes of state politics placed me in the Senate several years before he was promoted to its membership. When he came here and was put on my committee, our positions were reversed. This was not particularly comfortable for either of us. He was a good soldier under that difficult situation. However, it was evident that he was not altogether happy. Quite naturally, he became less a committee man and more a floor man.

"This is only another way of saying that his attitude toward all legislation, whether framed by his own party organization or by the Democrats, became more and more critical. His committee work did not, I think, greatly interest him. On the other hand, he occasionally gave those interested in certain pet measures a most uncomfortable time by unloosing his critical batteries. He was watchful of government expenditures and vigilantly determined that the funds of his country should not be squandered."

The weeks following his announcement of withdrawal from public life evidently were spent by Senator Burton in penitential reflections and in a detailed study of the changing political situation in Ohio. The skies which had looked so black when he had made his premature and impulsive decision to retire ultimately became bright with hope. Again in his home city, he promptly arranged for a conference with his friend and faithful political strategist, Maurice Maschke. As incidentally as possible, he reminded his former chief of staff that his retirement announcement had contained a contingent clause reading, "I am averse to becoming a candidate for re-election to the Senate and shall not be a candidate unless circumstances arise which I do not anticipate will occur."

Undoubtedly it was a shock to him to be interrupted by the statement from his former political manager that it was too late to "get back into the game again"; that their political friends had accepted his retirement announcement as final; that, only a few weeks before, the leaders of the Republican organization in Ohio had held a conference and pledged themselves to the support of Warren G. Harding for Senator and that it would be impossible to back down now and cancel their pledges to Harding and his friends.

In a word, Burton's former supporters were "sore" and not in a mood to break their new allegiance with a candidate whom they considered a great mixer and a leader of great popularity. Also, Mr. Burton was reminded that he himself had plainly indicated his satisfaction in the tentative selection of Harding as his successor.

This conversation was scarcely less embarrassing to Mr. Maschke than it was to Mr. Burton. In recounting it, Mr. Maschke once remarked to the writer:

"Of course, Harry M. Daugherty was brought into this a little later because an impression had gained acceptance that Mr. Daugherty had, perhaps deliberately, contributed to Senator Burton's discouragement regarding the Republican outlook in Ohio, early in 1914, when it was actually unpromising—this because of Mr. Daugherty's close friendship with Harding and his ambitions for his friend's promotion. This impression was without foundation in fact. It is a matter of justice to say that Mr. Daugherty was among the few party leaders consulted by Senator Burton before the

Senator's retirement announcement was issued and that Mr. Daugherty advised against it and expressed his readiness to work as hard for Burton's renomination and election as he had worked for his first election in 1908. On Mr. Burton's return to Cleveland Mr. Daugherty joined with me and with other leaders of the party and of the Burton organization in making it clear to the retired Senator that it was not politically possible for him to stage a comeback after new alliances had been formed and new pledges made."

Burton's most unhappy years in the Senate were those of his first term. Toward its close, problems of World War I weighed heavily upon him—more heavily, perhaps, than upon those of his colleagues who were less ardently devoted to the principle of the adjudication of international disputes by reason and arbitration instead of by war.

Burton's interest in international peace was crystallized while he was visiting in Paris in 1900. The second conference of the Interparliamentary Union was in session. Its announced purpose was "to study questions of an international character suitable for settlement by parliamentary action." This intrigued him. Then he learned that its delegates were all members of the lawmaking bodies of the various nations represented. It would be decidedly interesting, Burton thought, to take a look at so polyglot an assemblage of national legislators engaged in the discussion of ways and means for settling disputes between nations by civilized processes. Entirely as an unofficial visitor, he attended the session.

There was then no American group in the Interparliamentary Union. What Burton heard of the deliberations of this unique body interested him greatly—but not to the extent of moving him to take steps for the formation of an American arm of the organization. Bringing the United States into this strange parliament was left to one of his colleagues in Congress of a less cautious temperament, Richard Bartholdt, of St. Louis, who entered the House in 1893 and served until 1915.

Bartholdt attended the conference of the Union in Vienna, in 1903. He was so moved by what he heard there that, on his own initiative, he started a movement for the formation of a group to represent the United States in the deliberations of the Union. On his return to America he wrote an article urging Americans to do their share in helping to make the world peace-minded.

The day after its publication he called at the White House and had a conference with President Roosevelt. As a result, the President indicated that he was heartily in accord with Mr. Bartholdt's plan to secure an appropriation from Congress to finance a meeting of the Interparliamentary Union in St. Louis the following year. This appropriation was made and the Union accepted the invitation of the United States to call its 1904 conference in St. Louis.

Burton became Mr. Bartholdt's most active coadjutor, taking a prominent part in the deliberations of the conference and in the organization of the American group, which became a permanent and powerful arm of the Interparliamentary Union.

He attended the London Conference of the Interparliamentary Union in 1906, the Geneva Conference in 1912, the Hague Conference in 1913. Then, following World War I, he was present at the Vienna Conference in 1922, the Copenhagen Conference in 1923, the Berne and Geneva Conference in 1924, the Washington Conference in 1925, and the Paris Conference in 1927.

His activities were not confined to mere attendance at the conferences; he threw himself into the labors of the organization with characteristic thoroughness.

In all the deliberations of the Interparliamentary Union, Burton held to conservative ground. Many members of that deliberative body have borne testimony to the fact that this tall, scholarly American could not be carried off his feet by any burst of eloquence, any appeal to the emotions. All the leaders in the deliberations of the Interparliamentary Union came to understand that here was a man familiar with international leaders, problems, and affairs, who would not commit himself to a policy that could not be justified from the viewpoint of hard common sense.

His expectations of immediate results in the stabilization of international peace were much more modest than those of most of his associates in the Interparliamentary Union, but he believed in the necessity for a civilized adjustment of disputes between nations and had faith in the ultimate acceptance of this principle.

To Burton's great sorrow, then, war crashed down upon the world. It depressed him greatly although he had somewhat anticipated such a calamity. Judson C. Welliver said that long before 1914 Burton had told him that such a cataclysm as World War I was almost inevitable unless heroic measures were taken to avoid it.

Because of his policy of consistently fighting extravagant naval programs, Burton was often accused of being a pacifist. Burton *was* a pacifist; that is, he was a person who favored the policy of settling international differences by peaceful means. But Burton was also a patriot. He believed in defending his country.

During the early days of the war, he was asked to address the Cleveland Advertising Clubs, who were entertaining the Sons and Daughters of the American Revolution at their annual convention. He said, in part:

"It is hardly probable that such an elaborate system of military training as Switzerland has would be necessary in the United States, but something like it will likely be required. We have the raw material, but if an emergency comes to us we do not wish raw recruits to stand up as helpless targets for an enemy. A certain amount of military training is necessary. . . .

"Possibly even before this trouble ends we may be drawn into the conflict. That all means, however much we may love peace, that we must be ready for all eventualities. By all means do not let us stir up strife; do not let us indulge in bluff or bravado. Let us have a diplomatic policy which at the same time is without bluster and without cringing.

"Enlargement of the army, a more efficient navy are the immediate steps before us. The most important of all is to maintain a great reserve force."

He was somewhat more explicit in a later speech regarding our position at the close of the war. "We should immediately prepare for every emergency of the future, so that on sea and land we may be able to worthily maintain the honor of the American name, to protect our borders against assault and defend our rights wherever they may be challenged. This should be with no spirit of aggression or desire to pick a quarrel or to take up arms on light occasion, but with a proper sense of responsibility and a high resolve to be righteous as well as fearless."

After his retirement from the Senate, Burton expected to spend a year in travel. But in an informal address in Cleveland he said: "I feel like an old man who has passed things on to others. Perhaps my service might be useful as a private citizen. Suppose a boat were to be sunk, with a loss of life, and thousands would rise up and demand war. In such a time as that I would not want to be away from the United States."

CHAPTER 20

An Adventure in Presidential Politics

WHEN ON MARCH 3, 1915, Theodore Burton surrendered his "toga," he was not sorrowful or depressed. Quite the contrary.

The press of the country was then acclaiming him for the success of his filibuster against an overstuffed Rivers and Harbors Bill. High Republican medicine men were saying that he was a peculiarly available man for the Presidential nomination in the coming year. He had reached the moment of his greatest popularity; he was from the strategic state of Ohio; he would make an ideal candidate in the convention after the favorite sons had been given their brief hour in the spotlight. Burton himself felt that no other candidate then in sight was in better situation to be drafted to lead the Republicans against Woodrow Wilson. But he believed that so great an honor should not be the result of a bargain-counter scramble.

He had been selected to make an important good will visit to the countries of South America and, instead of prudently staying at home to tend the political pot, dashed away on this mission. The instant his feet touched the deck of the ship, his rosy political dreams were promptly dismissed from mind, as his diary discloses.

With him on the trip was Judge Otto Schoenrich, a distinguished New York lawyer representing the Carnegie Endowment for International Peace, who records that, although at the moment Burton was a private citizen, he was accorded the reception of an accredited Ambassador of the United States. He visited nearly every important city in South America and, according to Judge

Schoenrich, the results of this journey were important in promoting a better feeling and understanding between Latin American countries and the United States.

Burton believed that the situation as to his Presidential candidacy had in it an element of natural inevitability and he did not worry about it. However, he was destined to learn, on his arrival home, that Presidential booms are delicate growths which cannot safely be left to the care of destiny, but require constant individual nursing at the hands of those most interested in their development.

When the history of American politics is fully written, it will contain a chapter of great dramatic interest dealing with Burton's candidacy for the Presidential nomination by the Republican Party. Equally interesting and vital in its ultimate results to his party was his failure to receive the Vice-Presidential nomination—that traditional consolation prize of the defeated.

The turn of fate which denied him the position of running mate with Charles Evans Hughes, in 1916, was of minor importance to the Ohio Senator, but it was an event of first magnitude in the history of the nation. A searching post-mortem of that Presidential campaign and election compels the conclusion that, had Burton been either the Presidential or Vice-Presidential candidate, his party would have been successful.

The morning following the election, the Republicans of the country relaxed under the soothing assurance that their national ticket was elected. It had been a tight squeeze but, with California, they were victorious! Then followed a nerve-racking day of belated returns from the remote voting districts of the Golden State which turned their assurances of triumph to despair. California had gone Democratic! The reason of its revolt was soon apparent. Senator Hiram Johnson had taken revenge upon Hughes for what he regarded as a personal insult at the hands of the Presidental candidate.

The story is familiar. Unwisely responding to urgent invitations from groups of Republicans in California, Mr. Hughes visited that state as a climax of a western speaking tour. All Golden State Republicans looked alike to him and he considered that a brief appearance in their state would be a gesture of respect on his part which could scarcely be avoided without giving offense. Some of his wisest advisers counseled him against this. However, he was determined to make his smiling contribution to the glory of California's sunshine. There he innocently fell into the hands of the anti-Johnson wing of the Republican Party.

Senator Johnson happened to be at the same hotel at which Mr. Hughes and his party were stopping, but his anti-Johnson Republican hosts threw a cordon about Hughes and prevented him from calling upon the powerful and independent Senator, who was fully justified in expecting this act of courtesy and respect. Senator Johnson regarded the occurrence as a deliberate insult. The California Republicans into whose hands Mr. Hughes had fallen were as much Johnson's political enemies as if they had been outright Democrats. Instantly Senator Johnson took the warpath to avenge the insult—and so the Democratic national ticket won in California and in the nation as well.

Would this misfortune have befallen the Republican national ticket had Senator Burton been nominated either for President or Vice-President? There are reasons for believing that the answer to this question is "No."

Months after the election, in a talk with A. N. Rodway, of Cleveland, Burton dissected the fateful California episode in substantially these words:

"You know that if I had been given even the Vice-Presidential nomination the ticket would have been successful. I was familiar with political conditions on the West Coast and I am sure that what happened out there with such disastrous results to the national ticket never would have taken place."

Mr. Rodway was in a peculiar position to understand the accuracy of this analysis. "I know of my personal knowledge," he asserts, "that Senator Burton had a close insight into California Republican politics, for he had investigated it with characteristic thoroughness, and I was present at these conferences. I agree with Senator Burton's deduction that, had he been in first or second place on the Republican national ticket, it would have been elected."

To this should be added the supporting testimony of the late Maurice Maschke, who writes:

"I recall distinctly that after the election Mr. Burton told me that, had he been nominated for Vice-President, the blunder in California would not have been made; but, through his friendship with Senator Johnson, he could have straightened out matters there."

The fact that Burton enjoyed personal popularity in California is not to be overlooked. As Chairman of the Rivers and Harbors Committee, he had dealt fairly and liberally with proposed waterway improvements in that state. He regarded the businessmen of California as remarkably reasonable in their requests for the improvement of their harbors and streams; therefore he seldom denied them an improvement which had the backing of the business public.

This popularity of Burton with Californians is confirmed by Joseph H. McGann, who became Secretary of the Rivers and Harbors Committee under Burton's chairmanship and repeatedly accompanied his chief on official trips to the Pacific Coast. Mr. McGann notes that the first newspaper in the country to advocate the nomination of Theodore Burton for the Presidency was one published in San Pedro, California.

Says Mr. McGann: "There was a prevailing sense of gratitude to Burton throughout the state for his understanding of the importance of California's harbors, not only in relation to her commerce but also in connection with the problems of national defense. He met with expressions of this feeling wherever he went."

If the assumption is granted that, as candidate for Vice-President, Burton would have pulled through the national Republican ticket in California, then the spotlight of public interest shifts to the problem of why he was not nominated for second place.

There was one reason only why Burton was not made the Vice-Presidential candidate. This has never before been made public and has been known to only a small group of men who played a prominent role in the Republican National Convention of 1916. They have remained silent out of kindly consideration for the feelings of one person who was responsible for the political blunder that, in the opinion of the shrewdest political observers of that day, cost the Republicans the Presidential election which gave Woodrow Wilson a second term.

An offer to nominate Senator Burton for the Vice-Presidency was made by Frank Hitchcock to Granville Mooney, the Burton campaign manager, and was declined.

This was the night when the ruling powers of the convention reached an agreement upon the nomination of Hughes on the following day. The combination had the votes to enforce this decision. Burton was not present at headquarters, holding that it was a violation of political proprieties for a candidate for the office of President to appear in the open and personally dicker with convention strategists for such a supreme party honor. However, he was where he could be quickly reached by telephone.

The refusal of Mr. Mooney to accept, for his chief, the second place on the national ticket is said to have astounded the bearer of this consolation gift both by its abruptness and its firmness. There was no hesitation about it, no request for time in which to consult Senator Burton. The offer was instantly and flatly declined.

Mr. A. N. Rodway gives this account of the incident:

"I know this positively to be a fact, that at this convention in 1916 Senator Burton could have been nominated for the Vice-Presidency. The night before the nomination for President was made, when it was certain that Governor Hughes would be chosen for the Presidential nomination in the morning, the powers that were in control agreed that, if Senator Burton would accept the nomination for the second place on the ticket, he could have it.

"This information did not reach the Senator until later, when I told him of it. He remarked that to him it seemed 'incredible.' I added: 'Sometime when you meet General Frank Hitchcock ask him about it. He is in a position to tell you.' The Senator's reaction was that he would have been gratified with the nomination."

To those who knew Granville Mooney and his relations with Senator Burton, this offhand and peremptory refusal of the Vice-Presidential nomination on behalf of his chief is entirely understandable. Mooney regarded Burton with feelings akin to adoration. In his eyes Ohio's "distinguished Senator" was the greatest statesman of his country. Apparently he was dazed by the realization that the President-makers had not, with one voice, chosen Burton to head their ticket.

A niece of the Senator's who called at his convention headquarters on the evening preceding the nomination gives her impressions:

"I was dismayed and disheartened at the attitude of Mr. Mooney, who appeared to be existing in an exalted and glorified haze as if waiting for the chief strategists of the convention to appear and announce that the obvious superiority of Senator Burton's qualifications for the office of President compelled his nomination by acclamation. There was no sign of activity in the Burton headquarters; its atmosphere was one of complaisant and dignified receptivity.

"If the sentiment 'The Honor Should Seek The Man' had hung upon the walls of that room, it could not have emphasized the impression which I gained from Mr. Mooney's attitude. When the news that the ruling forces of the convention had agreed upon the nomination of Governor Hughes to head the national ticket reached the dignified quiet of the Burton headquarters it could not, from what I observed, have been received by my uncle's political representative as anything less than a bewildering blow, a miscarriage of obvious political justice which instantly fired his resentment.

"As to his reaction to the offer of the second place on the ticket —that is as clear to me as if I had heard Mr. Mooney exclaim: 'What? *Senator Burton* accept the nomination for *Vice-President?* No!' Such an 'honor' was utterly inadequate for so great a man as Senator Burton. That Mr. Mooney's adoration for Senator Burton moved him to repulse the proffer of the Vice-Presidential nomination I have not the slightest doubt. This makes his ill-considered action entirely forgivable—but none the less unfortunate. The fact that it involved disaster to the Republican national ticket of 1916 seems conclusive."

Burton took an option on defeat for first place on the ticket at the very start of the pre-convention campaign, when he failed to secure as his political general the experienced and adroit Frank Hitchcock, who had managed Taft's first campaign successfully and had been rewarded with the Cabinet seat of Postmaster General. Also he had served as Chairman of the Republican National Committee.

Mr. Snell Smith, who represented a Cincinnati newspaper in Washington and who knew Ohio politics and politicians intimately, made this statement to the writer:

"While Granville Mooney was a charming gentleman and a scholar, in the field of national politics he was a pathetic figure, a helpless babe-in-the-woods, who had virtually no idea of what it was all about. If he were living this could not be said with propriety; but he did not long survive Senator Burton and is now beyond the wounds of candid criticism. The Senator's friendship for him placed him in a position of great responsibility for which he was pre-eminently disqualified both by nature and experience. He was a guileless lamb in the hands of the shearers!

"It is only fair to qualify this estimate of Mr. Mooney by saying that, to a great extent, he reflected the attitude of Senator Burton, who leaned backward waiting to be pushed into the Presidential chair by popular demand. Mooney, I repeat, faithfully reflected this attitude of his chief. They were a pair of political innocents. If history is to justify itself, it must be honestly and frankly written and this is the plain truth."

Several weeks after the convention, Senator Burton told his personal physician, Dr. Robert W. Baker, of Washington, D.C., that he believed that, if the convention had been held one month earlier, he would have received the Presidential nomination.

Senator Burton took his defeat for the nomination philosophically. He reproached no one for failing to do all that could have been done in his behalf. Even after he learned that Granville Mooney had cost him the Vice-Presidential nomination by an officious and blundering act, he never mentioned his astonishment or regret. Mr. Mooney died in the comfortable belief that his management of that ill-fated campaign had been highly satisfactory to the Senator.

CHAPTER 21

Out of Step in Wall Street

WHEN PRESIDENT WILSON was keeping his country "out of war" * with one hand and preparing for war and re-election with the other, private citizen Theodore E. Burton was packing his books and furniture for removal to New York City to assume the presidency of the Merchants National Bank on Wall Street.

Cleveland's "most distinguished citizen" could not be permitted to take his departure from that city without being given a suitable farewell. He had been president of the Hughes League which gave an annual Lincoln Day banquet. Apparently, there was a general conspiracy to steal this show for Burton. Governor Charles S. Whitman, of New York, was virtually the only speaker who stuck close to the Lincoln theme. Early in the proceedings local orators spoke feelingly of the former Senator's service to his city, his state, and his country.

The presentation from the League of a loving cup preceded a response from Burton, the retiring president, who recalled his first visit to Cleveland, as a boy, when he "drove a flock of sheep down Euclid Avenue" and did a very poor job of it. Then, abruptly, he left the field of reminiscence and turned his attention to the present and the future.

"We are on the verge of a crisis now," he said. "What if, in a few days, we are engaged in a conflict with a nation superior to ours in a military way? This great war may be one in which we will take part. In this emergency we should sink partisanship deep in the earth. . . . Our duty is to stand as a phalanx behind the President and sustain him in preserving the rights and honor of our

* Of course the reason for Wilson's deliberation is obvious—the United States was absolutely unprepared for war and this delay gave the country a chance to make ready.

country. I fear that in some hour not very far distant we will read of the sinking of some ship of ours by a submarine. It will arouse the country from the Atlantic to the Pacific and drive us into war."

Then Burton raised the question: "If there is war, will the people respond? I know they will. There is a spirit which would respond to a call for duty no matter what the consequences. There is a devotion to country here that is a living fire and would lead to sacrifice to bring victory. We will perpetuate the principles of Lincoln and make our land the hope of the world."

This, in brief, was Burton's farewell to his Cleveland friends. They were greatly moved to hear from his own lips this call to military duty if our national honor demanded our entry into the great European conflict. Now they knew to a certainty that this ardent apostle of peace would fight if the occasion demanded.

Fate has used Wall Street as the stage for many strange dramas, but for none more bizarre than that suggested by a statement as brief as an epitaph:

BANK OF MANHATTAN, ESTABLISHED BY AARON BURR, 1799.

MERCHANTS NATIONAL BANK, FOUNDED BY ALEXANDER HAMIL-
TON, 1803.

ALEXANDER HAMILTON KILLED BY AARON BURR IN A DUEL
FOUGHT ON JULY 7, 1804.

MERCHANTS NATIONAL BANK AND BANK OF MANHATTAN
MERGED, 1920.

A world of romance is suggested by the mere mention of these two brilliant figures in the formation of the Union—Hamilton, the financial genius of the Revolutionary period, and Burr, Vice-President of the United States and grandson of the great Colonial preacher Jonathan Edwards. Destiny seemed to have marked Hamilton and Burr as congenital enemies but time and the impersonal pressure of financial changes united these two earliest of New York banks.

There was a fitness in the call to Theodore Burton to become the head of the financial institution founded by Hamilton. Throughout his life Burton had been a student of Hamilton's policies and regarded him as almost a miracle of financial wisdom. No other figure of the group immediately surrounding George Washington when the Union was formed so challenged Burton's interest and admiration. He was therefore pleased when he was called to head the bank established by Alexander Hamilton in the first administration of Thomas Jefferson.

A heavy mortuary atmosphere pervaded the Merchants National Bank when Burton was called to its presidency. Its ownership was held in "dead hands," entombed in the vaults of estates. Scarcely a share of its stock was owned by a living person. Far richer in traditions than in deposits, the Merchants National was the aristocrat of New York banks, often referred to as the "Tiffany of Wall Street." This distinguished old institution lived largely in the past and was considered by its more lusty and modern competitors as tangible proof of "life after death," an example of immortality in the realm of business institutions.

There were, however, some who realized that "dead hands" were powerless to build business for a modern bank and that customers could not be lured to deposit windows by the specter of even so distinguished a financier and patriot as Alexander Hamilton. If only the clutch of dead hands on the bank's certificates of ownership could be broken, it could be made one of the great, going, financial institutions of Wall Street.

Granville Mooney, a close associate of Burton throughout his banking experience, is my authority for the statement that, although Burton failed in his ambition to perpetuate indefinitely the identity of the Merchants National, he did succeed in breaking the grip on its stock of hands long since at rest in the burial grounds of Manhattan.

Mooney made the statement that, although Burton failed to achieve the reputation as a practical banker which many of his Wall Street friends had expected him to make, he performed the difficult task of working out conditions which forced considerable blocks of the bank's stock into the market. This allowed them to pass into the hands of owners interested in building the deposits of the institution to natural proportions.

The Bank of Manhattan had been fortunate enough to escape this paralytic inheritance which afflicted its rival and it had grown into an aggressive and prospering institution. But let Mr. Raymond E. Jones, Vice-President of the Bank of Manhattan, relate in his own words the story of the convergence of these two institutions:

> The Manhattan Company was founded by Aaron Burr in 1799 as a water company to "supply pure and wholesome water to the

City of New York," and the Merchants Bank, with Alexander Hamilton as its organizer, opened for business in 1803 in an adjoining building. As early as 1836 it was suggested that these two institutions be housed under one roof, but evidently their directors did not approve of the idea so the matter rested until 1838, when it was again reviewed with the same result.

However, in 1883 a committee was appointed to consider the feasibility of erecting one building to house these famous financial neighbors. This time the project went through and the new structure, known as the United Bank Building, became their new home in 1884. There they remained until March, 1920, in adjoining offices with nothing but a partition separating them. At that time the banks were consolidated, the partition was removed and the larger bank occupied the whole space until May, 1929. That year the old building was demolished to make room for the present seventy-one-story skyscraper in which the Bank occupies six floors.

As to our corporate title—it is "The President and Directors of the Manhattan Company," but as we are engaged in banking we are permitted to so inform the public by using Bank of the Manhattan Company as our trade name.

One reason why the Merchants National was able to continue so long under the heavy handicap of its entailed ownership was the fact that many of its original customers were the rich textile houses of New York. Not without reason they regarded themselves as the aristocrats of New York's trade and were proud of their connection with the bank founded by Alexander Hamilton. Natural conservatives, they were opposed to change on general principles. The traditions of the Merchants National were their traditions.

This important group of the bank's customers was influential in having Senator Burton called to its presidency. They knew that he was a statesman of international reputation, a personal friend of the foremost financiers of Europe, and they believed that his ability as a public speaker would be invaluable to the institution. Subordinates could attend to the details of making loans and putting out issues of securities, while Senator Burton made impressive addresses to important gatherings of businessmen.

He made the speeches—scores of them—and captivated his audiences, but those who expected him to figure largely as a "banquet banker," a platform financier, underestimated his industry and appetite for details. He simply could not keep his fingers out of the routine of the bank's operation. He had to know about everything—and the more he knew of how Wall Street banks made their profits the less he liked his general environment. It was small consolation to him to reflect that probably the business of the Merchants National was conducted with greater scrupulousness than that of competitors.

The thumbscrew methods which he saw in operation in daily transactions revolted him. The actualities of routine loaning transactions were shockingly at variance with his preconceived notions of dignified banking. The handling of "big deals" in the flotation of stocks and other securities also offended his sense of responsibility to the public. The fact that he received a salary at least equal to that of the President of the United States did not soothe him into acquiescence with the prevailing practices and moral standards of the Street.

His insistence that the security issues put out by the banks should be above challenge made him unpopular with important customers. He could not be diverted from considering the "ultimate consumer," trustfully buying securities for investment and income.

It was not in his nature, however, to quit an undertaking without a fair trial. Therefore, he stuck to his job and exerted all his influence to correct what he regarded as the abuses of an inherited situation. He realized that reforms require time, patience, and persistence —but he was far from happy! His high position had somehow "turned sour."

On Christmas Day, 1917, every employee of the Merchants National Bank below executive rank received a present of ten dollars. Not a charwoman, porter, or messenger boy was omitted in this remembrance from the private funds of the bank's new president. This act of generosity brought him great personal satisfaction and popularity.

The entry of the United States into World War I, on April 6, 1917, marked a decided change in the activities of Theodore Burton. Although he continued to keep a guiding hand upon the policies and the larger transactions of the bank, his main interest focused upon the grave affairs of the nation and the support of his government in the great "war to end war." In particular, he swung wholeheartedly into the Liberty Bond campaign. There was scarcely a day when he did not address one or more public gatherings in an appeal for the sinews of war which had to be forthcoming in vast volume to raise, train, and equip the American Expeditionary Forces for the European battle front.

In these speeches he was at his best and few of the thousands who listened to him forgot the power of his appeals. He was a torch-bearer of the flaming spirit which, in his farewell address to his Cleveland friends, he had said would sweep America if some great act of violence forced this country to enter the European conflict.

His appeals for money had good effect. In his diary is laconically noted: "At five o'clock went to New Rochelle . . . At the meeting . . . gave an address of about twenty minutes. Audience not large but they subscribed over $100,000 before I left."

In addition to these Liberty Loan speeches, advisory duties made large demands upon his time. He had abandoned partisanship and his support of the Administration was complete as to the prosecution of the war. His attitude was greatly appreciated by President Wilson. While they later differed upon many points, they had much in common and understood each other well.

Senator Burton was disappointed in his career as a banker. According to Wall Street standards, he was unsuccessful in that role. A former high Treasury official, who later had his fling in Wall Street banking, once told the writer that, in his opinion, Senator Burton "hadn't much business being associated with the financiers of Wall Street—he was too deeply rooted in his old-fashioned honesty to make a Wall Street bank grow."

Apparently, this was the prevailing impression among Senator Burton's old friends, especially among newspaper men who had been in close contact with him in Washington over a long period of years. These writers had a clear-eyed vision of the "practical" methods and "liberal" business morals characteristic of the Street and were amused at the picture of Senator Burton struggling to adjust his ideals to those of his new environment.

From their viewpoint, due allowance had to be made for the peculiarities of Wall Street's high-tension business in which the ups and downs of the stock market brought to the banks thousands of speculators begging for call loans and eager to pay exorbitant premiums to get them. This was the atmosphere of Wall Street which suggested that of Monte Carlo. The same considerations of taking high chances extended to its great financial deals. The question was not whether they were economically sound but whether they would get across, and win immediate profits.

One of the keenest and most conservative of these observers, in

THEODORE E. BURTON

a discussion of Senator Burton's unhappy experience as a head of a Wall Street bank, remarked to the writer:

"The sins and defects of the Wall Street system, as Senator Burton encountered it, may be left to the judgment of history. Banking as it was actually conducted by the 'practical' financiers in New York in the epoch preceding the collapse of 1929 led down to the day when every bank in America was locked up tight and the entire profession of banking fell into disrepute in the eyes of the public. The kind of banking which brought about this catastrophe was not the sort to which Senator Burton had given his allegiance. He stubbornly resisted it and refused to yield to its subtle and disintegrating influence. He could not bring himself to surrender either his ideals or his convictions as to what constituted sound economics and he applied his standards to every transaction of his bank. It was simply impossible for Senator Burton to eliminate from his consideration the ultimate good of the country.

"While I understand that Wall Street, generally, felt that Burton failed to achieve distinction as a banker, I am inclined to the conclusion that he did succeed in impressing his high ideals upon the policy of the bank to a considerable extent. Had he remained at the head of the bank for a long period of years, I have no doubt that his achievement would have stood out much more sharply. Very few men in the country knew more about the principles of banking and finance and how they ought to be conducted."

In April of 1919, his close friend Professor Arnold B. Hall, of the University of Wisconsin, sent him an article which he had prepared on the League of Nations and the Monroe Doctrine. Burton replied:

"I regard your article as one of the best which I have ever seen. The possible developments in violation of what we call the Monroe Doctrine are prepared with a great deal of ingenuity and with a grasp of the whole subject. Personally, I am not much of a believer in this doctrine, largely because of what I have seen in South America. They fear it as a means for keeping them in subservience to their big neighbor on the North, and refer to the North American peril."

Evidently in the same letter Dr. Hall requested Burton to write an article for the La Salle Extension University. In postponing this work Burton made the interesting explanation: "I am giving most of my time to the revising and putting in shape of my lectures at

Princeton [on Modern Political Tendencies] under the Stafford Little Foundation. These are to be published in book form and will inevitably be compared with very formidable competitors such as Grover Cleveland, Theodore Roosevelt, Senator Root, Mr. Choate, and others who delivered these lectures."

He closed his letter by urging Dr. Hall to go with him to the Orient and Australia and remarked: "I know of no one whom I should more enjoy having go with me." (In this connection it should be said that in 1916 Dr. Hall had made a valiant fight to secure the Wisconsin delegation to the National Republican Convention for Burton.)

These were very busy days for Senator Burton. In addition to Liberty Loan speeches, bank director meetings, and concentrated work on the Princeton Lectures, there were a multitude of other matters. Many of these were the pleasant social functions that come to an affable New York bachelor with an apartment on Park Avenue—parties at the Opera followed by suppers at the St. Regis or some other conservative restaurant, dinners and receptions at the homes of friends or at exclusive clubs. Here and there in his journal are references to shopping for ties at Sulka's. Certainly, Park Avenue and the presidency of an important bank were having their effect—sartorially speaking.

Burton also found time to solicit funds—he always found time for that—for the Lincoln Memorial University, of which he was a member of the Board of Trustees. This is a coeducational school in Harrogate, Tennessee, in which he was especially interested.

He was also on the Executive Committee of the Roosevelt Memorial of Columbia University, a fact which reveals the tolerance and lack of animosity in Burton's character. Theodore Roosevelt had done about everything possible to hinder Burton's Presidential nomination in 1916, even going so far as proclaiming that he was the least promising of the candidates. Yet Burton was glad to do his part toward perpetuating the President's memory, for he recognized and admired the strong qualities in Roosevelt's nature and generously overlooked his weaknesses.

The League of Nations Union was also claiming his attention at this time and there were meetings to determine whether or not other peace organizations should join forces with the newer one.

So crowded was his schedule, in the spring of 1919, that he had to decline many of the invitations to speak which came in every mail from all over the country. However, he did wedge in a lecture on "Immortality" before the Rose Croix in Brooklyn and another address in New York on the railroads before the National Institute of Social Science. In May he attended the American Academy of Political Science in Philadelphia and went directly from there to Bowdoin College at Brunswick, Maine, where he was scheduled to speak.

In his journal Burton characteristically fails to note the title of this lecture or the way in which it was received. But he does mention the more notable fact (to him) that between New York and Boston he read two books—*From Isolation to Leadership*, by Professor John H. Latané, finding it "especially valuable," and *British-American Discords and Concords*, compiled by the History Circle.

The next week saw him on the train again, this time en route for Kansas City, Kansas, where he addressed the Kansas Bankers Association on "The Present Outlook and the League of Nations."

This engagement gave Burton an opportunity to revisit the Iowa of his youth, and his relatives—his brother Phil and his children—who still lived there. He was interested in everything—the location for the new house of "Will and Jenny," their new baby, the meeting in Grinnell of "Arthur and Grace" and other relatives, and, particularly, the ride to the old farm, where he found the house in which he had lived just as it was when he had left fifty years before. At the college he gave an address in the chapel, then revisited the room of the Grinnell Institute, of which he had been the first president in 1868.

This had been a spring of family reunions. In March, Burton had been called to Lincoln, Illinois, because of the death of his brother Edward. It was a sad errand that brought him but, as is so often the case, it drew the family together. Burton loved his family and kept in touch with them. Among those who had come to Lincoln were Keith Burton and Burton Liese, grandsons of his brothers Philander and Edward.

The youngsters interested Burton and he arranged that they accompany him back to Chicago. In spite of the fact that time was precious, that there were many important persons whom he wished to see in the city, he spent the day giving the boys a good time. They went to the Navy Pier, visited the Lincoln Park Zoo and the Board of Trade and the movies. After a dinner with his sister Mary's daughters, Laura Shurtleff Price and May Shurtleff Storey, Burton put the boys on a train for Danville, Illinois, in the care of a porter.

Late that night he was en route back to New York and the grueling grind of a Wall Street banker. Here he found in the pile of mail awaiting him an urgent request that he head an important financial institution. But, though he was importuned several times to accept this flattering offer, Burton could not make up his mind to continue his Wall Street career. Already he was beginning to let go. In January he had resigned the presidency of the bank, though he still retained his membership on the Board of Directors.

Occasionally an old Washington newspaper friend called on Burton at the bank to pay his respects and talk over the old days in Washington. Among these was Snell Smith, whose scholarship and political acumen had resulted in an unusual intimacy with Burton. Of his call on Burton the banker, Mr. Smith said to the writer:

"One did not need to be clairvoyant to see that he was unhappy in the atmosphere of Wall Street and that his heart was really back in Congress. Our talk was brief but long enough to leave with me the conviction that the old Senator would not long remain a voluntary exile from the scene of his great activities under the dome of the Capitol. When I heard that he had left Wall Street and was going on an extended cruise I felt certain that his return to America would shortly be followed by his return to Washington as a Representative or Senator."

One day after the Armistice he surprised Raymond E. Jones, his chief executive in the bank, by confessing his dissatisfaction with his life as a Wall Street banker and by declaring his ambition to return to the House of Representatives unencumbered by heavy committee responsibilities and the restraints they involved. He declared that he wanted to be free to stand on his own feet and oppose or support any measure as his conscience might dictate. The most important legislative measures must originate in the House and therefore membership in that body offered peculiar opportunities of service to anyone of his convictions and experience.

In later confidential talks with Mr. Jones he revealed the grip which this new ambition had upon him, naming distinguished Senators, dating back to post-Revolutionary days, who had returned to the floor of the House to exercise a great and salutary power upon national legislation. In this connection he mentioned John Quincy Adams who, after being a United States Senator and a President of the United States, served for almost twenty years in the House of Representatives. Adams exemplified the idea that service in the House was not beneath the ambition of one who had held the office of President.

In the meantime, Burton continued his round of activities. It was a strenuous life for a man of his years but release was in sight. In July he resigned as a member of the Board of the Merchants National Bank. He was free at last.

CHAPTER 22

Again an Unofficial Ambassador

T HE INSTANT HIS CONNECTIONS as a Wall Street banker were severed, Theodore Burton prepared to celebrate that happy release by a trip to Australia and New Zealand, and Japan, China, and other Oriental countries. As originally planned, this journey was to be purely a pleasure trip. But as soon as his intentions became known to President Wilson he was handed the following letter:

> The White House
> Washington, D.C.
> 19th July, 1919

My dear Mr. Ambassador:

The bearer of this letter, the Hon. Theodore E. Burton, so long one of the distinguished representatives of Ohio, in the Senate, really needs no introduction to you, but I want to give myself the pleasure of putting into his hands this formal introduction, in order that I may ask what I am sure you will be more than willing to accord, that every possible assistance and courtesy be shown him, in his present errand to Japan.

> Faithfully yours,
> Woodrow Wilson

To Hon. Roland S. Morris
Ambassador of United States
Tokio, Japan

Once more Burton was back in his old role of unofficial Ambassador of the United States. This document reveals the personal relations between President Wilson and Senator Burton. It is proof of the President's confidence in Burton's influence and trustworthiness as an unofficial representative of his country.

At this time (1919) Japan was showing considerable irritation toward the United States, resulting from restrictions on the freedom and privileges of Japanese residents in California. Influential groups in Japanese politics gave evidence that Japanese sentiment was not as amiable toward the United States as formal diplomatic notes indicated. President Wilson drafted Senator Burton to iron out this sensitive situation by conferences and public speeches. It was a delicate task but one which greatly appealed to him.

He was accompanied by his old friend and physician, Dr. Robert W. Baker, of Washington. The boat sailed from Seattle where, looking over his luggage before embarking, Burton turned to Baker with evident embarrassment and confessed that he had left his passport papers in Cleveland! The doctor chuckled. The man who could astound his listeners with his feats of memory left a trail of personal belongings behind him wherever he went.

"It is virtually impossible," said Dr. Baker, "for anyone not having had the privilege of traveling from one nation to another with Senator Burton to realize the extent of his acquaintance with the leaders of thought and action in those countries. His personal distinction and graciousness, together with his intense interest in what he heard and saw, inspired an unfailing courtesy from those in the highest stations."

It will be remembered that the war had only just ended, the Armistice having been signed the preceding fall. In January President Wilson had gone to Paris to negotiate the Peace Treaty. After six months of heartbreaking compromises he returned to this country to lay the results of his negotiations before the Senate, almost on the very day that Burton left New York for his journey to the Orient.

The Senate, under the leadership of Senator Henry Cabot Lodge, would not ratify the Treaty and the President's League of Nations, to which Wilson had affixed his signature in France. The now famous Articles 10 and 11 were the greatest stumbling blocks. The United States was sick and tired of Europe. Under no circumstances would she contemplate a treaty which might again draw her into a foreign conflict. These debates in the United States Congress held the attention of the world. Everywhere Burton was asked the American point of view on the treaty and when it would be signed.

Also, it will be recalled that Japan had risen during World War I into a world power and had seized Shantung, ostensibly to hold it for China against the Germans.*

It was time for Japan to get out of China but she had no apparent intention of doing so. The world looked on anxiously. Particularly did the United States voice its disapproval of Japan's disregard for the rights of China and the Open Door policy.

The militaristic attitude of Japan was one of Burton's chief anxieties. The main purpose of his visit to that country was to promote peaceful relations between her and the United States. He wanted to determine the strength of this militaristic feeling and the likelihood that it might develop into active hostilities against the United States over some particularly irritating occurrence in connection with Japanese inhabitants of our Pacific Coast. To this end he talked with everyone. His journal shows how full were his days with calls and interviews, from each one of which he gained knowledge of Japan's problems and aspirations.

Dr. Baker dictated this account of Senator Burton's narrow escape from mob violence:

> In an automobile belonging to a gentleman from California who sent his Japanese secretary along as interpreter, we were driven from Yokohama to Tokio along the crowded main highways through a string of villages swarming with children. While we were proceeding cautiously, a child darted out of an alley and ran in front of our automobile.
>
> The driver instantly jammed the brakes and brought the car to a dead standstill—but not until we felt a distinct bump. Of course the thought occurred to me, as it did to the Senator, that if the child was hurt we might be in for a riot. Our situation looked bad. I got out of the car at once, pushed my way through the crowd to the child, whose mother had grabbed it and started up an alley. It required only a moment to discover that the little boy was simply stunned by the bump.
>
> While I was making this examination, the crowd about us quickly increased and there was an ominous murmuring. I could hear the Senator shouting: "Come out of that alley!"
>
> Then I heard a Japanese voice saying: "Better drive around to my house; you'll be safer there. I'll show you the way."

* In an interview, the ex-President of China, Yi Wuen Hung, told Senator Burton that, contrary to report, China had not been requested by the Allies to drive the Germans from Shantung. A demand had been made upon Germany through diplomatic channels for the evacuation of the Province and, while that was pending, Japan invaded Shantung.

The speaker's appearance was most reassuring. As he walked to the car, he spoke assuringly to some of the nearest members of the crowd. We were permitted to get into the car and go to the Police Station to report the accident.

The Senator was shaken by the experience. Later he would sometimes exclaim: "That was a close call, Doctor, a close call!"

At banquets, luncheons, and receptions held in his honor, Senator Burton spoke with candor. Before the Bankers Club he said that although it appeared, from reading the papers, that the situation between the countries was serious, it should be remembered that in the United States there was great freedom of expression. Articles were published that were not truly indicative of the real sentiment of the people.

"I am not sure," he went on, "but that some newspapers in Japan manifest the same freedom that prevails in America," but "it would be a source of real regret" should these outbursts disturb the friendly relations between the two peoples.

He declared that "in this era there must be no secret treaties or hidden agreements. What America asks of Japan in the Orient is a fair field for competition in trade and no policy of aggression toward other countries. The recognition of the special interest of Japan in the Orient does not mean to us a paramount interest, but rather a peculiar relation due to your nearness to the hundreds of millions of inhabitants of China and other adjacent countries. We ask for the Open Door as promulgated by Secretary Hay . . .

"It is easy for us also to see that in the trade of China and nearby countries you will have certain advantages over us, in that you understand more thoroughly the customs of the people and their language and tastes; also that you are nearer and have more ready access, and again that in the cost of production in many lines you have greater opportunities by reason of your abundant supply of labor and its cheapness. We only ask that no political control or special privilege shall exclude us from entry to the ports and to the trade of the Orient."

If the Senator's colleagues could have seen him at one dinner in Japan, they would have rocked with mirth. The invitation indicated that the dinner would be in Japanese style. But this did not tell the story to the Senator—his inference was merely that native food would be served. When he found, however, that he was expected to sit cross-legged on the floor and eat rice with chopsticks, he felt a little dismayed. He probably had not attempted that posture since he was a boy. But he was a good sport and took the merriment which his efforts provoked in good spirit.

A few days later Burton spoke before a meeting held under the auspices of the American Peace Society and the Japanese Peace Society. Among other things, he said: "The object of the League of Nations is to prevent war, which it proposes to do by limiting armaments and arranging for the settlement of disputes by other means than war. . . . Another most important source of trouble is the matter of secret treaties. Furtive diplomacy must go. All negotiations between nations must be made under the light of publicity.

"The objections raised in California to the Japanese are ascribed to racial differences, but this is only an excuse. The real reason is the demand of a powerful element to monopolize the labor of the state, and for purposes of political expediency. My advice regarding California is, first, to avoid excitement, and, second, not to take too seriously the loud talk and attitude of the jingoes."

Baron Sakatani's reply was equally frank. He said that one of the things which served to "irritate the Japanese mind was the frequent introduction into the California legislature of anti-Japanese measures." If the United States should take away the acquired rights of the Japanese in America, he would say it was cruelty. Morality and humanity would not permit such acts.

Senator Burton's visit in China was much like his experiences in Japan. He was greeted cordially and deferentially by everyone and was constantly asked to speak on international questions. At Peking an unusual tribute was accorded him when he was asked to make an address at a reception given him by the presiding officers and members of the two houses of the Chinese Parliament. In part he said:

"In the political situation America has always contended for the Open Door in the Orient, by which we mean no special privileges for any nation, no land-grabbing, no attempt to secure by the exercise of might or political power economic advantages in any part of China. With equal earnestness we insist that repeated promises by other nations for the maintenance of the political integrity of China shall be observed. . . .

"If I may set forth the hopes that we cherish for China, I would say that first of all we desire to see a united country in which there shall be no North or South, that order and efficiency in government may be established throughout the land; improved means of transportation by waterways, highways and railroads are urgently needed. Looking to the more remote future it seems to us that a more helpful distribution of population would be accomplished by migration from the congested districts of China to those which have less population. . . ." *

Here was at least one early plea for the modern device of shifting populations.

Later, at Shanghai, the Senator was even more outspoken: "In this age of frankness," he declared, "there is no place for any secret agreement or secret diplomacy. . . . America expected a good deal of China, expected that China would assert herself, that the national spirit would develop, that she would develop her railways, her waterways, and follow up with better education; it was to be hoped that the Chinese would develop the spirit of organization on the political side, and if any members of the body politic were selling out their country for private profit, it was their [China's] duty to fire them out. Those are the conditions on which China can take her place among the foremost nations of the earth."

When Dr. Baker was asked about the effect of these utterances on Burton's Japanese and Chinese listeners, he answered:

> Senator Burton had a faculty for inspiring the confidence and admiration of the cultivated Orientals with whom he was constantly associated on this trip. He looked and acted the part of a visiting statesman; his personal appearance and manners apparently gave him something like a certificate of nobility in the eyes of the educated and aristocratic Orientals.
>
> At a dinner given by the Governor of the Province of Nanking, one of his aides studied the Senator's face for a moment and then made a remark to the man at his right, who evidently passed the comment along down the line. As a result, there were many sharp glances at the Senator, accompanied by smiles. The officer sitting next to me spoke English, and smilingly explained:
>
> "There is a tradition among our people, handed down from ancient times, that a man with large ear-lobes has a great mind and is born to be a leader of men. The gentleman across the table merely called attention to the unusual size of the Senator's ear-lobes. The remark was really flattering."

* The China (Peking) *Star*, October 19, 1919.

In Peking there was a considerable movement of troops, and trains were crowded with soldiers who were very pushing. In Peking, at that time, was the daughter of Burton's old friend, Senator Aldrich, who wished to go to Hankow on the same train with him and Dr. Baker. The suggestion was made that a private car for the trip would not be prohibitive in cost and that it would insure much greater comfort and safety. With the convenience and well-being of Miss Aldrich in mind as much as his own comfort, Burton proposed that the three friends follow this advice. Greatly to his surprise she responded that she could not afford the expense. The Senator was amused and remarked to Baker:

"Well, Doctor, I never expected to find myself more reckless in the matter of expenditures than a female member of a multimillionaire family."

The trip to Hankow was made in the usual manner and was apparently uneventful.

Dr. Baker did not complete the tour with Burton. He sailed for America sometime in November and Burton went on to the Philippines. While he was there, he received word that the Senate of the United States had refused to ratify the Peace Treaty, which included membership in the League of Nations. This Burton greatly regretted.*

Interviewing him in Manila on the Senate's action, the *Daily Bulletin* of that city quoted him as saying:

"I am strongly in favor of the Peace Treaty and the League of Nations, including Article 10, which is nothing more than an application of the Monroe Doctrine to the entire world. I regret to learn that since my departure from the United States the Senate has acted adversely on this matter."

Burton's ideas regarding the League of Nations later changed somewhat, as will be noted.

Australia was as welcoming to the Senator as Japan, China, and the Philippines. His stay there was limited, however, for he was now anxious to return to the United States. A quick trip to New Zealand, ten days in Hawaii, and then home. He arrived in Cleveland on March 12, 1920.

His trip must have had considerable influence in shaping public opinion and in educating Americans on the Far East. Even before

* The resolution for a separate peace with Germany, vetoed by President Wilson, was passed by both Senate and House and signed by President Harding on July 2, 1921.

his arrival in Cleveland, Burton had begun a series of articles on conditions in the Orient in the New York *Times*. They were reproduced in the Washington *Evening Star* and the Cleveland *Plain Dealer*. Also he was constantly in demand as a speaker on the Orient.

In a talk at Cleveland he said that war between Japan and the United States would be "senseless" and that the way to cope with Japan was to "first open our entire trade resources to China, not for our own benefit but for the supreme justice to a nation which has been the football of the world. Then if we put our foot down and say to the rest of the nations, 'Cease exploiting China; cease impinging on Chinese territory,' not a nation on the globe would dare disobey. To fail in our obligations to the rest of the world . . . is to neglect our greatest opportunity and to be faithless to our duty."

CHAPTER 23

House Mentor and Floor
Free Lance

SOON AFTER BURTON'S RETURN from the Orient, in 1920, he was asked whether or not he would run for the Senate. This was certain to be a Republican year. President Wilson was ill and maintaining his office from his bedroom. Government affairs in Washington were more or less at a standstill. In the meantime the Republicans were organizing their forces and office seekers by the score were making ready for the impending struggle.

Among the important candidates for President were General Leonard Wood, Governor Frank Lowden, of Illinois, Senator Hiram Johnson, of California, and Senator Warren Harding, of Ohio. Before Burton could make up his mind what to do about his candidacy, it was necessary to learn whether or not Harding was going to file again for the Senatorship.

Early in March Burton's close friend Harry T. Hall, who after being Superintendent of the Division of Banks and Banking in Ohio had become Vice-President of the Merchants Bank of New York, wrote him as follows:

My dear Senator:
    Harding's managers have made strenuous efforts to stack things up so that he could keep his hands on the Senatorship and still be a candidate for President. As you know, in Ohio the law requires a candidate to file a declaration and petition sixty days before the primaries. Harding's crowd attempted to have this law amended to make it forty-five days so that it would allow Harding to file his petition after the convention. Cox vetoed the bill and his remarks upon the occasion of doing so were rather pertinent.
    I am just as anxious as I can be to see you get back to Washing-

ton. The next few years will provide an opportunity which has not existed in our history for a man like you to serve his country . . .

The only man who might give you any trouble I know of would be Willis. He is not competent for that place at all, but he is pretty popular and a good campaigner.

In your deliberations, I think you should keep in mind that you are under no obligations whatever to Harding, Harry Daugherty and that crowd.

With personal regards, I am

Very cordially,
Harry T. Hall

In spite of this advice that he need feel no encumbering allegiance to Harding, Burton still hesitated. And in the meantime, while he pondered, a more immediate problem arose. Should he accept an appointment to the Tariff Commission offered to him by President Wilson? If he did so, he would be shelved as an active political power until 1928, when the term expired. His niece and most intimate personal adviser, Grace C. Burton, vigorously opposed his acceptance. His place was in Congress! Her sensible advice prevailed.

Weeks went by and still there was no definite word as to what Harding was going to do. Burton, always a stanch party man and loyal to Ohio, already had named Harding as his choice for President. But, if Harding did not have a chance for the Presidency, he wanted to run again for the Senate.

Harry Daugherty, who later became his campaign manager, assured Harding that he had a very good chance at the Presidency. He said Wood could not win because he was an army man and the country was sick of uniforms. Lowden was out too because, having married Miss Pullman, he was too close to the railroads. Johnson had no chance, because the Republicans held him responsible for Hughes' defeat in California. Harding, said Daugherty, was "the man of the hour." *

By June 11, the last day in which to file for Congress, neither Harding nor Burton had signified his intentions. About eight o'clock that night, into Republican headquarters sauntered a loyal Harding man. He joked and visited with the other men in the room for

---

* Harry M. Daugherty in collab. with Thomas Dixon, *The Inside Story of the Harding Tragedy*. New York, 1932.

the next four hours without divulging the purpose of his call. At two minutes before twelve someone announced the time. Not until then did the Harding man pull out of his pocket a copy of his chief's petition to run for re-election to the Senate.

Two hours before, A. N. Rodway, who had helped Burton through so many political battles, had filed Burton's petition—not for the Senate, however, but for the House of Representatives.

Evidently, Burton knew what was going on in the Harding camp: that Governor Willis, who a few days later at the Republican convention made Harding's nominating speech, had been promised Harding's support in his race for Senatorship should Harding be nominated for President. Perhaps Burton thought he could not win against so powerful an opponent, although he too had been urged by many influential persons to try for the place. Among these was William Howard Taft, then in New Haven, Connecticut, who had sent him this wire:

". . . I hope you will become a candidate for the Senate. Any time that is possible you would greatly strengthen the ticket if you did . . ."

But Taft was equally delighted with Burton's decision to run for the House of Representatives, for immediately upon its announcement he sent him the following letter:

My dear Senator:
  I am delighted to hear that you are going back to Congress. You can be most useful there in the coming administration and Harding will rely on you, as he properly may. . . .
                                        Sincerely yours,
                                        William H. Taft

In the course of the Harding Presidential campaign, Taft wrote another letter to Senator Burton too characteristic and revealing to be omitted. It reads:

PERSONAL & CONFIDENTIAL

My dear Senator:
  I agree with you exactly about Harding's speeches and Lodge's. Harding has been bent on holding [Hiram] Johnson from a bolt and has ignored his natural friends and left them in an embarrassing and disappointed condition. He is going to lose a great many so-called "high-brow" votes on account of it but not enough

to turn the election. I am bound to say, however, that he has not helped himself in Massachusetts, New York, and some other eastern states. . . .

My impression is that Cox is going to find that the League issue will not win in the Middle and Far West and that he will begin an attack on the Republican Party and Harding as the representatives of wealth, capital, the railroads and against labor. He has already indicated a disposition of this sort. Harding and Coolidge make a shining mark for a demagogue pro-labor attack and it is likely to come and to shock a good many League people back to Harding. Harding will, I think, in the end put himself in Root's hands. I think Harding has it distinctly in mind to make Root his secretary of state. . . .

Root is for the League without article ten and with a court and will bring Harding around to it. Harding told Irving Fisher who came to me directly from him that he was as much in favor of the League as he (Fisher) was but that he proposed to embody the Lodge Reservations into amendments to the League and secure them by preliminary agreement with the Nations and then submit the result to the Senate. If this can be done we could not object to that. It is only another way to the same result. . . .

Harding will turn to Root to help him out and there will be the chance to secure what you and I desire. Harding's speech on Saturday will, I understand, exalt Root's court feature. Of course, that can only work inside a League. But Harding is weakly anxious to secure a patent on a new device and to rid himself of Wilson's claim of earlier invention.

I am delighted that you are O. K. in Congress. You can do great good there and not the least will be to help Root with Harding.

Sincerely yours,
Wm. H. Taft

Burton was opposed in his campaign for Congress by Henry I. Emerson, who was much in favor of the soldier bonus. Burton had made a number of speeches against it. Said he: "If patriotism and all the impulses of our better nature are to be melted into dollars, it would indeed be difficult to resist the claims for a bonus . . . There is a staggering weight of debts and taxes resting upon the country. Whatever the method to be chosen to provide for some billions for this bonus, whether by tax on sales or upon profits, all the people must ultimately bear the burden and such an additional weight threatens not merely a check but destruction of the prosperity which we now enjoy."

Later, on the floor of the House, he went on to say that he was aware of the dangers threatening the political fortunes of those voting against a bonus bill, but that no desire for political support would count with him against what he regarded as a duty to his constituency and his country.

For once Burton seemed to enjoy fighting for a place in Congress. "He sailed into the eleventh political battle of his career, at the Western Reserve Republican Club," said Nathaniel Howard in one of the Cleveland papers, "with his new straw hat at a sportive angle, with a beaming smile and a vigorous handshake."

Then he told his Cleveland friends some of the things in which he "hoped to wield a potent influence" if elected. He wished to make the United States a "leader in the cause of peace," to aid in revising the revenue laws of the country, to prevent "wasteful expenditures," to promote harmony and justice between employer and employee, to strengthen the laws which were "initiated by President Roosevelt for punishing dishonesty and fraud but at the same time to protect and stimulate honest business in all lines of effort." It is interesting to note how vigorously he followed this statement of his aims and ambitions during the next few years in Congress—fighting for every one of the points mentioned that hot July night in Cleveland.

The campaign, while comparatively tame, nevertheless had its own pleasantries. Emerson declared, "Burton has no right running in a district against a good Republican—an old man of seventy stirring up a fuss. He ought to be ashamed of himself!"

But far from being ashamed of himself, Burton was very much pleased when he was re-elected by a flattering majority. Newspapers all over the country acclaimed his return to Washington. The Columbus *Dispatch* remarked that it was likely "to take some prestige from the younger fellows who, in his absence, have edged along toward the top of the pile." After a complimentary reference to Nicholas Longworth, of Cincinnati, and Dr. Simeon Fess, this newspaper continued: "But Burton goes ahead of them both as to seniority and mental voltage."

When Congress convened the next April, Burton was appointed to the House Foreign Affairs Committee under the chairmanship of Stephen G. Porter. It was where he belonged, and almost from the opening day he assumed his old position—that of special mentor to Congress. With precision and thoroughness he would explain legislation presented for the attention of members. His school-master attitude may have been irritating at times, but on the other hand he "knew his stuff" and members paid close attention. At this time he remarked to the writer, "I am enjoying my return to the House. My colleagues listen to me with respect—and, I hope, sometimes with benefit."

Even the hard-boiled newspaper reporters listened with consideration to this gray-haired Congressman. A veteran of the press galleries in Congress, Walker Buel of the Cleveland *Plain Dealer*, told the writer:

"I have never heard a Washington correspondent make a cynical wisecrack about Senator Burton. And he is the only member of either house of Congress, prominent enough to draw comments from the press gallery, of whom this can be said.

"When Theodore Burton arose to speak, neighbors in the press gallery have remarked to me: 'There's a real one.' 'He's enough to make the most disillusioned of us believe that the United States once had statesmen as big, able, and honest as they appeared to be in the pages of the school readers and histories when we were boys.' "

Warren G. Harding's estimate of Burton was once expressed to Rodway, when this Cleveland friend was paying a social call at the Senate Office Building. In the course of that chat President (then Senator) Harding exclaimed:

"Rodway, the longer I'm down here the more I appreciate Theodore Burton. He is one of the biggest men with whom I have ever come in contact. If he were to die I wish that I might inherit his brain! . . . I will tell you what Senator Foraker said of him to me. I had just taken my seat in the Senate when Foraker called to pay his respects and offer me the benefits of his experience. Before concluding he said, 'Warren, if you ever get up against it, go to Burton for help. He knows more than any other man in Washington.' That from Senator Foraker!" exclaimed Senator Harding. "And I believe he's right."

Burton's first important act upon re-entering the House was to introduce a resolution "for negotiating with Great Britain and Japan with a view to decrease in naval expenditures." It eventually resulted in the five-five-three naval pact, the most signal diplomatic accomplishment of the Harding Administration.

On the following Congressional day, Burton gave a carefully prepared address on the "Burden of Military Expenses." He said it was time "for international negotiation or conference for the sake of stopping this mad competition for the construction of armaments.

"I have always been a lover of peace and am reluctant to vote for this [Naval Appropriation] bill, but on the other hand I cannot see my way clear to vote against it. In our declaration of 'America first' there stands in the very forefront our protection against all foes, foreign or domestic. We must appropriate for an adequate Navy and at least the nucleus of a strong Army."

He declared the bill on the whole was in the "right direction—a plan under which we can continue adequate preparedness." And he ended with his usual exhortation that the United States be a leader always for peace.

A few weeks later he again took the floor with regard to increasing American shipping. As he confessed, he had many times, both in the House and the Senate, talked against a ship subsidy. As noted in an earlier chapter, it was the subject of a bitter fight he had had with Hanna.

But now, Burton admitted, conditions were different. Moreover, he had always favored liberal provision for mail lines and development of passenger lines, and now the question to be considered was whether or not the Government "should be compelled at least to pay the difference between the cost of the operation of foreign ships and our own." Whoever could suggest something that would allow the United States to retain her position on the seas that she had attained during the war would be doing his country a real service.

This question of a ship subsidy came up a number of times during the next few years. In August Burton referred to it again in connection with an appropriation for the Shipping Board. He said that every principle of sound business management and proper organization had been neglected by this board. But regardless of the colossal waste—the building of 789 wooden ships which had been universally condemned for years and which could not be given away—there was on hand a fleet of 1,798 vessels. These were too valuable an asset to be scrapped and gave the United States a chance to see the fulfillment of a supreme desire—the establishment of a merchant marine.

The first step toward realizing this dream was to abandon the policy of granting charters under which those to whom government ships were leased received a compensation of 5 per cent of gross receipts. The next step was to transfer these ships to private ownership as soon as possible.

"We have had enough of government ownership and management," said Burton. "The object lesson may have been a frightfully expensive one but its teaching has sunk deep into popular thought."

And as to a future policy for maintaining a merchant marine, Burton strongly advocated subvention or subsidy.

No important bill was presented on which Burton did not express an opinion. His honesty, his logical marshaling of facts, his scrupulous accuracy, his long service, all gave him prestige and influence. Moreover, he was not partisan in his viewpoint.

One of these early discussions of the Sixty-seventh Congress concerned public utilities. The pending bill happened to come from Ohio where two competing lines wished to consolidate. Burton was for it, not because his own state was involved but because, he said, it was proved by the railroads back in the eighties that competing lines made for higher rates and inefficiency.

"Public utilities," said the Representative from Cleveland, "are or should be under an entirely different set of rules from ordinary investments of capital. They are natural monopolies. It is desirable that one consolidated organization should occupy one field. A failure to recognize that fundamental economic fact has cost this country billions of dollars." Of course, he continued, public utilities must be under the strictest regulation with regard to service and charges and the larger the organization the more it should submit to the control of the state.

Burton would unlimber his guns of criticism at the most unwelcome and embarrassing moments. There was his speech, for example, regarding appropriations for administering Indian affairs—a routine matter, surely. But not for Congressman Burton! He asked for twenty minutes in which to present his views and in this short time he demonstrated that the Indian was an absurdly expensive national pet. He said that the per capita wealth of the Indian was $7,000, very unequally distributed, and that the per capita wealth of Americans was $2,000 (before the war); that keeping Indians on reservations in a system of bureaucracy was demoralizing and that they should be allowed to become citizens, given whatever was due them at twenty-one years of age, and then be permitted to work out their own destinies.

His recital recalled to some of the older Congressmen a similar incident of his younger days. It was toward the close of the Sixtieth Congress, in 1908, after Representative Burton had been elected Senator from Ohio and a few days before he took his seat in that Chamber. James S. Sherman, Representative from New York, was at the same time preparing to go to the Senate to preside over it as Vice-President of the United States. He was Chairman of the Committee on Indian Affairs and one of the last of his acts as a Representative was to report a bill from that committee. Evidently he regarded it as a mere formality which would be passed as a matter of course and was surprised when Burton, who would soon sit under his gavel in the Senate, announced that he had quite extensive remarks to make on the bill.

This Indian bill of 1908 was a masterpiece of legislative absurdities. It provided the Indians of the Chicago region—all wooden tobacco signs!—with a blacksmith shop. This item had been carried in each appropriation since Chicago was a frontier trading post. But the measure had its modern features; the provision for band instruments was generous! In general this was also true of agricultural implements.

But why, Burton asked, had one populous tribe, which had been moved years before to the great open spaces of the Western frontier, been denied the civilizing influence of plows, cultivators, and other agricultural implements?

He was, he indicated, particularly interested in one tribe of Southwestern Indians who appeared to be not only the high favorite of the gods but of Uncle Sam also. The discovery of oil on the lands of these Indians suddenly had made them the richest group of agricultural people in the world. But to make their magnificence complete, Uncle Sam, as this bill witnessed, was still supplying them with liberal government rations, to the distribution of which they rode in expensive vehicles bought with oil money.

In the end, Chairman Sherman accepted his critic's suggestions and withdrew the bill to be rewritten.

This incident had a more than passing influence. It became a Congressional tradition and made legislators more cautious in leaving to their secretaries the drafting of routine measures. "Getting past Burton" was a standing problem among the national lawmakers. Often the Republican Speaker, the floor leader of the House, or the

Senate whip would suggest: "Better sound out Burton on that bill before it's too late. You can't afford to have him hit the warpath."

One interesting Burton characteristic yielded unfailing surprise to his colleagues—his ability to devour mountains of details and extract from them the broadest views and conclusions. To those on his personal staff a large portion of these details appeared insignificant and irrelevant.

He was a veritable magpie for hoarding pamphlets, documents, reports, and newspaper clippings. He could not bring himself to throw away a scrap of paper on which was written or printed anything which challenged his momentary interest. His office and his apartment overflowed with these hoardings. One of his secretaries makes this amusing confession:

"At a time when every filing case, cabinet and table in the Senator's office was loaded with a chaotic assortment of data which his assistants regarded as so much trash, he said good-by to us and started on a short journey. Promptly, gleefully, we began heaping the waste baskets with the accumulation of these papers. We were laughing at the joke we were playing on the Senator and assuring each other that he would never miss these hoarded treasures when the door opened and he reappeared.

"His keen eyes instantly caught sight of a treasured pamphlet topping a well-heaped waste basket. Then they shifted to the other waste baskets and he quickly took in what had happened. He seldom showed anger—but this time he was furious. When he finished expressing his mind to us, we felt that we were fortunate to retain our positions."

In the midst of arduous legislative duties, it was a pleasant interlude for Burton to be invited, in the spring of 1922, to give a lecture at the University of Rochester. This was one of the "Cutler Lectures" founded by James Gould Cutler "to promote serious consideration . . . of certain points fundamental . . . to the permanence of constitutional government in the United States."

Although Burton had discontinued his lucrative law practice rather early in his career to devote himself to national legislation, throughout his later life he secured a considerable income from the delivery of lectures and addresses. "Extra money" is always the sweetest brand of income and he relished it. If any program committee chairman hoped that Senator Burton would decline compensation for an address or would be content with mere traveling expenses, he figured without his thrifty guest of honor.

On the other hand, Burton did not, like his friend William Jennings Bryan, or like the senior La Follette, join the staff of a lecture bureau and make public speaking a profession. This was in conflict with his ideas of senatorial propriety. He considered only those requests for addresses which came to him unsought.

Into each of these speeches he put an unsuspected amount of research and preparation. Usually he dictated two or three versions of them. This process fixed them so firmly in his memory that he delivered them virtually verbatim, with only a few topical notations on a small slip of paper held in his left hand as he spoke.

One of the most ambitious of these lectures was a series on "Corporations and the State" which he delivered near the close of the first decade of the new century at the University of Pennsylvania. They were published by D. Appleton & Co. in 1911, in a volume which was at once recognized as a classic on this subject. Its brevity gave no indication of the extent of the research upon which it was based. The procedure of attacking this task was characteristic of all Burton's adventures in the field of authorship.

Calling his staff of secretaries and assistants—numbering about a half-dozen capable young men—into consultation, he informed them that he was about to prepare a series of lectures on corporations and that they would proceed to the Senate's special rooms in the Library of Congress, where he would assign them to their several tasks. There he asked the reference librarian in charge to have placed upon a long table "all of the books, pamphlets, and magazines in English, French, and German relating to corporations, ancient and modern."

The librarian smiled at this request but made no comment. While a procession of heavy-laden book-bearers began depositing their burdens on the table, Senator Burton assigned the work to his staff. One of his young men was a Rhodes scholar, who had majored in Roman and Phoenician law. To this assistant he delegated the research into the ancient history of corporations and the laws governing them. To another, who read French fluently, he assigned the French branch of the research; and to still another, equally proficient in German, he gave that field of inquiry. His group of assistants contained two or three young men who had considerable training in law and to them was given the English field of research.

Then he directed that they start reading in their several lines, making brief summaries of the most interesting and important materials which they encountered. Before the meeting dispersed, the huge table was heaped with a mountain of books, documents, and magazines. The task of searching them seemed almost insuperable to Burton's staff, but he gave no sign that he was surprised by its magnitude. In fact, his countenance suggested that of a hungry man facing a feast. Later, as the excerpts and comments of his staff came in, he read them avidly. He made almost no notes, but occasionally asked a few questions. By one of his research staff the mass of information submitted was described as "prodigious and appalling."

"He swallowed it whole," relates this secretary, "like a boa constrictor. Then he began dictation and amazed us with the thoroughness of his feat of mental digestion. It was a great experience and those who fed the materials to him were amazed at the results."

It was an honor to be asked to contribute to the Cutler series of 1922 on which William Howard Taft had previously talked on "Constitutional Law." Burton's subject was "The Constitution of the United States—Its Origin and Distinctive Features"; it was published the following year in book form. Not only is this small volume a valuable analysis and history of the Constitution, but it also gives interesting sidelights on some of Burton's views. In speaking of the ways by which the rights of the minority may be infringed, he mentioned taxation.

"Just now there is a delusion prevalent in the country which is contrary to the most elementary principles of economics, and that is that there is a kind of mysterious fund in existence somewhere owned by the government. Some think that you can issue millions and billions of paper money that bears the stamp of the government, and spend it . . . But this fact should be borne in mind—that it is not those who pay the taxes to the tax collector in the first instance who bear the burden. It is diffused over the whole community."

Taxation was a favorite theme. He often spoke in the House on this subject, so important to the welfare of the people. He said repeatedly that, while the rule was not of universal application, the imposing of all taxes tends to raise prices and to increase the cost of all facilities.

Opposing a proposed surtax of 50 per cent, he said that he believed in graded taxation—a surtax on those of larger incomes—but that there was a limit beyond which there was not only "injustice but danger to the economic structure." He also observed that high surtaxes had become a farce because of the many tax-exempt securities available.*

* See Congressional Record, 67th Cong., 1st sess. (Aug. 20, 1921), vol. 61, part 5, and 68th Cong., 1st sess. (Feb. 18, 1924), vol. 65, part 3.

CHAPTER 24

On the Foreign Debt Commission

IN SPITE OF ALL THE sorry events of the Harding Administration, it accomplished at least two things of great importance.
The more important was the Limitation of Armaments Pact
with Japan and England. The treaty remained in existence for ten
years and while it lasted proved a constructive step toward amity
among nations.

The second important act of the Harding Administration was the
treaty of peace with Germany, signed on July 2, 1921, the resolution for which Burton presented to the House in June. Because no
peace treaty had been signed between Germany and the United
States, there was no commerce between the countries, and there
were no diplomatic relations except through Spain.

It seems incredible that so long after the Armistice there should
have been such haggling over the passing of this resolution. Objections to it were on the grounds that it was unconstitutional for
Congress to make peace, that it must be made by the President
under a treaty to be ratified by the Senate.

During this controversy in the House, Burton said: "We have
come to realize that in this great expanding country the Constitution must be a flexible document. . . . Are we so bound by constitutional limitations that Congress, which declared that war
existed, can not now declare, as a statement of fact, that war does
not exist?"

With the declaration of peace came talk about settling the war
debts. It was proposed that Congress stipulate that the amount of
interest on the loans to be funded be set at not less than 5 per cent,
the same rate of interest carried by the Liberty Bonds. This
alarmed Burton. He argued that such matters should not be settled

by Congress, but should be left to a commission to be appointed by the President.

It was gratifying to Burton to be appointed by Harding in February, 1922, to this World War Foreign Debt Commission, authorized "to refund or convert and to extend the time of payment of the principal or interest, or both, of any obligation of any foreign government arising out of the World War." There were, of course, certain definite specifications: the rate of interest was to be not less than 4¼ per cent and the principal was to be paid off within a period of twenty-five years.

This was a task of tremendous responsibility and complexity which required the highest order of diplomacy and an amount of patience and detailed labor difficult for any layman to appreciate. Burton looked upon it as perhaps the greatest opportunity for world statesmanship placed in the hands of a group of Americans since the Versailles negotiations. Its results would in a large measure determine future relations between the countries of the Old World and the United States. In particular he saw in it an opportunity to further his desire for universal peace.

After years of service as an unofficial ambassador to the Old World, he had at last been honored with an official opportunity to participate in a most delicate and complex diplomatic enterprise. Although he realized in advance that his labors on the commission were predestined to result in criticism, he threw himself into this work with the ardor of youth.

The other members of the original committee were men of outstanding abilities. The Chairman was Andrew C. Mellon, Secretary of the Treasury, and the other members were Charles E. Hughes,* then Secretary of State; Herbert C. Hoover, Secretary of Commerce; and Senator Reed Smoot. Eliot Wadsworth, who was then Assistant Secretary of the Treasury, acted as Secretary of the Commission.

Later, to make the commission nonpartisan, three prominent Democrats were appointed by President Harding. These were, to quote a speech made by Senator Reed Smoot in Congress at the time of the funding of the English Debt, "Congressman Crisp, of Georgia, a practical American of a family notable in American public life and long a distinguished member of the House of Representatives; former Congressman Richard Olney, of Boston, a suc-

* Replaced by Frank B. Kellogg, who became Secretary of State in 1925.

cessful wool merchant of broad vision; and Edward N. Hurley, of Chicago, formerly chairman of the Federal Trade Commission, at one time chairman of the Shipping Board, and one of President Wilson's trusted advisers at the Peace Conference at Paris. And I may say to the Democratic side of this body that no members of the commission have been more loyal, none have worked harder, and none have been more conscientious in the performance of their duty."

In announcing Burton's appointment to this Commission, the Cleveland *Plain Dealer* said:

Appointment today of Representative Theodore E. Burton, of Cleveland, to be a member of the Foreign Debt Refunding Commission may have an important bearing on the contest in Ohio for the Republican Senatorial nomination. . . . It is realized that this work will consume a great amount of time, and Mr. Burton has been of the belief that if he is to announce himself a candidate for the senatorial nomination this year he should act soon. An active speech-making campaign from now on has been urged by some of his supporters. As a member of the Foreign Debt Refunding Commission he must remain in Washington much more than would be necessary if he had only his congresssional duties to look after. He would have little opportunity to stump the state.

Burton had been considering running for the Senate, but he hesitated. It was hard work and a bore. In his indecision he sought advice and was told that no doubt he could win, but that it would be an ordeal for a man over seventy. He decided to pass the opportunity up to Simeon Fess, who battled with Willis for the nomination.

With the Senatorial temptation put resolutely behind him, Burton squared himself to the task of his work on the Foreign Debt Commission. As the *Plain Dealer* had predicted, the commission demanded a great amount of time. Meetings were held almost daily. The commission began its task under serious disadvantages. Nothing had been done toward collecting the enormous principal of $10,337,000,000 owing to the Government. The European countries were in a chaotic condition, bordering on bankruptcy. Budgets were not balanced and currencies were depreciating.

In this country there was a strong opposition to our demanding these payments. Many urged that it was not only an unfriendly thing to do but would work to our ultimate economic disadvantage. In Europe, also, there was sentiment against payment of the debts.

The attitude of the United States Government, however, was that the loans, made to the Allies during and after the War,* were actual loans and never considered by this country or the debtor nations as subsidies. The money loaned was borrowed from the people by the selling of Liberty Bonds, and therefore this country owed its taxpayers the duty of obtaining as good terms as possible on these foreign notes.

In the face of all hostile criticism, including petitions from such men as President Hibben, of Princeton, and a group of professors at Columbia, the commission went steadily forward trying to make the best settlements possible for the United States, consistent with a just and generous spirit to the debtor nations.

Incidentally, although this commission had the settlement of approximately ten billion dollars of debts in its hands, not one cent was appropriated at the time of its foundation for expenses.

Immediately after the first meeting of the commission in April, 1922, the Secretary of State asked foreign nations to appoint representatives to negotiate with it. France was the first country to respond. Jean V. Parmentier was sent almost immediately for a conference, but soon departed for Paris to take up the matter with his government.

Burton, however, was not at these conferences. He had once again gone to Europe—his sixteenth visit—where he interviewed the prime ministers or chancellors of six prominent countries and two of their presidents. It was far more important to the success of the commission that he renew his acquaintances abroad and ascertain for himself the financial status of these countries than that he be present during the preliminary negotiations.

In London, Burton learned to his consternation that two prominent members of the Democratic Party, James M. Cox, Democratic nominee for President in 1920, and Henry Morgenthau, had been making speeches, just prior to his visit, in which they said in effect that the United States did not care at all about the collection of the debts.

He decided it was time to do something to counteract the effect of these "friendly but immaturely considered statements." **

* Approximately three tenths of the debts were incurred after the Armistice.
** Congressional Record, 69th Cong., 1st sess. (Jan. 13, 1926), vol. 67, part 2.

Consequently, a luncheon was arranged at the Hotel Cecil by the American Chamber of Commerce. Among the guests were Sir Robert Horne, M.P., Chancellor of the Exchequer, who came to this country the following January to confer on the debt; Sir George Paish, with whom Burton held interesting debates on this subject some years later; H. L. Simonds, the Chairman of the Council of the London Chamber of Commerce; a number of directors of British banks, and other prominent London businessmen.

Burton first answered the question of why the United States had kept aloof from the League of Nations. He said, firstly, it was because of our geographic isolation; secondly, because of a conviction carried down from the founders of our nation that we should keep away from the antagonisms and ambitions of European countries; thirdly, because the United States more than any other nation, perhaps, was self-sufficient.

"Fate," he said, "had decreed that the United States was to be one geographical and political entity with the promise of colossal wealth and power. This land, stretching from the lesser to the greater ocean, must be one country with one purpose and one destiny.

"How incalculable would be the benefit of a similar union of a large part of the continent of Europe organized on economic lines within which, whatever the political boundaries or barriers, there might be free interchange of commodities. Such a *Zollverein* or economic United States of Europe would surely go far to remedy the distress now pressing upon the world.

"There is another subject on which I will speak frankly. That is upon the Allies' debts in the United States. I must say that the disposition of the people of the United States is to require the payment of these debts."

Burton's speech on the American attitude toward the debts was commented on in an editorial in the London *Times*. The true lesson of his speech, said that famous newspaper, is for England "to recognise its indebtedness to America and to arrange to pay it off in such time and by such means as the American Funding Commission may agree to hold just and feasible. Then, with some prospect of greater harmony in European political and economic affairs, and with a consequent prospect of assured peace and reduction of armaments, the average American view of Europe and of American relations to Europe may develop in so salutary a direction as to bring within the range of practical solution problems which today seem intractable."

In commenting on his speech some years later, Burton said that he was listened to "very respectfully but not very responsively."

Burton had not been home long before he entered Johns Hopkins Hospital in Baltimore for a slight operation. According to one newspaper he was actually on the operating table when he asked the doctor how long he would be confined to bed.

"Possibly a week or ten days," answered the doctor, motioning the nurse to give the patient the anesthetic.

"That will never do; that will never do!" Burton exclaimed. "I have to speak in Cleveland the 17th, and there is an important meeting of the Debt Funding Commission on the 20th."

With that he fairly leaped from the table. And regardless of any inconvenience he may have caused in hospital routine, he kept his Cleveland appointment, talking before the Chamber of Commerce on "Europe As I Saw It." In this speech Burton urged leniency and generosity toward the suffering abroad.

"I have no hesitancy," he told his Cleveland friends, "in saying that the burdens imposed on Germany in the way of reparations are altogether beyond what she can carry and that the attempt to collect those reparations is an injury not only to herself but to the economic, the social, and I may say the political life of the world."

The conferences of the Debt Funding Commission with England in January were productive of satisfactory results. The settlement finally agreed upon amounted to about 83 per cent of the amount owed.

As in the case of every other settlement thereafter, Burton was the one who presented the plan to the House for its approval. When he arose to explain the funding of the English debt he was surprised and pleased at the thunder of applause which greeted him.

"It is with a profound sense of responsibility that I approach the discussion of this bill," Burton began. "No measure has been presented in this House of more far-reaching importance since the days when our armies were battling in the field."

And he went on to say what he had said many times before—that he did not believe the United States should release the principal of these foreign debts, yet he would be "unmindful of the interests not only of our own country but of those vast interests which pertain to the whole world" if he did not advocate also a "reasonable degree of concession and leniency in the terms of payment."

He then told his colleagues just what problems had confronted the commission during the past year. He said the terms of the original law—that the duration of the loan should not be more than twenty-five years nor the rate of interest less than 4¼ per cent— were "manifestly impossible at the outset."

"I will say right here that so great a transfer of capital as would be involved in the payment of these debts or even in the payment of the debt of Great Britain inside of twenty-five years would be disastrous to our own people as well as to the United Kingdom. . . . Our stock of gold in the United States, though it affords us most sincere gratification, is not altogether an asset; it would be far better for us if a part of this gold were distributed among the nations of the earth, loaned on adequate security, because its presence here tends to create inflation, raise prices, and stimulate injudicious enterprise."

For the first five years, Burton went on to explain, the commission thought it best to make very moderate terms. The principal was to be paid in full at 3 per cent interest for the first ten years. After December 15, 1932, it was to be 3½ per cent. Another departure from the original stipulations was in the duration of the notes, extending the period of payment from twenty-five years to sixty-two years. Moreover, all settlements were to be based on the ability of the debtor country to pay.

Prolonged applause greeted Burton's careful explanation. The commission had done a fine piece of work and Congressmen felt that no small part of it had been accomplished by their colleague from Ohio. Their satisfaction was voiced by James A. Frear, of Wisconsin.

"If there is one thing of which we may well be proud," said Mr. Frear, "it is the distinguished member whom the House furnished as a part of that commission and of the fine work that he did." Whereupon the entire House arose to its feet with another outburst of applause.

For four years the Debt Funding Commission gave most careful study to the questions involved. It held long consultations with the experts of Europe, including prime ministers, ministers of finance, and prominent bankers.

In an article in the *Kiwanis Magazine* of November, 1927, Burton went so far as to say that it would be "quite impossible for another commission or for any private organization, however competent the members might be, to give the careful consideration to the capacity for payment of foreign countries that was given by the commission during the more than four years in which it functioned."

The settlement with England formed a basis for the settlements with the other countries, except in the cases of Belgium and Italy, where even greater leniency was shown. In each case the facts were carefully summarized and presented to the House, and after some hours of questions and answers the bills went through without a hitch. Occasionally, however, trouble arose.

When the funding of the Estonian debt came up for the confirmation of the House, there ensued the usual interchange of Congressional repartee. This was possibly brought on by the somewhat superior attitude of Burton who, for once, showed irritation and impatience because he felt that the House could not afford to spend time on obtaining a roll call on this bill when so many other important matters were pressing, but should accept the findings of the commission without delay.

Said Blanton, the rough and ready Congressman from Texas: "However discourteous he [Burton] may be to the gentleman from Wisconsin here on the floor when he gets exasperated, he is all right when he is cool and calm in his office. The gentleman from Ohio is a real American when it comes to Americanism. But when it comes to politics and he is exasperated he is almost as mean as the devil." At which everyone was unkind enough to laugh. Then Blanton went on: "I want to say to the gentleman from Ohio that expediency is not going to keep me from asking for a roll call on the important questions coming up this afternoon."

And Burton, very dignified, replied:

"The question of expediency is never considered by me in passing on any legislation."

There were fireworks, too, when the terms with Italy were discussed. It was Henry T. Rainey, afterward Speaker of the House, who caused most of the trouble. The terms decided upon for funding the Italian debt were very generous. The settlement, based entirely on Italy's ability to pay, was immediately ratified by the President and then presented, according to the statute, to the House.

Rainey thought the findings were entirely too generous to Italy and protested, bringing out in his arguments that Italy had greater "capacity to pay"; and to prove his point, in true Congressional fashion, he produced magazine articles denouncing the government of Mussolini, concluding with the statement that the Debt Commission represented "a lack of statesmanship unprecedented in the history of the commercial nations of the world."

Again, Burton indignantly replied to these statements—not with his old-time patient and suave enumerating of facts, but with sarcasm and bluntness.

"I want to say of his [Rainey's] remarks today, that I never heard so long a speech in the House of Representatives in which there was so much not pertinent to the issue. And I never heard a speech in which there was so much muckraking. Our bargain is with the Italian people. Our settlement is with them. What is involved here is good relations with those 40,000,000 of people in the years that are to come . . . but you are not going to settle this question by a discussion in which facts are disregarded, in which economic principles are cast to the winds, by comparisons which are not applicable. . . . Cut it out! That is not the question before this House. The question is, shall we make this settlement? . . . Will we seek to insist on the uttermost farthing when such insistence would not only degrade ourselves but would defeat the very object that we are seeking; because, if we had sought a settlement more severe, it would have meant that all of our prospects would have vanished into thin air."

Burton presented the last settlement to the House on June 4, 1926—that with the Kingdom of the Serbs, Croats, and Slovenes, which was funded at approximately 32 per cent of the indebtedness. Altogether the commission had effected settlements with thirteen countries. The total settlements amounted to nearly ten billion dollars, or 97 per cent of the total principal amount of the obligations held when the commission had been created.

There was no question as to the leniency of the terms for the earlier years, but what of the future? The commission believed a "true balance" had been held between the "duty of the Debt Commission to the American taxpayer and fairness toward those nations to which was extended aid during and after the war. They had not canceled the debts but neither had they demanded the impossible." The result of the adjustments were: Britain, 81 per cent;

France, 50 per cent; and Italy, 26 per cent of their total indebtedness.*

The commission ended officially on February 9, 1927. If it was notable for nothing else, it was notable for its lack of partisan politics. As Mr. Crisp said, "We were all influenced by the sole desire to serve our country as best we could."

With regard to Burton's work on the War Debt Commission, Former Secretary of the Treasury Mellon wrote:

"By reason of his long service in Congress and experience in affairs of government and also his acquaintance with men both in this country and abroad, he was able to render most useful service as a member of the Commission. As Chairman, I always valued his suggestions and relied upon his sound judgment."

Former Senator Reed Smoot also wrote the author concerning Burton's work on the commission:

"Senator Burton was a very dear friend of mine. I served on conferences with him while he was a member of the House and I a member of the Senate. We were together daily during the settlement of the foreign war obligations. He had a splendid mind and was wise in all matters pertaining to the affairs of our nation."

Not all of Burton's colleagues in the House agreed with him. One of his adversaries was Col. A. Piatt Andrew, who had worked so closely with Aldrich on the framing of the bill presented by the Monetary Commission in 1912.

Under the auspices of the Foreign Policy Association, on March 12, 1927, in New York City, he and Burton held a joint debate on "The War Debts—Status Quo or Revision?" Burton first reiterated his belief that the leading motive of America's participation in the war "was one of altruism—a desire for the maintenance of popular government and for liberty in the world." He then went on in his characteristic style to state the facts regarding the settlements.

"The loans," he said, "were not made from an overflowing treasury. The amounts were obtained from the people by intensive campaigns, by sacrifices on the part of our citizens. In some communities a quota was assigned to all the citizens as to how much they should subscribe. So, in a very important sense, the Government of the United States is a trustee for the people of the United States for the payment of these loans.

* *U.S. World War Foreign Debt Commission* in the report for the fiscal year 1926. Washington, 1927.

"If anyone who has bonds advocates cancellation, he ought immediately to bring them to the Treasury and surrender them."

Then Mr. Andrew declared: "The best argument that I know in justification of the debt settlements is the fact that my friend, Mr. Burton, is willing to defend them. It is a strong, and for me a very appealing argument, and I may add that is almost the only argument that I know that carries much weight." He then proceeded in his brilliant way to present the opinions of the other side of this much-debated question, the main issues of which were the "capacity to pay" stipulation of the commission and the sixty-two-year term of payment. On these points he scored telling criticism.

This was but one of a series of debates staged that spring in various large cities by the Foreign Policy Association, in each one of which Burton presented the arguments for payment of the War Debts. In three of these discussions the opposing side was taken by Sir George Paish, of England, who had been at the luncheon in London in September, 1922.

In at least one of these debates Burton came out clearly ahead. In Cleveland, in order to judge the influence of these two orators, a poll was taken before and after the speeches, as follows:

Before the debate—For cancellation	16%
Undecided	18%
Against cancellation	66%
After the debate—For cancellation	12%
Undecided	2%
Against cancellation	86%

Possibly Burton never discharged an official responsibility of greater service to his country than as a member of the Foreign Debt Commission. That his work contributed greatly to adjustments which kept payments coming in over a period of years is admitted by American statesmen most familiar with the facts.

CHAPTER 25

America's Busiest "Old Man"

BURTON HAD BEEN SO BUSY at his work in Congress that apparently he gave little thought to national politics until early in 1924. He then announced that he would like to be an Ohio delegate at large to the Republican National Convention in June. This did not please the bosses of the party. They wanted Burton to eliminate himself so that he could be named as "second choice" for the Presidency.

But Burton refused to budge. The Ohio Senators Fess and Willis added their voices to the clamor. Willis reminded Burton that he had been his candidate for President back in 1916 and that he was the "greatest Republican in Ohio."

President Coolidge himself entered the controversy and asked Burton to the White House for dinner, where they could have a confidential chat about political affairs. But nothing persuaded Burton to change his mind.

There was only one thing to be done about it. When the Republican leaders named the delegates at large, Burton's name was omitted. Thereupon Burton issued a tactful statement to the effect that the object to be attained rather than the persons who accomplished it should be the first consideration. But as to running for second choice, he was adamant. He would not allow his name to be used.

Nor would he accept a Cabinet position. In March Secretary of the Navy Denby resigned, following the Teapot Dome exposure, and Coolidge wished to give Burton the place. But a Cabinet position held no more charm for him in 1924 than it had back in the days of the Taft Administration. He liked the House of Representatives. He had important work to accomplish there.

The work at that particular time was preventing Henry Ford

from acquiring Muscle Shoals, the proposed sale of which "would make Teapot Dome look like a bagatelle."

Although Burton became engrossed in Congressional matters following his fight for appointment as delegate to the Republican convention, the party leaders did not forget him. They asked him to become temporary chairman of the convention and to deliver the keynote address for Coolidge.

Burton was exactly the type to express the conservative views of Coolidge and he had been a loyal party man for many years. But it was not because of his conservatism or loyalty that he was chosen as keynoter. It was because he was thought to be the man who could draw Ohio's rival Republican factions together for Coolidge.

The situation confronting Burton as a keynoter was by no means ideal. Not only had the oil scandal just been brought to light but Congress had only recently, in the case of the Japanese Exclusion Act, shown itself quite independent of the President's wishes.

As the newspapers had predicted, Burton delivered a good orthodox Republican recital, an informative speech on the achievements of the past four years, characteristically interspersed with bits from Shakespeare. The Teapot Dome scandal, which caused so much embarrassment to good Republicans, was squarely faced. "Our highest duty," Burton said, "in the midst of all these rumors of iniquity is to punish the guilty but at the same time condemn exaggeration and protect the innocent." On the whole, the consensus was that Burton had done an able job under difficult circumstances.

This convention was unusual in three particulars. It was the first in which women were admitted as Republican delegates, it was the first in which radio was employed, and it was the first in which there was an uncertainty as to a Vice-Presidential candidate. It was a surprise to everyone, including Burton himself, when New York on the first ballot gave him practically its entire vote. However, the convention adjourned soon afterward and on the following day Dawes was nominated.

Although it would have been a nice compliment, Burton did not want the Vice-Presidency. In 1916 it would have been different, but now he was deep in work on the Debt Commission and other international affairs.

In the midst of all this political hubbub, only a few days before the convention Burton learned of the death at Oberlin of his sister, Mary Burton Shurtleff. Perhaps not even his mother's death some years before had brought him such sorrow.

Burton went back to the political melee and then on to Kenyon College, at Gambier, Ohio, where the honorary degree of Doctor of Laws was conferred upon him. There was a touch of sadness for him about this occasion. His sister Mary would have been happy to witness this honor. She had taken great pride in the fact that both Dartmouth and New York University had given him this same degree.

Ohio politics continued to seethe. The right candidate for governor—one to please all factions—did not appear. Periodically Theodore Burton was proposed as the man most agreeable to all sides but he steadily refused the position.

Feeling certain of his return to Congress in the fall, he sailed in high spirits for Europe. He went on behalf of the Debt Funding Commission, to sit in on the League of Nations and, as was his custom, to attend the annual meeting of the Interparliamentary Union.

Returning to the United States early in September, he was forced into the turmoil of both national and local politics. His own election was not such a foregone conclusion as he had anticipated. While he was gone Albert F. Coyle, an editor of the *Brotherhood of Locomotive Engineers Journal,* had filed as candidate for Congressman on the Progressive ticket. Upon his return Burton found himself the object of much vituperation.

Coyle's main contention was that Burton supported the Teapot Dome scandal. This charge was based on the Congressman's reply to Burton K. Wheeler, who, while running for Vice-President with La Follette on the Progressive ticket, had declared that the Government had lost a billion dollars by this famous contract. Such exaggeration was too much for the factual Congressman Burton. He therefore denied the charge, saying that actually the Government made money on the contract. He did decry the lack of bids, the secrecy of the transaction, and the part played by Secretary Fall.

Then, to fill speaking engagements on behalf of Coolidge, Burton took a train for the Middle West, where he campaigned vigorously for the Republican Presidential ticket, leaving his own election in the hands of his Ohio friends. His optimism concerning his success at the polls was well founded, for he was returned to Washington with twice as many votes as the combined totals of his opponents.

Coolidge was grateful for Burton's help in this campaign and wrote him as follows:

> My dear Senator Burton:
> As a whole, the Ohio result is a tremendous achievement, and I want to thank you for the large part that I know you played in making it possible.
>
> Very truly yours,
> Calvin Coolidge

Once Senator Burton confided to his close friend A. N. Rodway, of Cleveland, his estimate of both President Coolidge and Mrs. Coolidge.

"He told me," said Mr. Rodway, "that, in his opinion, Calvin Coolidge was, in some respects, the ablest man who had occupied the White House in his Washington experience. 'I never saw a man,' Senator Burton declared, 'who could sit at a council table, listen to the statements of a number of men on intricate problems and then more ably summarize their statements than he could. And the conclusions which he drew from his summary were singularly clear and sound. In this faculty President Coolidge was remarkable.'

"His characterization of Mrs. Coolidge was equally crisp and interesting. He declared her to be representative of the ideal type of American womanhood and a keen politician in the best sense of the term.

"Once Senator Burton told me that he considered Lloyd George about the ablest politician he had ever encountered anywhere. Again, in a casual chat, he once unwittingly gratified my curiosity as to his opinion of Theodore Roosevelt, which was this: 'A very able and strenuous man with a tremendous ambition.' "

Although normally the position of Speaker of the House would not be filled before December, 1925, a fight for it began as soon as the House convened in the fall of 1924. Frederick H. Gillette, of Massachusetts, who had been Speaker for the past three Congresses, had been elected to the Senate. When his re-election as Speaker had come up in 1922, Burton had been mentioned for the place, but he would not run against his old friend Gillette. Now, however, he wanted the honor. It would be a nice rounding out of his career. But while Burton had an assured place in the country generally, his fellow Ohioans were inclined to criticize him. They thought him too independent, too determined to follow whatever course he considered right, too nonpartisan—and, possibly, too dogmatic.

When the assigning of places on committees came up, there were vacancies on both the Rules and the Ways and Means committees. Burton asked for both, feeling that his length of service, his ability, and his age warranted his having what he wanted in the House. This created a storm from his Ohio colleagues and it ended by giving him merely the Rules Committee.

The Ohioans also were disturbed by Burton's desire for the Speakership. Nicholas Longworth coveted that position and announced his candidacy. Burton evidently was waiting to see how the land lay for when he was approached by newspaper men he would not admit seeking the honor but only said: "It is an office that no one will decline."

Representative Martin B. Madden, from Illinois, was another who wanted the position and had a chance to win it, not only because of his able record but also because he was Chairman of the Appropriations Committee and therefore had plums to give.

Burton had many friends outside his own state who wished him to have the Speakership. He also had the friendship of Coolidge— and still he would not commit himself. The reason was characteristic. A year before, he had pledged his support to Longworth, and unless Longworth agreed to his candidacy there was nothing to do but to let matters take their course. Many others in a similar position would have forgotten the pledge. Not so Burton! When he gave his word, that ended it.

Longworth, fearing that if Burton did become a candidate it would so divide the vote that Madden would be elected, finally got Burton to make a statement. He said he was not a candidate but would do all he could for Longworth's election, admitting, however, that, if Longworth had not been a candidate, he would have enjoyed the support of his Ohio colleagues. When Longworth was formally named as a candidate in March of the following year, Burton was asked to make the nominating speech.

No matter how strongly he might have felt on a certain subject he never lost his balance. He could always see the question sanely. This trait was evidenced in that spring of 1925 when he rose in the House to protest a resolution on calling an international conference on the reduction of armaments, though it was no more than a request to the President to hold such a meeting.

"I do not rise to oppose this amendment," said Burton. "But I am not cordially in favor of it."

His colleagues were startled. They thought of the times he had wrecked naval appropriation bills, of his criticisms of army appropriations, of his invariable cry for peace. Yet here he was on the floor of the House saying:

> It is an amiable but very futile gesture. In the first place, it is entirely unnecessary because whenever the time is opportune this House would vote with substantial unanimity for a conference to consider the question of the limitation of armament. More than that and more important, the President of the United States, with whom rests the responsibility for conducting our foreign relations, has over and over again, by messages to the House and in addresses elsewhere, signified his intention when the time is ripe to call such a conference.

> But let us recognize what the situation is. A plan was proposed at the last meeting of the League of Nations and submitted for signatures in the form of a protocol on the second of October last, which suggests a more advanced step for the assurance of peace than has ever been brought forward in any international official gathering.

> It provides for security, it provides for peace and for compulsory arbitration; and security may be said to rest upon that compulsory arbitration. If the dispute is of a legal or judicial nature it is to be left to the Permanent Court of International Justice. If it is on another subject, if the nations do not agree to arbitrate, it goes to the Council of the League. The Council of the League seeks to induce the warring or contending nations to arbitrate. If they do not succeed in that, then the Council by unanimous vote comes to a conclusion that is binding upon the two nations. If the members do not agree unanimously then the Council shall select arbitrators. This goes further toward outlawing war than any proposition which has been brought forward by the League of Nations on any other occasion.

> The United States, it is true, is not expected to sign this protocol. The problem of peace or war is primarily and principally one that pertains to the Old World. If they have peace there the world will be at peace. In the New World, partly by reason of treaties recently framed, there is every assurance that any controversy which may arise will be settled amicably.

These are the reasons why the President cannot call such a conference at this time. If he were to do so it would mean a forecast that this proposition embodied in the form of a protocol was doomed to certain failure. It would be a reflection on the sincerity of the nations that have joined in this protocol. The Premier of France, the most powerful military nation in Europe under the labor government, also signed it, and it would be little short of an insult for the President of the United States to comply with this request and ask for a peace conference at this time.

With this admonition Burton asked the House to pass a resolution framed by the Foreign Affairs Committee, urging the Senate to dispose of the question of joining the World Court, which had been pending since early in the Harding Administration. Initiation in such matters usually emanated from the Senate. To defend the position of the House of Representatives in this action, Burton appended an exhaustive report which he had laboriously prepared, not only explaining what membership in the World Court would mean but also showing that the House had a right to advise the Senate on the matter since it would have to pass an appropriation bill for such membership.

The resolution was passed by the House with enthusiasm. It read as follows:

Whereas, A World Court, known as the Permanent Court of International Justice, has been established and is now functioning at the Hague; and, whereas, the traditional policy of the United States has earnestly favored the avoidance of war and the settlement of international controversies by arbitration or judicial processes:

And, whereas, This Court in its organization and probable development promises a new order in which controversies between Nations may be settled in an ordinary way, according to the principles of right and justice, therefore be it

Resolved, That the House of Representatives desires to express its hearty approval of the said Court and an earnest desire that the United States shall give early adherence to the Protocol establishing the same, with the reservation recommended by President Harding and President Coolidge.

Resolved further, That the House expresses its readiness to participate in the enactment of such legislation as will necessarily follow such approval.

This question of joining the World Court had been pending

since Secretary of State Hughes had presented it some four years before. It had been a plank of both the Democratic and Republican platforms of 1924 and still the matter lay dormant in the Senate.

Burton had always been in favor of the Court. He had somewhat changed his mind about whether the United States should join the League of Nations (although with certain reservations he would still have favored it), but on the World Court he had never altered his opinion. In fact, as early as 1909 he had advocated a similar court in a speech before the American Society of International Law.

He had also told the Ohio Society of New York:

"I do not say that this International Court is all that it might be, but it is the entering wedge. It is the beginning which gives promise of development which in time will exercise jurisdiction in international controversies. The final goal to be reached is a means of settlement of controversies between nations in the same manner as those between individuals and states of the American Union are now settled."

Late in March, 1925, Burton went to Cleveland to attend a banquet held in honor of the fiftieth anniversary of his admittance to the Ohio bar. This gave his many friends the opportunity to let him know in what esteem he was held. Letters and telegrams came in by the score. Among them was the following message from Coolidge:

> I wish it were possible to participate in the recognition which the Cleveland Bar Association is extending to the Hon. Theodore E. Burton on the fiftieth anniversary of his admission to the Ohio bar. . . . He is one of the long line of public servants who has brought distinction to the State of Ohio, and I strongly feel that the Cleveland bar in paying honor to him is also doing an honor to itself.

And another from Taft:

> I should be glad to attend the dinner and testify to my gratitude for the presence of such a man as Theodore E. Burton in politics. He is a real statesman and a practical one. He is always for the better things and he makes up his mind only after thorough knowledge of the facts.

In his response to a toast, Burton claimed, as he said, "an old man's prerogative"—that of rambling, and in these "ramblings" told perhaps for the first time how, in 1901, Theodore Roosevelt, then Vice-President, had seriously considered entering a Washington law school as a freshman.

Roosevelt told Chief Justice White that he had made up his mind to enter a law school. White advised against it, as hardly becoming to a Vice-President. "If you really wish to know more about the law, I have some excellent law books I can let you take," he said.

Roosevelt promised to begin the study of law the following September. But in September McKinley was assassinated and Roosevelt became President.

After other reminiscences Burton concluded with the advice:

"Don't be too quick to enter public life. A political career, in the words of Macaulay, offers 'hope without realization, labor without accomplishment, and devotion to duty without reward.' " After which Burton gave six rules for arriving at old age in good health.

1. Avoid all excesses.
2. Cultivate regularity and punctuality.
3. Don't give way to the emotions; especially, don't let any antagonism become permanent.
4. Don't get grouchy, or don't begin to think that society was much better when you were young.
5. Work to uplift humanity and to upbuild the state, so that you may feel you have done some good in the world.
6. Cultivate variety, love the state and cherish it, love your community and work to make it better; champion every movement that makes for the welfare of mankind.

He returned to Washington after a few days to find the inevitable pile of mail heaped high on his desk and a call to be at the White House that night for dinner.

Because of the importance of that dinner to Burton, on this day he began another of his inconstant journals.

Tuesday, March 31, 1925:
Invited by phone to the White House for dinner at seven. Present: the President and Mrs. Coolidge, Mrs. Goodhue, her mother, John and myself. Talked with John, at my right, about his studies in Latin and Greek and in mathematics. The President jokingly asked John what the Odyssey was about. He replied: "The same as when you were a boy."
Spent an hour and a quarter with the President in his study. He

asked me to go to Geneva as a delegate to the Conference for Control of the Traffic in Arms and suggested that I see Secretary Kellogg.

The conference was called for May 4. There was not much time. Burton called a meeting the following day at which Allen Welsh Dulles, Admiral Long, General Nolan, General Ruggles, and Major Strong were present.

"We went over the Draft Convention," writes Burton, "particularly in the early portions. There was a manifest intention to give, as I thought, undue importance to the interests of private manufacturers. Called on Secretary Hoover late in the afternoon. He was very favorable to the Convention and inclined to make light of the petition of the manufacturers, saying they would be in a better position under the convention than they were at this time."

For the next two weeks the American delegation held daily meetings. Burton was to sail on the fifteenth of April and had to work day and night in order to be ready in time. It is interesting to note that he jotted down in his journal that while he was away his secretary was to "work at Cleveland on material for biographies of Clay, Blaine, Sherman, and Hay." He had written a limited biography of Sherman years before which the Houghton Mifflin Company published in 1906, but this was evidently to be a more ambitious work.*

In a meeting at the White House regarding the various propositions of the conference, Burton suggested a provision against the use of poison gas to which President Coolidge, Hoover, and Kellogg readily agreed. Just prior to the Congressman's departure Coolidge again summoned him to the White House for a few last words of counsel. Burton told the President that he was "not at all pessimistic as to the outcome of the conference." Coolidge, with characteristic terseness, answered this only by impressing upon Burton the importance of making a good record for the country.

The Traffic in Arms Conference in Geneva was a grave responsibility, but it was only one of Burton's important duties. There was work on the Debt Commission to be done. France had not yet signed an agreement and it was rumored that she never would. It

---

* Another of Theodore Burton's ambitions which was not realized was his desire to write a biography of David Ross Locke. During the Civil War and just preceding, Locke wrote numerous satirical articles under the pseudonym of Petroleum V. Nasby, illustrated with caricatures by Thomas Nast. These were very forceful antislavery propaganda.

was necessary to see Ambassador Herrick regarding the present situation immediately upon arrival in Paris.

Burton wrote in his journal:

> Talked with Herrick about French debt. He evidently favors large concessions. Said he had made reference to the ten-year moratorium granted by France to the United States after the Revolutionary War, also to devastation in France and her inability to pay. This in talks with Briand and others. Had suggested moratorium and nominal interest for 10, 20, or 30 years. Read memorandum sent to the Department about Herriot when he became Prime Minister. Very discriminating. Described him as a scholar, idealist, lacking in experience, having been only Minister of Public Works for a short time during the War, patriotic, and honest withal. . . .

The following three or four days were devoted to attending sessions of the Interparliamentary Union, to which Burton was a delegate, as was also Senator William B. McKinley, of Illinois. Burton admired McKinley very much. They thought alike on many subjects, particularly on the World Court.

At Geneva, Burton was joined by Hugh Gibson, then United States Minister to Switzerland, an experienced diplomat who had been conducting preliminary negotiations for the United States.

On May 4, Burton wrote in his journal:

"Made elaborate preparation for the meeting which occurred at 4 P.M. in the main assembly room of the League of Nations Building. . . . There was a reference to the failure of the Treaty of St. Germain * which grated upon me a little as the responsibility was placed upon the United States. . . ."

When the Executive Committee of the Conference was chosen on the following day, Burton received 38 of the 39 possible votes— far more than any other delegate received.

The days which followed were crowded with conferences and meetings. There was no time for relaxation. Every evening someone gave an elaborate dinner, following which the American delegation quite frequently held a meeting far into the night.

Burton enjoyed these social functions although they were an added exertion. It gave him an opportunity to meet the delegates

---

* A treaty was signed at St. Germain, a suburb of Paris, on September 10, 1919, between the Allies and Austria in which Austria recognized the independence of Hungary, Czechoslovakia, Poland, and Yugoslavia.

away from the formality of the council chamber and to become acquainted with their wives. Among these distinguished persons were Paderewski and his wife, who urged that he visit them at their villa near Lausanne. Mme. Paderewski, whom he sat beside at dinner one night, "expressed unusual loyalty and attachment for her husband." She spoke of her desire to get back to their estate in California.

After the dinner, as was so often the case, Burton met his delegation to urge it "to adhere to the American proposition in regard to the use of poison gas." He wrote in his journal that he had "to use more firmness than on any other occasion as to our stand—referring to the policy of our country, the Washington Treaty, our instructions on leaving, and the recent cablegram received from the State Department."

Burton held his delegation in line, however, and eventually a protocol was signed outlawing poison gas and bacterial warfare.

Many times during the six weeks of the conference matters seemed to be at an impasse. There was one day when the smaller states moved "that the Convention should not be effective until a convention controlling private manufacturers had been elaborated."

Burton opposed this viewpoint strenuously, stating that prohibition of private manufacturers would be ineffective, especially in a country like the United States. He said that the delegates from the small states were too much influenced by the threat of war. They should rely on hope and faith. "The speech was greeted with enthusiasm," he wrote in his journal.

On the whole it was a successful meeting, although Burton confessed to his niece, Mrs. Laura Shurtleff Price, that there were too many military men present to make a conference for the purpose of disarmament ideal.

Besides the prohibition of poison gas, through the influence of Burton and his delegation, the conference also made decisions regarding the use of publicity on international trade in arms and regarding the regulation of their international shipments.

It was a weary statesman who took the train on the night of June 17 for Aix-les-Bains. Burton had been there before. He enjoyed taking the baths and resting in this beautiful little resort town. However, this particular interlude of relaxation was far from happy. It rained almost every day and was unbelievably cold for June in the south of France. He notes, with evident exasperation:

"Lost umbrella just purchased." Losing umbrellas was one of his failings. He scattered umbrellas right and left, and as they invariably were vast cotton tents his aggrieved accusations that they had been stolen caused his friends amusement.

For diversion at Aix-les-Bains, Burton conjugated French verbs under the guidance of an instructor at the Berlitz School and in the evening read a biography of Shakespeare.

But there is a strain of lonesomeness running through his journal. He bewailed the lack of congenial companionship. Burton never went abroad alone again but took with him one of his nieces for companionship.

His spirits revived when he got back to Paris. From the train he went immediately to call on Ambassador Herrick to learn what the developments were with regard to the French debt. Although the hour was late and Herrick had already gone to bed, he and Burton held a long conference, the result of which was the arrangement that Burton would see Caillaux the following day.

Again quoting from Burton's journal:

> At 7:15 went to the Louvre and had interview with Caillaux. Fortunately I was not asked to commit myself in any way about the attitude of the Commission. Caillaux spoke English perfectly, understood all about the story of the Commission.
>
> We talked first about Morocco and I stated to him that the American attitude was one of sympathy with French policy, provided they sought no expansion of territory.
>
> We then spoke of the debt. He said it was the intention to send a commission of about seven or eight members, including representatives from Senate and Chamber—those representing Foreign Affairs and those representing finance; that Franklin-Bouillon would go, if possible, but his total absence must be limited to three weeks. I suggested that he might go later, after other members of the Commission had taken up the subject.
>
> I called his attention to a prevalent impression that France was not as heavily taxed as the other nations and we talked of the form of statement to be made, I suggesting that one general statement briefly drawn should set forth the case and be accompanied by exhibits. He spoke of the necessity of brevity. . . .
>
> July 9: . . . In the afternoon went with Whitehouse [Sheldon Whitehouse, a counselor in the American Legation in Paris] to the Chamber of Deputies, heard Marshal Cachin, Communist and advocate, for half an hour, 3:30 to 4:00.

Most disorderly scene I ever witnessed in a legislative body, though Whitehouse said it was often worse; some twenty Communist deputies at the extreme left were clapping hands and shouting approval. Most of the rest were noisy in disapproval. He was speaking against the war in Morocco.

A few days later Burton was in London where he called on Premier Baldwin. Burton asked him if his government would make any objection if a settlement more favorable to France should be made than that which had been effected with England. Baldwin answered that the British probably would not object to a different treatment but that primarily it was for Winston Churchill, the Chancellor of the Exchequer, to decide.

Again quoting from the journal:

> July 20: At 1:30 went to 11 Downing Street. First met Mrs. C. [Churchill], who seemed to me to be a lady of charming manners. Afterwards the Chancellor, Grigg, and Niemeyer. We talked of the Geneva Conference, of the use of poisonous gas, which C. mildly defended. He was suffering from an attack of lumbago and had difficulty in rising from his chair. . . .
>
> Coming to discussion of Debts, it was evident he had talked with Baldwin, for he said promptly: "We have no objection to a more favorable settlement for France than that with England but England would insist upon a settlement of French indebtedness as favorable to them as that with you." After rising from the table he expressed the opinion that France would make no proposition which either country could accept. I had said that if Caillaux visited the United States he could not return empty handed unless he could say the terms offered were altogether too severe. He responded that neither can he afford to return with an empty purse.
>
> From Downing Street at three, went to call on Lady Bryce. She asked me to furnish letters and such materials as I could for his biography. [Lord Bryce, who had been a close friend of Burton's, had died in 1922.] She expressed herself very freely about English public men, said young men were not coming forward because they had been lost in the war. There were no great leaders whom the people trusted. Baldwin was of limited capacity, Lloyd George was discredited—he always had been an opportunist—Churchill was clever but volatile. The Liberal party had gone upon the rocks, their natural leader Asquith was now too old.

This time, upon returning from Europe, Burton had a comfortable, well-ordered home awaiting him. There he was well looked after and warmly welcomed by his niece, Grace Burton. It had not always been so, however. Laura Price often recounted how she and her sister had been summoned one time by a cable to meet "Uncle" at the dock. He wished to have the feeling that a member of his family would be waiting to greet him on his return from Europe. Before going to New York to meet him, Mrs. Price went first to his bachelor apartment to see that it was put in order for his occupancy. She relates:

"It was a pathetic sight—a revelation of bachelor desolation! The kitchen of the apartment would have thrown any of his New England 'female' forebears into hysterics. Not only were the china cupboards filled with books, but the oven and drawers of the gas stove were crammed with them. But this incongruous scene seemed thoroughly characteristic of Uncle Theodore. Books were his 'bread and cheese.' Intellectual food came first with him."

On the whole, this European trip of 1925 had been of value. Soon after Burton's arrival in Washington, President Coolidge summoned him to the White House and, as Burton noted in his journal, "he commended my action in Geneva very strongly."

On August 6 Burton wrote in his journal:

"First meeting for some time of the Debt Commission and the thirty-ninth meeting held. All members present except Crisp. Wadsworth's resignation accepted and Garrard B. Winston appointed Secretary in his place."

Later on in August Burton was back in Ohio, where he presided at a convention of postal clerks in Cleveland. Following this engagement he toured his district attending Old Settlers' picnics, greeting friends, making speeches, and seeing ball games.

There was no rest for Burton. The French Debt Commission was due in Washington in late September. Caillaux headed the group as he had half promised Burton he would do. There followed the usual meetings and finally an agreement, and the commission departed with the hope expressed on both sides that a ratification by the President and Senate of both countries would immediately follow.

In discussing this matter in the House, Burton said:

> Consider the fact that our sales to France were made at a time when prices were at the top; enormous profits were realized by our own people; great amounts of taxation from excess profits and otherwise poured into the coffers of the Federal Treasury by rea-

son of our doing that business with France and, that being so, must we play the part of selfishness at a time like this? I say no. Let the distinction of our country be that it has due regard for the disability and for the suffering of other lands. Let us first of all be generous, as we have been in the past.

As will be remembered, the settlement was duly authorized by both Coolidge and Congress.

Between meetings with the French Debt Commission, Burton was making arrangements for the session of the Interparliamentary Union that was to be held in Washington in October.

Before he sailed for the Traffic in Arms Conference in April, he had made a most unusual request of Congress. The United States delegates of the Interparliamentary Union had invited the Union to hold its next meeting in Washington. The invitation had been accepted and as there were to be a large number of important representatives of practically all the countries of the world at that meeting, he sought permission from Congress to use the Hall of Representatives. After all, it was no more than the other countries had done. In every country in which meetings had been held, he said, the greatest deference had been shown the Interparliamentary Union. The United States should not be outdone in courtesy by other nations.

All precedents were against such a procedure; no other legislative or deliberative body had ever been permitted to hold its sessions in this historic hall. Only one circumstance favored the plan —the House would be on vacation at the time of the session of the Interparliamentary Union.

It was a compliment to this veteran member of Congress that his extraordinary resolution was passed by unanimous consent.

The meeting in Washington had an excellent effect. Many Congressmen had never before had the opportunity of attending the sessions of this organization. Some could not see its purpose nor why the United States should be a member. Some even worked against the appropriation of the fifty thousand dollars necessary to cover the expenses of the meeting, saying that it was a waste of taxpayers' money; that this group of individuals with no official authority would come to this country and talk peace and do nothing to effect it.

To this, Burton made a patient reply, recounting the history of the organization since its founding in 1889. In part, he said:

It accomplished substantial results in the first decade of its existence. The members met here in the year 1904. Perhaps their greatest accomplishment was at that meeting, when delegates from the United States and from a number of foreign countries in a body called on President Roosevelt and urged him to ask the other nations to meet again in a second Hague Conference. President Roosevelt gave heed to that request, consulted diplomats of the different countries with a view to a second conference, which, as a result, was held in the year 1907. It was an important step, a milestone in the history of better and more friendly relations between nations.*

The great benefit of these meetings is primarily the coming together of representatives of the different parliamentary bodies for consultation. This was very well expressed by Senator McKinley, the President of the American group:

"The advantages of such an organization readily suggest themselves. Freed from the domination of any government, it represents a universal and democratic aspiration. Nothing in it savors of particular interest or privilege. Composed of officials, holding its conferences in the houses of parliament, it is itself only semi-official. Perhaps its main service is its opportunity for parliamentarians from all parts of the world to meet, to confer, to educate one another. . . . For parliamentarians from so many different countries just to meet, officially or unofficially, at conference, at table, at social gatherings, is in itself not without benefit."

A multitude of questions have been discussed at these meetings, including economic and financial subjects, reduction of armaments, problems of social policy, the rights of minorities, the burden of high rates for passports and visas, and improvement in international law.

Perhaps nothing definite was accomplished at the Washington meetings along the lines discussed—the codification of international law and the elimination of economic barriers between nations. However, they had one important result. They helped to make the American legislators think internationally. After the meetings were over, many who had scoffed the most at this peace organization were the loudest in its praise.

When Congress again convened in January, Burton resumed his role of critic. One of the bills which were pending early in 1926 was the Haugen Bill for farm relief. Burton in rising to oppose the

---

* At the 1925 meeting in Paris, Burton suggested a third Hague conference but he said the suggestion "was coldly received."

measure said he was willing to go far in rendering aid to farmers provided "it was within the scope of our constitutional powers" and provided the action was "fair to the whole country and helpful to the farmer himself." But he did not believe the Haugen Bill was constitutional.

He declared that he felt, regarding all classes of citizens, that "the less they are coddled the more strength they have in the elements that enable them to go ahead." He declared that "largely because of circumstances arising out of the [First World] War, we have departed from those old principles of independence" which have proved themselves the "chief bulwark of American progress and American institutions."

There was another important bill pending at this time—the Rivers and Harbors Bill—which Burton strenuously opposed. He said it was the first time in Rivers and Harbors legislation that provision was made for one project that would do serious injury to another. He referred to "the Illinois River item, which seeks for the first time to authorize by legislation diversion from waters of the Great Lakes." Although Burton never made a more impassioned appeal, the bill was carried. He said there was a diversion of water at Chicago which diminished the level of the lake six inches and this, together with a "cyclical decrease of thirty-four inches" because of deficiency in rainfall since 1917, caused serious injury to harbors, to foundations along water fronts, to shippers, and to many summer resorts.

There was one bill pending, however, on which Burton had nothing to say. It was the fight instigated by Martin L. Davey, a leading Ohio Democrat, who had represented his district in Congress for ten years, to secure a contract for the Goodyear Tire & Rubber Company, of Akron, Ohio, to build two dirigibles.

One of the first things Mr. Davey did in starting his campaign, he told the writer, was to try to secure the co-operation of the entire Ohio delegation. Burton was in sympathy with the project but said he could not possibly take an active part in the fight for the legislation.

"You see, Mr. Davey, it would not be ethical," said Burton, "because I am a stockholder in the Goodyear Tire & Rubber Company."

Burton was glad a few months later to pack his trunks and set sail once again for Europe. This time he took with him his niece, Laura Price.

She said she could not at first understand the change that apparently had come over her uncle. When she met him at the dock he was surrounded with luggage. He must be growing vain, she thought, to take so many clothes along. Later she discovered that his luggage was crammed with books. Even his hatbox was filled with them.

He was on his way to another meeting of the Interparliamentary Union, which was to be held at Geneva just prior to the session of the League of Nations. He was also a member of the American delegation to the League of Nations Conference on the Control of Opium.

Upon his return he was, as usual, interviewed by the Cleveland *Plain Dealer* as to conditions in Europe. His remarks show perhaps for the first time a pessimistic view of the future.

> The outlook for another arms limitation conference in the near future is unfavorable. At the meeting of the Interparliamentary Union, which I attended in Europe, it was hard to get an agreement on any subject, whereas, at the meeting of the Union held here in Washington a year ago, the other nations were willing to yield to the judgment of the United States on everything. Militarism is the handicap of Europe today. It is the crushing weight of militarism that is keeping the people back.
>
> I have never known such a propaganda in Europe as there is now in favor of cancellation of debts. That propaganda extends somewhat into this country. . . .

In November it had been rumored that Andrew Mellon would resign as Secretary of the Treasury as soon as the next tax bill passed the House and that Coolidge's choice of a successor was Theodore Burton, "who had been taking such a prominent part in the settlement of foreign debts." This rumor appeared again and again in the newspapers and finally drew a denial from Burton himself. "I am very well satisfied where I am," he said.

In the Congressional campaign of 1926 he had no opposition. Regardless of party affiliations, the twenty-second district of Ohio was for Theodore Burton. The esteem with which he was regarded by his Cleveland friends was shown in an elaborate dinner which they gave him in Cleveland on his seventy-fifth birthday.

His old friend, Paul Howland, was the toastmaster and the guests included poor men and rich, judges and merchants, old neighbors and political opponents. There was a speech on "Senator Burton and the City of Cleveland"—he was always "Senator" to Clevelanders—by the City Manager, William R. Hopkins; one on "Senator Burton and the Press," by E. C. Hopwood, Editor of the *Plain Dealer*, who said that his paper was Democratic except during one month in the year. The Vicar-General of the Catholic Diocese of Cleveland, Monsignor J. F. Smith, talked on "Senator Burton and his Influence for Good"; Judge John J. Sullivan on "Senator Burton and the Legal Profession"; Rabbi Abba Hillel Silver spoke of Burton as the "Scholar in Politics." And lastly, that good Democrat, Senator Atlee Pomerene, discussed "Senator Burton and Congress." Pomerene closed his remarks by saying that Congress will always be better for the Burtons who are selected to serve in it.

When the silver loving cup was presented Burton responded:

> It is a good thing to be seventy-five. Usually we have a good many eulogies on persons who are seventy, and then again a less number, because there are less of them, on those who are eighty, but as regards seventy-five, it is a little bit like a way station on a railway where the fast trains do not stop.
>
> I have occasion for gratitude to Heaven because I have been permitted to live so long and to enjoy such good health. . . .
>
> It is indeed my hope to live for years yet to come, and with the preference that I may be engaged in the public service. . . .
>
> But as far as satisfaction to myself is concerned, the good will of this community, which has reached its very climax tonight, is a greater satisfaction than any act of legislation with which I have been connected, and if I have endeavored to instill into the minds of men that there is something better than war among nations, it is because I believe that honesty, charity, tolerance for all races and creeds, for all nations, are the crown of all the achievements of a public man. . . .
>
> We had all hoped that, after the terrible suffering of the war, the minds and hearts of men would be softened, that an era of peace and co-operation would begin. . . . I fear that hope has not been altogether realized. . . The statesmen of the different countries cannot see eye to eye, and while I could put first and foremost the maintenance of the right of our country and its standing, I fear that we are not taking that place in the leadership of the nations which we ought to take, because of our supreme

might and power, our resources, and the confidence which the rest
of the world should vest in us. . . .

I have lived long. Of the twenty-nine Presidents of the United
States my life has been contemporaneous with seventeen. I have
been familiar with eight of the Presidents of the United States, with
perhaps all of the leading men of the last forty years, and I cannot
feel like breaking away from this work which I have done. I do
not know where I should go or what I should do if deprived of the
opportunity for doing something which I think to be best in the
public service. . . .

This dinner was held on the twenty-seventh of December because on the twentieth, his birthday, Burton had to be in Washington. But here, too, he was greatly honored. When he arrived at his
desk in the morning he found many congratulatory telegrams and
messages, and photographers besieged him for pictures.

At the House, the members arose in deference to him. Representative John Q. Tillson, the Republican floor leader, addressed
Burton as "our ablest, most respected and best beloved colleague"
and one who is "honored, admired and loved by us all, a veritable
tower of strength in our midst."

It was a day for reminiscence. Burton gave an interview to the
press comparing the Congress of 1889, when he entered at the age
of thirty-seven, with that of 1926. He first mentioned the difference in appropriations. In 1889 there was approximately $500,-
000,000 appropriated for the business of the country. The 1926
bill asked for $4,000,000,000.

Said Burton:

> I would say that the standard of intelligence is quite as high now
> as in 1889. The fault with Congressmen and Senators is not the
> absence of a desire to give faithful service to the country but a
> supreme anxiety to be continued in office. This causes many of
> them to vote in a manner contrary to their convictions. The influ-
> ence of a multitude of telegrams and letters often sent by those
> who have no sense of responsibility can hardly be exaggerated. . . .
>
> In giving you an opinion as to the outstanding American in
> public service during the past forty years, I must say that the
> qualities and capabilities of those who have served here at Wash-
> ington have been so varied that it is impossible to answer this ques-
> tion. For real intellectual ability I would place Thomas B. Reed
> well in the forefront. I would say of one of our Presidents, Ben-

jamin Harrison, that he had the qualities of a great executive—firmness, quick decision, and excellent judgment of human nature. For really lovable qualities and a spirit of conciliation which gave him a leadership no one surpassed, McKinley. . . .

Burton's humor was quiet and well controlled. He was too much concerned with world problems to indulge in levity. But he made a speech at this time in which he let himself go in a way that delighted his listeners, the Republican women of Ohio. He said the country was too demoralized by its concern with scandal and such to consider great subjects affecting national welfare.

If Burton's talk upon his seventy-fifth birthday had a plaintive, wistful note, a hint that perhaps the time had come to let go, it was unwarranted. He was still outstanding in Congress. He still could sway his listeners. One of the best examples of his power of persuasion over a recalcitrant House was in the 1927 contest over a bill calling for the immediate construction of three scout cruisers.

President Coolidge did not want the bill to pass. Neither did Burton, who was ably supported in this stand by Representative Blanton, of Texas, a Democrat and a man who in the past had often opposed him. Their reasons were those of President Coolidge, who said that the construction of these cruisers "would not be in keeping with our attitude toward the disarmament negotiations instituted by the League of Nations, in which we are now participating."

Representatives Longworth and Tillson fought on the opposite side and had a powerful following. But they reckoned without Burton.

"I rise to oppose both amendments that are before the House Committee," said the white-haired statesman who had successfully fought Theodore Roosevelt on the very same question many years before. "One of the main reasons why I am opposed to these amendments is the glaring inconsistency between advocacy of a conference for the limitation of armament and at the same time expanding our navy by the building of three warships."

The appeal of Theodore Burton had good effect. It strengthened the determination of uncertain Congressmen who hesitated between offending those powerful Republican leaders, Longworth and Tillson, and fighting the President. When the roll was taken the bill lost in the House 135 to 133—a narrow margin. But it revealed, said one of the papers, "that the power to sway votes by dint of persuasive argument is not a lost art beneath the Capitol dome."

The Senate, however, passed the bill with amendments which Longworth later forced through the House.

While this bill was pending Burton attended a meeting of the American delegation to the Interparliamentary Union at which he was elected president. The meeting was held in Geneva in August, and again Theodore Burton took with him his niece, Laura Price. For perhaps the first time in his life he neglected to make reservations in advance at his favorite hotel in Geneva, the Hotel de Bergues. There was not a single room available, so Burton insisted that Mrs. Price accept an invitation to visit his old friend, Miss Eliza Scidmore, a writer on Japan. He would not accompany her—did not want to be bothered—could find a room for himself; and went off to register in a dingy, second-rate hotel nearby.

When Miss Scidmore heard of it she went to the hotel, where she found Burton sitting dejectedly in the lobby, his ever-present umbrella clasped in both hands, while he waited for his room to be made up. This time he was not hard to persuade and was driven to Miss Scidmore's apartment on the Quai de Mont Blanc. Here he and Mrs. Price had a suite to themselves, with the use of a car and a chauffeur, and were altogether luxuriously looked after.

During the assembly of the League of Nations, which met after the close of the Interparliamentary Union, Miss Scidmore frequently took her visitors to ride along glorious Lake Geneva. The last afternoon as they drove along the shore past the League Building, Burton took off his silk hat, made a sweeping bow and said ironically, "Good-by, dear League of Nations! Good-by!" Did he realize that this was truly to be his last farewell to the League and his beloved Geneva?

When Burton arrived in London on his way home, he found awaiting him a membership in the Liberal Club, a great honor which afforded him much satisfaction. During the following two weeks he visited the club frequently, but in all that time not one member spoke to him!

This particular trip to Europe had given Burton an opportunity to extend a personal invitation to prominent Europeans to visit Cleveland the following May. This was to be the annual meeting of the American Peace Society of which Burton had been president for many years, which would at that time celebrate the one hundredth anniversary of its founding and at the same time would inaugurate the first Conference of International Justice.

CHAPTER 26

Moonlight Reminiscences

PROBABLY THE MOST POPULAR of all Senator Burton's public addresses was the most informal; it was an intimate, personal
talk, pitched in a confessional key. He was called upon to
deliver it in various parts of the country.

Regarding it, Robert Norton, long his chief secretary and friend,
said: "He called it 'Reminiscences' and delivered it in a conversational way which captivated his hearers. Once I had the good fortune to hear it delivered at the Coshocton Country Club, in Ohio.
Because the evening was extremely warm, the company went outside on the grassy terrace, which was flooded with brilliant moon-
light. The beauty and peace of the scene put the Senator in a happy
mood and he charmed his audience."

Burton reminded his hearers that his experience in public life
had been almost exclusively that of a national legislator, and that
he had found it "much more severe and wearing" than his work as
a lawyer, a teacher, or a banker. Then he told them the troubles of
a Representative or Senator in Congress who tries to do his duty
and to accomplish something for his country.

He discussed the insidious disease that reduced the usefulness as
well as the happiness of every national legislator, no matter how able
or how devoted to the public welfare. Not one of them, he declared, was spared the gnawings of the cancer of "home politics,"
of patronage manipulation, and of local logrolling necessary to hold
a seat in Congress. "A Representative," he reminded his listeners
"has a term of only two years. . . . Thus he has but a few months
of service until he must again plunge into the activities and worries
of a political campaign."

The demands of office seekers upon the time of a Senator or Rep-

resentative at Washington, confessed Burton, left him only a frag-
ment of his time for legislative duties. His efforts to achieve anything important must be made as a sideline to the routine business
of receiving and entertaining constituents hunting appointments
for themselves or for their friends or pressing for legislative favors.
"If there is any one thing," he declared, "that requires reform in
our system of government it is the method of selecting public
servants for nonelective positions. At Washington I was always a
strong advocate of what is called 'civil service reform,' notwithstanding the fact that it is easy to see that all manner of defects
would arise under a permanent tenure of office."

He confessed to his auditors that one of the keenest worries of
the Representative or Senator is to know what applicants are competent for a position and worthy of appointment. "I recall an instance when I had at my disposal an important office requiring
special ability. I consulted a man of standing and influence in his
community and asked him to suggest a good man for the place. 'My
son-in-law,' he promptly replied, 'is just the one for that position.'
Careful inquiry developed the fact that this son-in-law was a use-
less sort of fellow, who had been a burden to the family out of
which he married and a still greater burden on the family into
which he married."

On one occasion, Burton said, he had the appointment of a chief
census taker in Alaska. An applicant for it confessed that he was
actuated by a desire to get away from civilization to a place where
he could "live among the Indians." Another applicant, seeking a
minor position on a ship going to Sweden, admitted that this appointment would "solve a domestic difficulty."

Burton voiced his estimates of various public men, among them
James Buchanan. Following the census of 1910, which showed a
great increase in the population of the country, came propositions
in Congress to increase the size of the House of Representatives
by about fifty members. Thousands of men throughout the country thought they saw a chance of breaking into Congress by the
enlargement of the House membership.

"I opposed that with all my might," related Burton, "because the
physical proportions of the hall were too small for 435 men and
also because the larger you make a legislative body the less the influence of the individual member and the greater the influence of
bosses. In preparing to address the Senate on this subject I found

that far and away the ablest treatment of it was a speech delivered by James Buchanan, about 1841, following the 1840 census. Reading that speech greatly increased my appreciation of the abilities of Buchanan.

"Incidentally, I do not think that his qualifications for the Presidency have been fully realized by students of history, in which he occupies a very unfortunate place, as it is felt that possibly he might have prevented the Civil War. With the exception of John Quincy Adams, no President was ever inaugurated who had the preparation by experience that James Buchanan had. He was elected a member of the Pennsylvania legislature when twenty-two years old, served ten years in the lower house at Washington and was then sent as Minister to Russia and there negotiated a very important treaty. On his return he served nine years in the United States Senate and was then elected President.

"Also, I found that James Madison, in a plea to restrict the membership of the House, had said: 'Though every member of the Athenian assembly be a Socrates, the Assembly will be a mob.' When I first entered the House it consisted of 325 members and, incidentally, belonging to it was much more of a distinction than to be one of 435 members."

The most important phase of this problem, Burton told his hearers, was the fact that pressure for increasing the number of House members was bound to be felt following every national census, as the population of the country was steadily increasing and the time was certain to come, if it had not already arrived, when the membership of the House, if it followed the increase of population, would be unwieldy to the point of absurdity. In his opinion the usefulness of the House would have been increased had the deadline been drawn in the days of Buchanan.

Here he recurred to his original theme of the pest of office seekers, constantly descending upon Washington like a devouring cloud of grasshoppers, by repeating a story about a New York collector of customs who attended a White House reception when Abraham Lincoln was President.

A few days before, in a private talk, this New York politician had told a story which delighted President Lincoln. As the receiving line at the White House reception was passing before the President and Mrs. Lincoln, it was blocked for several moments while the President held a whispered conversation with this New

Yorker. The next day this man was besieged with office-seeking callers who had concluded that the reception incident indicated that he "had the ear of the President" and therefore had great influence with him.

Not until long afterward did the man reveal the nature of that conversation. Mr. Lincoln had whispered to him: "I can't exactly recall that story you told me the other day, but it was a good one and I want you to repeat it."

Lincoln's propensity for storytelling intrigued Burton and he described an incident revealing the purpose which actuated the President to tell amusing anecdotes on many occasions in the terrible days of the Civil War.

The battle of Malvern Hill marked one of the most discouraging days of the great conflict. Henry Wilson was that day admitted to the President's office, his face a picture of gloom and despair. Lincoln greeted him with the remark: "You look out of sorts this morning and your appearance reminds me of a little story."

"Mr. President," brusquely interrupted his caller, "this is no time for storytelling; it is an awful time in the history of our country."

With unusual severity President Lincoln responded:

"Mr. Wilson, do you think you take this situation any more seriously than I do? I know that if defeated not only would our cause be lost but I would go down in history disgraced. But suppose I were to appear on the streets with such a face as yours at this moment. The newspaper correspondents would telegraph all over the country that the cause of the North was lost and that Mr. Lincoln himself published that fact in his face. And I say to you, sir, it would be well for you to show more cheerfulness and hope in your countenance."

This rebuke, Burton declared, was a revelation of the fact that Lincoln constantly used his wartime stories as weapons of defense against the gloom of those dark days.

Said Burton of the Civil War President: "If there is any one feature in the career of Abraham Lincoln without a parallel, it is the increase of his reputation since his death. He was very bitterly attacked and criticized while President and did not then enjoy the reputation he now has, the world over, not only for his great qualities of heart but for his discerning interpretation of the currents of popular opinion and for his ability to suit his measures to the time and the occasion. There is every indication that his reputation is going to continue in the future, showing that there is for every man a today and a tomorrow—a today made up of what he does while living and a tomorrow of his influence after death."

Burton then drifted to comments on the picturesque character of Andrew Johnson and remarked: "No man who ever occupied the Presidential chair had such a stormy time as Johnson—and there was reason for it: he turned his back on what he had been professing and, regarding the proposal to call a Reconstruction Convention for the Southern states, said: 'Who shall take part in it? Shall it be the traitors whose hands are dyed in the blood of their fellow men? Let the traitor take a back seat in the work of reconstruction! Treason must be made odious. The great plantations must be divided up and given to honest and industrious men.' "

Commenting on General Grant as a President, Burton repeated a story related to him by a member of Congress in Grant's administration. A delegation called upon President Grant to urge the removal of one of his Cabinet officers. To this Grant responded: "The test of a man's friendship is not standing by a man when he is right, but when he is wrong." Grant, the speaker pointed out, showed the same courage as President that he did on the field of battle. "No man," declared the speaker, "who was not in the midst of it can recognize the strength of the movement for debased money which continued throughout Grant's administration. President Grant courageously and stubbornly put his foot on it."

Illustrating Grant's iron nerves, Senator Burton related an incident which occurred when, with a group of military officers, Grant was taking a trip on the James River. Suddenly there was a tremendous explosion and every one of the officers jumped to his feet. Grant arose quietly and remarked: "Gentlemen, it is out of order for any officer of the army to get excited."

Rutherford B. Hayes Burton regarded as perhaps the least appreciated of all our Presidents, declaring that the famous contest over his election placed him in a position of peculiar disparagement. "There was a sentiment of rebellion in the House, which had to determine whether Samuel J. Tilden, the candidate of the Democrats, or Mr. Hayes, the Republican candidate, had been elected at the polls. This contest had been stubbornly fought and was not decided until one day before March 4 when the President was to be inaugurated. As March 4 fell on Sunday, the inauguration could not take place until Monday. On Saturday, the 3rd, the session of the House opened with the contest undetermined, those favoring a decision for Tilden battling fiercely to prevent a vote. But Speaker Samuel J. Randall, although a Democrat, saw anarchy ahead if a decision was not reached. He had the courage to demand that the members go ahead and vote—and Hayes was inaugurated two days later.

"As President, Hayes did more to promote civil service than any of his predecessors, but his great achievement was that of settling the long-standing Southern question, which had become a cancerous sore—and settling it in the only way it could be settled, by courageously ordering the Federal troops out of the South. Sooner or later that had to be done.

"Then he established more just relations with the Indians and took the leadership in improving their conditions. Also our diplomatic service was brought to a much higher plane during his administration. But, above all, he took a courageous stand for sound money. There is no worse chapter in American history than the movement for a debased currency, by paper money or by silver coinage, which had so strong a hold on the people in those years."

Here Burton observed that President Hayes was the victim of perhaps the most shameful treatment from the public press of any man of his period. Hayes, he declared, was a gentleman—clean, intellectual, high-minded, and of judicial temperament. His private life, like his public career, was above reproach. This drove the pro-Tilden press, in its task of making Hayes so unpopular that the great election contest must be decided against him, to the lowest forms of personal ridicule. There was nothing to be said against his character, his private life, or his career; therefore ridicule was the only weapon left the hostile press and it hesitated at nothing calculated to make Hayes appear insignificant in the public eye. Cartoonists of great ability applied their art to him with unprecedented shamelessness. Political correspondents and paragraphers pitched their attacks in the same low key.

Senator Burton could speak most sympathetically; he had himself suffered from the cartoonists and the jibes of the paragraphers. He remarked that one might better "have a bad epitaph on his tombstone than the animosity of the public press while living."

A procession of other Presidents passed in review. Burton remarked that Garfield's Presidency was too brief to demand comment, but observed that:

"Within seven years after his graduation he had been a teacher, a college professor, president of a college, preacher, lawyer, member of the Ohio State Senate, Lieutenant Colonel in the United States army, Colonel, Brigadier General, and Major General."

This, Burton declared, was certainly "going some!"

In speaking of Grover Cleveland, Burton urged his hearers to realize that a President elected by a party other than that of his predecessor is in a position of peculiar advantage. Preceding Cleveland there had been Republican Presidents for twenty-four years —from 1861 to 1885. This detachment from the party long in power, observed Burton, afforded Cleveland opportunity to accomplish important reforms and gave him a place of high prominence in history.

Burton characterized Benjamin Harrison as a man whose great abilities were generally unappreciated because of his cold and repellent personality—his icy unresponsiveness to the enthusiasms and excitement of high moments in public life.

Said Burton: "I have seen him stand on a platform, with his hat on and as utterly unmoved as a statue, while a crowd of ten thousand men surrounded him, paying him lusty homage as the President of the United States. This acclaim did not affect him a particle; he appeared utterly unconscious of it.

"He always took the 'off side' of the argument. Once, when I was having some difficulty up at the White House, Senator Sherman cautioned me: 'Don't lose your patience or get offended. President Harrison will be of your way of thinking when he appears to be quite the opposite. We sat side by side in the Senate for six years. On almost every measure that came up he would ask how we ought to vote. The instant I would tell him he would give reasons why we should vote the other way. But in the whole six years he never voted on the opposite side of any question.'

"About the second day after Harrison was inaugurated, General John M. Palmer, then Senator from Illinois, escorted a constituent of his to the White House to present the man's claim for appointment to the position of public printer. Promptly President Harrison began to antagonize this candidate and bluntly said, among other derogatory things, that he did not consider him a sound Union man. When they were outside the Executive Office the chagrined candidate declared: 'I'm going to take the first train for home.' Senator Palmer remarked: 'Have no fear. The President will come around all right.' The following day the man's appointment was announced."

Burton recounted one of his own experiences with Harrison. "One hot July day, in 1889, I called on the President to ask the appointment of a constituent to a rather important position in the Treasury Department. At once President Harrison responded: 'I don't hear the best accounts of that man. Again, the present incumbent has made a good record and I'm inclined to think that he ought to stay.' Then the President took out his watch, glanced at it casually and remarked: 'Secretary Windom goes to luncheon promptly at 12 o'clock and if you want to see him you'd better go there.' Windom told me that the man's commission was already made out.

"Yet, despite his total lack of affability, Benjamin Harrison was a great man, strong of will, quick in decisions and possessing a remarkable judgment of human nature. He sized a man up the first time he saw him with a discernment that was seldom incorrect."

Senator Burton's hearers listened with special interest to his appraisal of Thomas B. Reed, Speaker of the first Congress of which he was a member. It had often been said that Reed had "made" Burton, but this was far from the truth. He had merely taken the measure of the raw young recruit from Cleveland and decided that he possessed uncommon ability.

Burton was not blind to Reed's faults. "He had a sort of contempt for the common man and took no pains to conceal it. Members of Congress have carried to their graves the smart of the barbed arrows of his wit. Reed was the peer of any man at Washington but he never could have been President of the United States. His capacity for making enemies was too great. Again, it was impossible for him to forget or forgive. Although he could be delightful in private conversation with a friend whose mentality commanded his respect, he had about as little affability with strangers or those whose mentality did not impress him as had President Harrison.

In this particular Reed was a startling contrast to William McKinley. In a national campaign there was great demand for Reed's services, as he was one of the most brilliant stump speakers in the country. However, his vote-getting appeal was confined strictly to his speeches. The genial and gracious McKinley would have his hotel room, from the moment he arrived, crowded with callers and he made a friend of every one of them. When Speaker Reed registered at a hotel he would give emphatic instructions that he was not to be disturbed by anyone. Callers were to be told the truth —that he was asleep and was not to be awakened. This habit naturally caused disappointment and resentment wherever he went in a campaign—a fact which did not cause him the loss of a single wink of sleep!

"When Reed revolutionized the House procedure by counting all who were physically present, instead of only those who chose to respond to their names, the Democratic attack on the Speaker was bitter and furious. Amos Cummings, of New York, a warm personal friend of Reed's, but a stanch Democrat, came to the Speaker's desk and asked to be recognized a little later. Reed said to him: 'Amos, don't you talk. You will say something for which you will be sorry.' In the evening session, however, Reed recognized him.

"Meantime, Springer, of Illinois, for whom Reed had a special contempt, had spoken and compared the Speaker to King Charles I. Cummings had not heard Springer's speech and, in his own speech that evening, made the same comparison. A little later the Speaker summoned Cummings to his desk and said: 'Now, Amos, I told you that if you insisted on speaking you would say something you would regret. This afternoon Springer compared me to Charles I and this evening you did the same thing. You have sunk to the intellectual level of Springer—think of it!'

"In the course of the same general debate, while I was at the desk to learn if I might be permitted to bring up a certain bill, a very able Democrat member of the House concluded a heated speech. 'That man,' commented the Speaker, 'never opens his lips that he does not subtract something from the sum of human knowledge.'

"The Speaker seemed to have a rather contemptuous opinion of a certain member from South Dakota. I happened to be close to the Speaker when this man asked for recognition. 'The gentleman from North Dakota is recognized,' drawled Mr. Reed. 'No, Mr. Speaker, from South Dakota,' the member explained. 'Yes, yes,' responded the Speaker, 'the gentleman from *South* Dakota. I beg North Dakota's pardon.' "

"There are," said Burton, "many justifiable attacks from the opposition and a member of Congress must cultivate a certain callousness. But if he keeps close to his constituents he will receive evidences of appreciation that he will treasure. For example, I once wrote a letter to a father whose son lost his life in Cuba. When the old man died, some time later, my letter was found under his pillow. That touched me.

"Defeats do not always leave stings and regrets. I have been quite as much in the right in my attitude on measures which have been defeated as on those which have carried and I recall many of these experiences with particular pleasure."

Many of Burton's hearers recall that talk on the moonlit sward of the Coshocton Country Club. Many of them that evening discovered in him a warm human quality which they had not before believed him to possess. It was in this period of his life that he achieved his notable social popularity. Hostesses in Washington, New York, Cleveland, and elsewhere engaged in spirited competitions to secure Senator Burton as a dinner guest. His affability was conspicuous on these occasions and his conversational charms were recognized everywhere.

He also took time during these years to indulge in two weaknesses—prestidigitators and mystery yarns. He never missed a magician's performance if he could avoid it, but was a highly critical observer. His interest was in attempting to figure out how each trick was turned. For the same reason he read with relish the most popular mystery stories of the day. This was a form of mental exercise most agreeable to him, as it has long been to famous members of the United States Supreme Court.

A performance, in Washington, by a magician of national reputation was an event in Senator Burton's entertainment program second only to a Shakespearean play by a star of international reputation. On one occasion, he invited his secretaries and their ladies to attend a performance by Thurston. One member of this party relates that throughout the performance Burton appeared "as completely carried away as a boy at a circus."

CHAPTER 27

Burton Sponsors Hoover

A VERITABLE CHRISTMAS PUDDING was the year of 1928 in the calendar of Theodore Burton. He could "stick in his thumb and pull out a plum" from almost any part of it. One plum was the award of the Cleveland Service Medal for distinguished service to his home city. But the sweetest plum of all was the success of his bold political adventure which captured the votes of Ohio for Herbert Hoover and thus insured his nomination. It revealed Burton's courage in choosing a course of action involving the certainty of charges of disloyalty and ingratitude by followers of Senator Frank B. Willis, who had placed Burton's name before the Republican National Convention of 1916 and had cast the vote of the Ohio delegation for him.

Senator Willis decided to become a favorite-son candidate and demanded the support of the Ohio delegation until he should choose to release it. This demand Burton rejected as unreasonable. He determined to do everything in his power to insure the nomination of Hoover by committing the Ohio delegation to him in advance of the convention by a victory in the Ohio preferential primary. His decision was dictated by the conviction that Secretary Hoover was better qualified by character, ability, and administrative experience for the great responsibilities of the Presidency than any candidate for that office since Abraham Lincoln.

Public knowledge that Hoover would enter the convention with Ohio's fifty-one votes behind him, Burton believed, would insure his selection in the convention. Therefore, he must be brought into the Ohio preferential primary at any cost. This move might easily involve Burton's own elimination from public life. To Walter Brown, who suggested that if Hoover were nominated and elected

Burton would be offered a high Cabinet post, Burton replied: "No, you will be in the Cabinet. My field is the legislative branch of the National Government. I have no taste for public service in any other branch. When the Republicans of Ohio will not return me to Congress I will retire from public life and accept my dismissal as final. This may happen. But if Hoover is nominated and elected President, I shall be content."

"Had he known for a certainty that his course would have ended his political career," commented Walter Brown, "he would not have hesitated to follow it. Of this I am certain."

No other living person had so vast an experience in the field of applied humanitarianism as Hoover. Every nation of Europe held him in an affection that was personal and unprecedented. Here was an asset that would be of incalculable value to a President of the United States in guiding the foreign relations of his country.

Another magnet which drew Herbert Hoover and Theodore Burton into a friendship of peculiar understanding was the fact that they were internationally minded and spoke the same language in world affairs. They were equally at home in the chancelleries of Europe; they knew the same leaders of Old World thought and understood the traditions which dictated their national objectives.

Still another bond which held Theodore Burton to Hoover was the conviction that the latter had a more profound and practical knowledge of economics than any other man of his acquaintance.

In Herbert Hoover Burton saw an intellect which absorbed a vast and complex array of facts and details and quickly reduced them to their simplest working proportions, to their sharpest focus as factors to be dealt with in a program of constructive action. Hoover, Burton believed, could think his way through any problem with swiftness and sureness.

These two men recognized the same high ethical standards, their mental processes were similar, and their resources of economic knowledge were both rich, varied, and international beyond those of most men.

Mr. Hoover's distaste for the indirections and intrigues of "practical politics" also appealed to Burton. Hoover, in fact, had even less patience with the necessity of "playing politics" than Burton had. As a mining engineer, as the head of relief work in Europe, as Food Administrator of the United States under wartime conditions, he had only one requirement placed upon him—to do the job. As Secretary of Commerce he also enjoyed considerable freedom of action. His task was to develop American industry and trade and Presidents Harding and Coolidge gave him their confidence and virtually a free hand.

Both Burton and Hoover shunned exposing their strong humanitarianism to public gaze. As a result, they acquired the reputation of lacking warmth. Burton, however, regarded Hoover as the incarnation of kindliness.

As he faced the preferential primary campaign in April, 1928, Burton felt a deep conviction that the nomination and election of Herbert Hoover would mark a departure in the process of selecting Presidential timber which would establish a precedent of value to the nation. It would recognize a new and nobler basis than political "availability."

Mr. Hoover's official home was in a state which had never given the nation a President. Then, too, his party attachments were rather vague and his party services were equally indefinite. He was in the novel position, as a Presidential possibility, of being almost devoid of party background—a political waif whose party legitimacy was certain to be challenged. Most of his adult years had been spent abroad in the pursuit of his profession and in the relief of suffering humanity. In party politics he was a novice, had never had his hands on the steering wheel of even the most insignificant local political machine.

His reputation had mainly been made in posts to which he had been appointed by a Democratic President and relatively few of his fellow citizens had specific knowledge of his party allegiance. To them he was a "citizen of the world."

True, when the campaign of 1928 approached, Hoover was serving in the Cabinet under a Republican President. However, since he knew the conditions of world trade as probably no other American knew them and since a major problem of the Administration was to build an increasing market in other countries for American goods, his selection as Secretary of Commerce was by no means a tribute to his partisan usefulness.

Burton was sufficiently familiar with the sordid complexities of Ohio politics, the details of national conventions, and the devious processes of President-making to realize that he had enlisted for the nomination of a man who had almost every possible handicap as a Presidential candidate in both the preliminary and the final campaigns. Yet he threw himself into the Ohio preferential campaign with a vigor and enthusiasm that belied his seventy-seven years. He believed that, if Ohio's fifty-five votes in the Republican National Convention were committed to Hoover at the outset of the pre-convention campaign, other states would instruct their delegations for the quiet Quaker humanitarian. This would avoid for him the uncertainties of a convention situation well equipped with favorite-son candidates and their managers maneuvering to prevent the nomination of the leading candidate and throw the great prize to the best trader among them.

In the forenoon of March 13, 1928, Secretary Hoover called at Burton's apartment and handed him two sheets of paper, remarking:

"I wonder if these letters will interest you?"

As Burton read them, his face lighted with a smile of almost boyish mischief. "Yes, I am sure they will prove very interesting," he replied.

Immediately after roll call in the House that noon, the speaker recognized Charles Brand, of Ohio, and the colleagues of this veteran member settled back in their seats to listen to what they knew in advance would be an attack upon Herbert Hoover and his distinguished sponsor in Ohio. Brand, a champion of Senator Willis, was about to carve and serve the leading candidate for the Republican Presidential nomination—a menu much to their liking.

Mr. Brand did not disappoint his hearers. As one newspaper correspondent expressed it: "He served them a full meal and served it piping hot." After accusing Secretary Hoover of using the organization of the Department of Commerce as a political machine to secure the Presidential nomination for himself, Mr. Brand struck into the main line of his attack, and declared:

"There is a great cause at stake in this nomination of a candidate on the Republican ticket for the Presidency of the United States. Agriculture is making a gigantic struggle for equality and she must have a President sympathetic with her needs . . . Mr. Hoover has been the supreme opponent of agricultural prosperity for the past ten years. He came back to this country in 1917 because the English nation wanted him to come here and secure cheap food for them and the Allies—which he succeeded in doing at the expense of the American farmer. Mr. Hoover represents those who have been against all practical relief measures."

After digressing to argue that Mr. Hoover's status as a citizen of the United States was open to question, that his Republicanism was still more doubtful, that his position as a tariff protectionist was vague and evasive, and that he was committed to the League of Nations, Mr. Brand swung back to his keynote theme of Hoover as the enemy of the American agriculturist and said:

"This blocking of the prosperity of agriculture is not the first effort Mr. Hoover has been guilty of against the farmer. When he came back from England to take charge of the food administration, he determined upon the policy of holding down the price of farm products. Who has benefited? . . . If you will think it out, you will find that the ones benefited were in Europe. England got her wheat and food supplies for the prices dictated by Mr. Hoover, and England supplied the money that bought the food for all the Allies . . . Mr. Hoover is the man who made the farmer pay all this burden and he had no authority in law for doing so. Mr. Hoover did that for the benefit of the English . . . In other words, a few captains of industry, with Mr. Hoover as their major general, are obstructing any actual relief for agriculture."

Burton made a brief and characteristic reply to this attack upon Mr. Hoover, answering each accusation with his customary precision and thoroughness. This done, he smilingly concluded:

"But it is said that Mr. Hoover has not been friendly to agriculture. On this subject I wish to read a letter from a Congressman . . . a prominent supporter of agricultural legislation in this House . . . I ask your special attention to this letter.

> Dear Secretary Hoover:
>
> I read your release of January 20th with a great deal of interest. You have the ideas that will put agriculture on its feet, and you have the confidence of the producers of the country of all kinds that would make your leadership easy.
>
> Although some of my friends have suggested my name to the President as Secretary of Agriculture, I am inclined to go to the President and urge your appointment. I don't know of anybody who fits the place so well as you do. It seems to me those under discussion have exhausted themselves in the past without result and the need for you seems to be very great.
>
> I am enclosing a copy of the letter which I wrote the President a year ago, showing you how strongly your ideas impressed me. . . ."

Mr. Madden, of Illinois, interrupted with a question: "Could the signer of that letter by any chance be Mr. Brand, of Ohio?"

"Wait a bit—look and listen!" exclaimed Mr. Burton. "Who wrote that letter? Charles Brand!" The House broke into laughter and applause.

Burton emphasized that Mr. Brand's letter was dated January 21, 1925. Then he resumed his unfamiliar but successful role as House jester in these lines:

"There is something more here. He was willing to cast aside the agricultural crown for himself, as his name had been suggested. Never a finer instance of self-abnegation since Julius Caesar refused to accept the crown [laughter] at the feast of the Lupercal. He said: 'I do not want it, because you are the man,' because he thought Mr. Hoover the best and ablest friend of agriculture. Then again, a few days later, he wrote:

January 27, 1925

Honorable Herbert Hoover
Secretary of Commerce
Dear Secretary Hoover:
    I have your favor of the 23rd. I did see the President since I called on you and told him I thought he ought to insist on your accepting the position of Secretary of Agriculture.
Very truly yours,
Charles Brand

"But Mr. Hoover declined, stating he could be of more service to agriculture in the Department of Commerce. My colleague makes the statement that for ten years Mr. Hoover has been unfriendly to agriculture and that for five years, or since 1923, he has known who were the friends of the farmer and who were not."

Burton then presented a review of the character and achievements of Herbert Hoover which became a classic in the Presidential campaign.

Another outstanding occasion in the primary campaign was the meeting of the Western Reserve Republican Club. In his speech before a large audience, Mr. Burton reminded the friends of Senator Willis that 1928 was not the year "for another 2:00 A.M. Convention"—a reference to the secret morning conclave of Warwicks just preceding the nomination of Warren G. Harding in 1920. Said Burton:

"Who is so bold as to believe in the possibility of Senator Willis's nomination? Admittedly the delegation from his own state will be divided, with possibly a majority against him. The press of the country outside of Ohio is, with almost unanimity, unfavorable to him. The same is true of the leading journals of his own state. He has not ventured to submit his name for an expression elsewhere than in Ohio. . . . The only result of Willis's campaign would be another '2:00 A.M. Convention' and this would defeat the desire of the Republicans of the country."

Next Burton dealt with the attitude of Senator Willis as Ohio's favorite-son candidate and quoted from circulars issued by Willis's men "stating that if he cannot be nominated, then they are free to use their own judgment in the choice of the Republican candidate. Just what do they mean by that?" asked Burton. "When can such judgment be exercised? Who is to decide that Mr. Willis cannot be nominated? If the supporters of Mr. Willis some weeks since had given liberty to the delegates to exercise their individual judgment as to the time they could leave him—if this liberty had been promised to half the delegates—this contest in Ohio would not have occurred."

The Republican board of strategy in Ohio saw in this split the possibility of an interparty feud which might continue for years and cost them many an important state office. Senator Willis had devoted adherents who refused to admit that their big, hearty leader had been a bit too greedy and had made unreasonable demands upon the Republicans of the state. As they saw it, he had been hampered in his chance to secure the Presidential nomination by Theodore Burton's championship of a man who had done nothing for the Republican Party or for Ohio. The Burton-Hoover crowd should be made to pay for this failure in loyalty!

Then, suddenly, on March 30, 1928, Senator Willis was stricken and died.

Probably no two political occurrences ever gave Theodore Burton greater happiness than Hoover's prompt nomination by the Republican National Convention at Kansas City and his election as President by a plurality of 6,471,473 popular votes and 357 electoral votes over his Democratic opponent, Governor Al Smith. Here was vindication of Burton's theory that the people of the country were eager to discard the old and shopworn considerations of "availability" and make their choice of a President on character, ability, and public service.

Mercifully, this political idealist was spared the unhappy spectacle of President Hoover's abysmal defeat in 1932 and his preceding struggle with a hostile Democratic House of Representatives.

Calvin Coolidge had been a sufficiently outstanding example of Presidential refrigeration, but he could understand a problem in practical politics without a diagram and had a dry New England humor; besides, he was the Rising Market President and the impersonation of national good luck—which made his lack of warmth less penetrating than the low temperature of this blunt, troubled engineer who had an increasing realization of why Mr. Coolidge "did not choose to run."

The national politicians in both major parties had found Hoover deficient in political tact and they passed this viewpoint on to their followers. Mr. Hoover might be the world's greatest political economist, but he was a bungler in his relations with members of Congress and stepped on their toes whenever he moved. The broadcast of this defect was industrious and bipartisan. Magazines and newspapers repeatedly carried articles ringing the changes upon the thesis that a President of the United States must be a practical politician in order to put over his policies.

Precisely how much of this failure of Mr. Hoover as a practical politician contributed to his humiliating defeat cannot, of course, be determined, but the extent of the triumph of the genial and smiling Franklin Delano Roosevelt would seem to establish the fact that Burton was decidedly in advance of his times in the belief that other qualifications in a President could outweigh lack of qualifications as a practical politician. Burton died in the faith that the nomination and election of Herbert Hoover had elevated the standards of Presidential selection.

"Practical politics" is quite as human a calling as horse trading —which will disappear only with the extinction of the horse. Theodore Burton, despite his long experience in public life, had much to learn about human nature. In his espousal of Hoover as a Presidential candidate, he displayed both his idealism and his ingenuousness.

Ohio politics was an arena for the most agile acrobatics in politics and its alignments changed with a rapidity which made the champion of today the opponent of tomorrow. This was confusing to Burton; he was unable readily to adjust himself to such hard-boiled reversals. He stuck by friends who failed him politically when to do so required extreme forbearance.

Burton's strenuous work in the Hoover campaign was exhausting and it is doubtful if he fully recovered from it. But in his judgment Hoover's triumph was worth the sacrifice.

There was still another plum in this 1928 Christmas pie for Theodore Burton. In view of the attitude of the Republicans of Ohio, who sustained him to an unexpected extent in their vote for Hoover, he decided that he would become a candidate for the seat in the United States Senate which had been occupied by Willis. In taking this step Burton was influenced by many offers of support from men active in politics who had been champions of Senator Willis in the preferential primary campaign against Hoover.

Burton's health in 1928 was not robust. His friends urged him not to make an active campaign. There was not a chance for his defeat. Yet, against the advice of his physician, he did make an arduous campaign which greatly depleted his strength.

CHAPTER 28

Burton's Great Peace Party

NOTHER EVENT OF 1928 stood out in glowing letters upon the Burton record. This was the First World Conference on International Justice, celebrating the one hundredth anniversary of the founding of the American Peace Society. This important conference convened in Cleveland at ten o'clock on the morning of May seventh. About thirteen thousand persons, including a large number of distinguished guests from foreign countries, attended. In the eyes of his fellow citizens, this was "Burton's big party," an international gathering which revealed his standing with statesmen of the great nations of the world.

Comparatively few residents of Cleveland were deeply concerned about what the World Conference might accomplish for International Justice—but they were proud that Cleveland had a citizen so respected in foreign lands that hundreds of visitors from remote countries were willing to make tedious journeys to honor Burton and his peace plans.

Up to this time, not many of his political supporters had taken the Senator's "peace tinkering" seriously. But when they saw the groups of distinguished delegates arriving from distant lands and read in the newspapers the names of the famous men and women attending, their attitude altered. Ohio's "Grand Old Man" had handed them a surprise and brought to Cleveland a crowd of strangers almost as great as that attending a national political convention.

However, an undercurrent of criticism was apparent. To many it was a "damn pacifist show." There was a note of hostility in the murmurs from the crowds which lined the streets along which the delegates passed.

When the moment came for the sponsor of the conference to go to the auditorium, his secretary, Robert Norton, hurried to the apartment they occupied.

"The apartment," related Mr. Norton, "was so still when I entered that I was almost startled. Then, stepping to where I could look through a half-opened door into the bedroom, I saw a sight I can never forget. The proud, dignified old Senator was down on his knees at his bedside, asking for guidance from God to the end that the peace conference might become a blessing to all humanity for generations to come. He never knew that his supplications were observed by human eyes or heard by human ears.

"This scene was doubly impressive to me because the Senator had never discussed his religious convictions in my hearing. Nothing could have so vividly dramatized to me the emotional depths to which Senator Burton was moved as this act of humble prayer which he thought was sheltered in privacy."

Burton's profound interest in the problems of international peace is not difficult to understand when his personal traits are taken into consideration. Unlike many other leading advocates of this cause, his approach to it was not emotional but intellectual. He thought as a jurist rather than as an advocate. He held civilization to be an evolution of law and every step in the progress of human relationships a proof that laws embodying principles of human justice must command increasing respect and acceptance because man is a reasoning being.

He believed that the settlement of disputes between nations by the peaceful processes of orderly adjudication could be increased by providing the proper machinery for such adjudication. This belief rested upon his recognition of the fact that millions of individual disputes are now settled by law instead of by personal combat, as was the practice in earlier days, and that violent differences between various political units of one country—cities, counties, provinces, and states—are constantly resolved by recourse to law instead of to arms. Those who regard the peaceful adjustment of differences between nations as a fatuous dream ignore the historic fact that, not far back in the development of civilization, virtually all quarrels between individuals, clans, tribes, and communities were decided by prompt resort to physical force.

The extension of the domain of law to the settlement of international disputes seemed wholly logical to Burton. For him to regard as visionary the expectation that disputing nations would increasingly accept the principles of adjusting their differences in a judicial tribunal was to admit the whole judicial fabric everywhere to be a failure. The system of courts in every civilized country of the world was the answer, in his mind, to assertion that national selfishness could not be restrained by any international tribunal.

Burton's profound respect for law and his familiarity with the history of its advancement and acceptance through the centuries made him unable to accept the assertion that civilization, as represented by the reign of law, was powerless to extend the frontier of its domain into the international field.

Among the many distinguished men who were present at this Cleveland Peace meeting were Sir Esme Howard, Ambassador to the United States from England, and Sir Austin Chamberlain, British Secretary of State for Foreign Affairs. Evidently there was a sprinkling of anti-British sympathizers in the audience who were bent on creating a disturbance. Burton gave them one warning and declared: "There will be order in this hall. The police will do their duty." And they did.

Probably a speech made that same day in the House of Representatives, by John E. Nelson, of Maine, gave Burton greater pleasure than anything in the Cleveland meeting. This Representative from the Congressional district in which the American Peace Society was born said:

> The thoughts of lovers of peace the world over are turned this morning to the City of Cleveland, Ohio, where there is now in session a World Conference on International Justice . . . a part of the centennial anniversary celebration of the American Peace Society, founded on May 8, 1828, by William Ladd, of Minot, Maine. The President of this Society today is our distinguished colleague, the Hon. Theodore E. Burton of Ohio, whose eloquent utterances on the floor of this House in behalf of world tolerance, world understanding, world sympathy, and world justice have repeatedly won our love, challenged our admiration, and compelled our respect. May God spare this man of magnanimity and vision for many years of useful service! We need such men as he in this House; for long ago it was written, "Where there is no vision, the people perish."

Probably no other figure in American history appealed to Burton's interest and imagination as did the relatively obscure William

Ladd, a graduate of Harvard University at the age of nineteen; at twenty, commander of one of the largest brigs putting out from New England when the seas were infested with pirates and priva- teers; a Georgia cotton planter operating with paid Negro labor as an adventure in constructive industrial philanthropy; and again a rover of the high seas until the War of 1812.

When he was forty-one years old, Ladd, under the inspiration of President Jesse Appleton, of Bowdoin College, and Noah Wor- cester, dedicated his life and fortune to bringing national leaders to recognize the possibilities of settling disputes between nations in ways more intelligent and civilized than recourse to bloodshed. He enlisted the interest and co-operation of John Quincy Adams, Webster, Emerson, and many others. Although he devoted him- self to the cause of international justice and peace with unsparing energy, he appeared to Senator Burton to have been far removed from fanaticism. He sacrificed his strength and his fortune to a great humanitarian cause with the courage and devotion which, as a younger man, he had given to adventures on the seas in pursuit of rich returns from long and dangerous voyages.

It was a matter of regret to Burton that he could not attend the ceremonies at Minot, Maine, on July 21, 1928, where a memorial tablet honoring William Ladd was unveiled and where the scholarly Dr. David Jayne Hill sketched the conclusions and objectives of that "First Apostle of International Peace" in these words:

> Stated in the briefest possible form, his plan proposed two separate but correlated organizations; the first, a mechanism for arriving at an agreement regarding a body of international laws; the second, a nonmilitary agency for rendering it effective, as follows:
>
> 1st. A congress of official representatives chosen by their respec- tive states to formulate principles of international law, afterwards to be adopted by treaty; and
>
> 2nd. A court to apply the law agreed upon in case of contentions regarding compliance with it, jurisdiction and judgment to be ac- cepted by mutual consent. . . .
>
> It should be clearly understood that in Mr. Ladd's plan there was no provision for the political control of one State by another, or of any State by the totality of States. . . . Force could be used only if necessary to resist aggression. William Ladd knew that self-defense can never be made illegal with any prospect of obedience.

After referring to William Ladd as "a man of hardheaded common sense, with no suggestion in his temperament of the visionary," Dr. Hill continued:

> William Ladd struck a clear note of what has proved to be the consistent policy of this Nation, complete co-operation in a strictly judicial organization of international peace, with no commitment to political or military entanglements. . . . If justice is possible between nations, then peace is possible. . . . There is only one way to terminate the spirit that leads to war, and that is the establishment of organized justice. . . .
>
> We must seek the means to abolish war, not by the threat of more war, but in the time of peace and by the agencies of peace. We shall find peace where, as a nation, we have found prosperity, in obedience to just laws to which we have previously assented after free collaboration, followed by submission, when necessary, to a judiciary whose sole functions shall be the interpretation of rules of action deliberately considered and mutually agreed upon to which a free nation can, with honor, pledge obedience.

Senator Burton might well have written those clear, unemotional planks of the platform of International Justice himself. The adventurous man born in 1778 and the "International Statesman" of 1928 held the same common-sense convictions as to principles upon which international justice must be founded and developed to be of service to humanity. Neither deluded himself that the progress of this great humanitarian enterprise would be other than slow, but both held to the conviction that no progress could be made in extending the frontier of law into the international field unless machinery for the peaceful adjudication of disputes between nations was established.

Burton abhorred war with all his soul and he lived to see war enthusiasm for any cause short of an attack on the United States by a foreign power become unsalable and to recognize in war veterans the largest body of antiwar sentiment in existence.

His addresses and articles of the late twenties indicate that in this great interest of his closing years his feet were firmly planted on the ground. He realized that the urge of nations—especially those having an acceptance of law less complete than that of the United States—to engage in war would not quickly yield to reason. But that the law would ultimately occupy the international field and delay hasty recourse to combat he had no doubt.

Theodore Burton took his seat in the Senate on December 15, 1928, having been elected by an amazing majority of more than 500,000 votes. His return to that body, which he had left so unfortunately fourteen years before, was a most unusual occurrence. No other American had ever served in the House, then in the Senate, returned to the House, and then served again in the Senate.

On the last day in which Burton appeared in the House he was given a remarkable ovation. A graphic picture of this was given in the Cleveland *Plain Dealer* by Paul Hodges:

> Streaming down the aisles of the chamber, members of the House of Representatives today gave Senator-elect Theodore Burton of Cleveland an ovation unsurpassed in House history. . . .
>
> They threw off every semblance of restraint and, regardless of party, creed, race, or section, cheered him with an intensity and sincerity that brought tears to his eyes and a happy smile to his face. His oldest colleagues said they could remember no greater tribute during their service. It was a truly notable speech that the veteran made in concluding the House career which he began forty years before. Again and again the legislative chamber rang with shouts. . . .
>
> When Burton had concluded he held open house in his little office on the first floor, receiving the congratulations and best wishes of congressional leaders, as a flock of porters carried out the files and furniture to the Senate office building where Burton served from 1909 to 1913.
>
> Tomorrow Congressman Burton will become Senator Burton. The Senate will meet especially to permit him to take the oath of office, and Burton will take his seat with Senator Simeon D. Fess of Ohio in the more august of the legislative bodies.
>
> Mr. Burton went to the House Chamber at noon undecided whether to say a formal farewell. He had prepared no speech.
>
> John Q. Tillson, majority floor leader, insisted on a speech. He asked Speaker Nicholas Longworth for unanimous consent to permit Mr. Burton to speak out of order. The consent was quickly given and Tillson, with Burton on his arm, moved down to the chamber "well" as the entire membership of the House rose to its feet and cheered.
>
> The Clevelander stood there, smiling happily at his noisy colleagues, many of whom were not yet born when he first came to the House. . . .

Burton's reason for going back into the Senate, he told his

friends, was because he could then "act in the larger sphere of activity in foreign affairs which belongs to the Senate and thus serve the ennobling cause of peace and international good will." This opportunity came early in 1929 when he made a strong plea in Congress against the hurried construction of fifteen cruisers.

At the close of the Seventieth Congress, on March 4, being worn and ill, Burton went to Atlantic City for a rest and change, but was back at his desk again in April when the President called a special session of Congress.

In accordance with custom, the first day of a first session is very short. Just before the motion to adjourn was made, Senator Burton's tall, spare figure slowly arose. His face looked tired. His voice, that once deep, clear, resonant bell, was husky and unsteady. He began to speak of Myron Herrick, his boyhood friend, who had died a short time before. There was no one present who had not understood the friendship between these two. Not always united in political interests, they were nevertheless held by bonds lasting through a long period.

This special session lasted for about two months. The heat of Washington was intense. It was hard on the Senator. He felt old and tired, though he seldom admitted it. But his work was as arduous as ever, as he was a member of the Civil Service, Commerce, Education, and Labor and Judiciary Committees.

When the Senate convened after a summer recess, Burton had to leave the Chamber in the midst of a session. He did not again return.

CHAPTER 29

Passing of a Statesman

PERHAPS ON NO OTHER public occasion had Senator Burton ever shown himself to be in better health and spirits than at the dinner given him in celebration of his seventy-fifth birthday anniversary, in December, 1926, by his Cleveland friends at the Hotel Hollenden. He then smilingly confessed that he had two ambitions: to die in public office and have a public funeral at public expense. Both these ambitions were realized.

Three years later, when he knew he was doomed by an incurable malady, with his friend William R. Hopkins, Cleveland City Manager, he planned every detail of his own funeral.

He was old and weary and he craved final and official public recognition by his government that his services to it had been long, faithful, and efficient.

Once he had been offered an appointment to the Federal Bench, when the Foraker Bill of 1901 created an additional United States Circuit Judgeship in the Cleveland district. Friends urged his acceptance and told him that it would start him on his way to the United States Supreme Court.

But Burton had started out to become a legislative statesman and he declined to be diverted from his course.

At the end of his life, after his long legislative service, he did not fully appreciate the esteem and affection in which he was held by the general public.

It had been planned that Senator Burton would accompany President Hoover to the dedication of the monument celebrating the completion of the nine-foot waterway project at Cincinnati. When it became known that he was too ill to leave his home, Dr. Joel T. Boone sent him a telegram suggesting that he turn on his radio and listen to the President's address. He did so, expecting to hear only the story of the fulfillment of one of his cherished dreams. Soon the voice of President Hoover came to him, saying:

"I personally feel deeply the absence of Senator Theodore Burton, at whose bedside in Washington I recently stood. His work as Chairman of the historic Inland Waterways Commission appointed by President Roosevelt in 1907 gave the foundation upon which this great development has been created. The report of that Commission in 1908 has been the 'Bible' of waterways improvement. Its first result was the act of 1910, with which began the present project, now brought to its successful conclusion.

"It reflected not only the clarity of mind with which Senator Burton has endowed public issues for a generation, but also the broad humanity of his spirit that dwelt with especial concern upon the problems of equity involved and upon the welfare of the whole body of men and women of the country for whose benefit the program was primarily undertaken."

In the earlier days of Senator Burton's long illness, President Hoover was a frequent visitor at his friend's apartment. As the fatal outcome of the malady became assured, the President was almost daily at Burton's bedside. Here was an old Spartan, of proved courage and devotion, knowing that his days were numbered and yet facing his end with serenity, who talked with easy and interested detachment of the problems of his nation to his President and friend. They crowded much into the companionship of those last visits.

Burton failed perceptibly after he left his chair in the Senate on September 4, but until a very few days before the end came he took short daily walks with Robert Norton, who lived in the house. Norton had been with him for about five years and had his affection as well as his confidence.

During these days of anxiety, letters, telegrams, and messages from friends and acquaintances deluged the apartment. They were from rabbis, bishops, Salvation Army officers, Supreme Court Justices, diplomats, bankers, and politicians. A most appreciative and sympathetic note was received from Ramsay McDonald. Persons of high rank and of low, all were concerned. From the Merchants National Bank in New York came a message from the entire institution.

Especially solicitous were the ambassadors of the foreign legations in Washington. They had known the Senator in their own lands as the unofficial ambassador of the American Congress.

A deep quiet reigned in the huge apartment house. The telephone operators sent written messages up to the Senator's apartment to avoid any ringing of a telephone bell which might break the patient's rest.

Any story of Senator Burton's life failing to present the picture of a personal relationship which contributed more than anything else to his comfort and happiness from the time he was forty years of age would be inadequate.

One September day, in 1891, when he lived at the Euclid, in Cleveland, he received a message from his niece, Miss Grace C. Burton, the daughter of his brother Edward, saying that she had secured a good position in the Cleveland School for the Deaf and would like him to advise her about a permanent boarding place.

At once he asked her to come to his apartment. There he listened to an account of her determined preparations to lead her own life in surroundings more appealing and stimulating than those of Lincoln, Illinois, where she was born and where her father was a leading merchant. She had responded to the urge felt by young people everywhere to make her own place in a new world of broader possibilities than those available at home.

Burton had always liked this daughter of the brother to whom he was devotedly attached. He knew that she possessed rare courage, determination, industry, and adaptability—characteristic Burton traits. Possibly she expected him to question the wisdom of her adventure into the life of a large city. Promptly he expressed his approval of her course, his satisfaction in her ambition, in the hard work which had gone into her preparation for her career as a teacher and in the courage with which she faced the future. He added: "Why not live here with me? The arrangement would be most agreeable. I think I understand you rather well and I am sure that we will get along together famously."

His niece found her greatest difficulty in getting his assent, under this arrangement, to her financial self-sufficiency. She was proudly on her own now and insisted that complete economic independence was essential to her. Eventually he surrendered to her terms.

From that moment, she became his homemaker and devoted companion. This close relationship was never interrupted while he lived. Inevitably, it was a thing of growth and expansion. More and more he came to appreciate her qualities of mind, her quick grasp of the problems of politics and of the legislative matters in which he was concerned. Gradually he learned to trust greatly her intuition both as to men and measures.

In all the stress and strain of Senator Burton's last illness, this devoted niece was tireless. She was rather frail of body, but her nearest friends were amazed at her endurance and strength. She, who had waited up long hours many nights in order to "talk over with Uncle" some tense affair of the moment, now kept herself ready through anxious days and nights to answer his call for her. Not once did she fail to respond with motherly tenderness, though the call came at increasingly frequent intervals. His comrade of many campaigns, of two trips abroad, of his fireside—the hostess of his social life as well as guardian of his domestic comfort— could not and did not once fail him in this last great battle.

The obsequies for Senator Burton were stately and impressive. At the home at 2101 Connecticut Avenue, a few of his intimate friends and relatives gathered for a short prayer service. Besides Grace C. Burton, there were his nieces, Laura Shurtleff Price and her sister, Mrs. Mary Storey, and a grandniece, Mrs. Elizabeth Hasell and her husband, as well as the Senator's nephew, Will Burton, of Omaha. They had all come to bid a last farewell to their beloved friend and relative.

Then the Senator was taken to the Senate Chamber. The services there were at the request of the Justices of the Supreme Court, diplomats, Senators, and others who wished to honor Theodore Burton but who could not go to Cleveland.

His friends came in throngs, for the last farewell, until the journey to Ohio began—Ohio, the home of his boyhood and young manhood. Arriving in Cleveland, the party, with an escort of mounted police and a detachment of National Guards, went to the City Hall, where the body lay in state for hours. Here again were old friends and neighbors and also those who knew the Senator only in his political and public life. In that reviewing line were men, women, and children from all walks of life.

When the cortege started for the final service in the Euclid Avenue Congregational Church, it proceeded through a double line of sorrowing townspeople. Every business house was closed. Streetcars and all traffic came to a dead stop. There was not a sound but the clatter on the pavement of the hoofs of the soldiers' mounts and the droning of airplanes overhead.

At the church the party of relatives was met by additional nephews and nieces: Margaret Starkey, of Jefferson, the daughter of Margaret Burton, an older half sister of the Senator's; Lynds Jones, who was his sister Lavinia's son, and his wife; Will's son, William; and Phil's son, Arthur. Thus all those of the Austinburg parsonage were represented here through their children.

Bishop McDowell, of Washington, complying with a request Burton had made, delivered the address. In closing, he said, "His place is secure. 'The work of his hands is established.' "

At the end of the service, the Grand Commandery of Ohio, Knights Templar, took charge of the journey to Lake View Cemetery. There, at the top of a little knoll only a few feet from the imposing Garfield monument and near the last resting place of his friend Herrick, Theodore Elijah Burton was buried. From this little hillside one may look over the city and see the blue waters of Lake Erie, one of his waterways, and all about are familiar names of those who were friends of the young lawyer of the seventies and eighties. A stately monument, erected by Grace Burton, now marks the place of his rest.

INDEX

THIS BOOK WAS SET IN

JANSON AND BULMER TYPES BY

BROWN BROTHERS LINOTYPERS.

IT WAS PRINTED AND BOUND BY

THE HADDON CRAFTSMEN.

THE PAPER IS PERKINS AND SQUIER COMPANY'S

RRR WOVE ANTIQUE

MADE BY THE P. H. GLATFELTER COMPANY.

TYPOGRAPHY AND DESIGN ARE BY

ABE LERNER

DATE DUE